PEACEFUL RESISTANCE

Ethics and Global Politics

Series Editors: Tom Lansford and Patrick Hayden

Since the end of the Cold War, explorations of ethical considerations within global politics and on the development of foreign policy have assumed a growing importance in the fields of politics and international studies. New theories, policies, institutions, and actors are called for to address difficult normative questions arising from the conduct of international affairs in a rapidly changing world. This series provides an exciting new forum for creative research that engages both the theory and practice of contemporary world politics, in light of the challenges and dilemmas of the evolving international order.

Also in the series

The Ethics of Refugee Policy
Christina Boswell
ISBN 0 7546 4519 3

Justice and Violence
Edited by Allan Eickelmann, Eric Nelson and Tom Lansford
ISBN 0 7546 4546 0

Global Ethics and Civil Society
Edited by John Eade and Darren O'Byrne
ISBN 0 7546 4214 3

In War We Trust
The Bush Doctrine and the Pursuit of Just War
Chris J. Dolan
ISBN 0 7546 4234 8

Cosmopolitan Global Politics
Patrick Hayden
ISBN 0 7546 4276 3

Understanding Human Rights Violations
New Systematic Studies
Edited by Sabine C. Carey and Steven C. Poe
ISBN 0 7546 4026 4

Peaceful Resistance

Advancing Human Rights
and Democratic Freedoms

ROBERT M. PRESS
University of Southern Mississippi

ASHGATE

Published by
Ashgate Publishing Limited
Gower House
Croft Road
Aldershot
Hampshire GU11 3HR
England

Ashgate Publishing Company
Suite 420
101 Cherry Street
Burlington, VT 05401-4405
USA

Ashgate website: http://www.ashgate.com

British Library Cataloguing in Publication Data
Press, Robert M.
 Peaceful resistance: advancing human rights and democratic
 freedoms. - (Ethics and global politics)
 1.Passive resistance – Kenya 2.Human rights workers – Kenya
 3.Political activists – Kenya 4.Democracy – Kenya 5.Human
 rights - Kenya 6.Kenya – Politics and government –
 1878–2002
 I.Title
 323'.044'096762

Library of Congress Cataloging-in-Publication Data
Press, Robert M.
 Peaceful resistance: advancing human rights and democratic freedoms / by Robert M. Press.
  p. cm. -- (Ethics and global politics)
 Includes bibliographical references and index.
 ISBN 0-7546-4713-7
 1. Government, Resistance to--Case studies. 2. Government, Resistance to--Kenya. 3. Human rights--Kenya. 4. Democratization--Kenya. 5. Political activists--Kenya. 6. Human rights workers--Kenya. I. Title. II. Series.

 JC328.3.P74 2006
 322.4'4096762--dc22

2005037637

ISBN-10: 0 7546 4713 7

Printed and bound in Great Britain by Antony Rowe Ltd, Chippenham, Wiltshire.

Contents

List of Tables

About the Author

Robert Press grew up in Missouri where he graduated from the University of Missouri with a degree in journalism. After working in Africa for the U.S. Agency for International Development, he and his wife, Betty Press, hitch-hiked and flew around the world for two years. He then worked as a staff writer for *The Christian Science Monitor* in various locations, including eight years based in Kenya (1987-1995), traveling across East and West Africa with his wife, a photographer.

He is the author of *The New Africa: Dispatches from a Changing Continent*, published in 1999 by the University Press of Florida, selected as one of the best 40 books published by any university press in the United States in 1999-2000. He was a Visiting Professor at Principia College in Elsah, Illinois and an Adjunct Professor at Stetson University in DeLand, Florida before moving to Mississippi. He is currently an Assistant Professor in the Department of Political Science, International Development and International Affairs at the University of Southern Mississippi. He may be contacted at bob.press@usm.edu or The University of Southern Mississippi, 118 College Drive # 5108, Hatttiesburg, MS. 39406-5108.

Preface

The idea for this book stems from eight years living and working in Kenya as a correspondent for *The Christian Science Monitor* from 1987-1995. My wife and I traveled many times across East and West Africa and saw first hand examples of the most significant moves toward democracy that most African states had ever experienced. Except where there were civil wars or revolutions, most of the changes were peaceful, at least from the side of activists: regimes often used brutal force to try to stop or slow change.

In 1999, the University Press of Florida published my account of these turbulent years: *The New Africa: Dispatches from a Changing Continent.* It focused on the democratization process, civil society, and the civil war in Somalia and genocide in Rwanda. My account of Kenya featured some of the activists in the current work.

I never examined the process by which democratization occurred in Kenya or the dynamics behind human rights and democracy activism. When I returned to Kenya in 1999 for initial research for this book, my plan was to focus on human rights organizations. I learned, however, that the human rights groups were only part of an array of organizations that had pushed for greater human rights and democracy. I also realized that not just organizations, but individual activists had played an important part in the early stages of the overt resistance. When I returned in 2002 for the major research for this book, I was able to locate most of the key activists and interview them and others about their efforts, cross-checking their claims with archival accounts. They helped start a process that led to establishment of what I call a *culture of resistance*. This consisted of widespread disagreement with a regime and open efforts to force it to make reforms. The resistance involved not only organizational activism but also *individual activism*, an important but over-looked phenomena in the study of human rights and democratization.

Much of the current literature on social movements and democratic transitions describes activism as highly dependent on external circumstances, so-called structural and institutional constraints. In Kenya I found that activists, including individuals activists, organizational representatives and visible segments of the general public forged ahead despite such constraints and despite the risks. Their efforts won key advances in human rights and democratic freedom through a process that was fairly loose, not easy to predict, and involving a high degree of human initiative.

I make no claims that activism results in an election as in Kenya, where the ruling party was defeated after a long reign. But without the activism, it is unlikely that changes would have come when they did. Once in power themselves, there is no guarantee that former activists will not resort to some of the same repressive tactics they once opposed. But a population awakened to their human rights and democratic freedom will be less tolerant of those who come later and try to reverse those gains.

Activism for human rights and democracy has played an important role in the transition of many countries around the world – from the Philippines to South Korea, in the Ukraine, across much of sub-Saharan Africa, and in South America. The Kenya study shows how an aroused citizenry can help establish a *culture of resistance* and provides fresh analytical tools for examination of other cases of activism, both past and present. If the activism in other authoritarian settings occurs despite great obstacles, as it did in Kenya, then we political scientists and others need to raise our estimates of just how much a people determined to advance their human rights and democratic freedom can accomplish.

Acknowledgements

Only one name is on the title sheet of this work, but many people in Africa and the United States have shared their time, energy, and wisdom in making it a reality. Here are some of them.

First, the more than 70 individuals I interviewed for this work in 2002, mostly in Kenya, but also in Washington and London, generously set aside other tasks to provide their insight on a dramatic period in Kenya's recent history. The interviews were generally planned to last one hour but many lasted several hours. For many of the activists it was the most thorough review they had ever made of their contributions to the efforts to advance human rights and democracy to Kenya.

Second, numerous academicians and other professionals provided inspiration and guidance. In Kenya, Political Science Professor Peter Anyang' Nyong'o managed to find time to help provide important theoretical overviews in the midst of running for re-election to Parliament (he won) and helping bring opposition presidential candidates together behind the scenes for victory in December 2002. Activist Attorneys Gibson Kamu Kuria, Pheroze Nowrojee, Willy Mutunga, and my friend Chiuri Ngugi, gave me many hours of help. Historian Macharia Munene and analyst Nguyi Mutahi, among many others, provided me with valuable insight. Also in Kenya, Harold and Annetta Miller, Donald and Ruth Thomas, and Damian and Elizabeth Cook, shared their friendship, hospitality, and ideas based on their long association with the country and its people. In London, long-time Amnesty International researcher Martin Hill provided his personal perspective.

At the University of Florida, a number of professors deserve acknowledgement. Goran Hyden tirelessly guided me through several revisions of this work; Michael Chege and Professor Hyden shared their long experience and passion regarding Kenya and Africa in general, as well as their knowledge of comparative politics. Even as they travelled abroad they continued to help me refine and clarify my draft chapters. Dr. Philip Williams first introduced me to social movement literature and shares my interest in the developing world. Dr. Larry Dodd helped me think more creatively, to question theories and the way we acquire knowledge; and he introduced me to the concepts of institutional "learning" and of changing political and social dynamics over time. Anthropologist Dr. Paul Magnarella, whose own work encompasses human rights in Africa, listened patiently to my many early thoughts on this project. Ken Mease helped me with a conceptual framework in the early stages of research.

Others professors at the University of Florida helped me prepare for this research. Historians Hunt Davis and Jeffrey Needell, and political scientist Rich Conley were among my first teachers and models for scholarship and advanced research. Leslie Thiele encouraged me to engage political theorists directly, not through layers of interpretations; a process he said helps "sharpen the mind." Peggy

Conway and Leslie Anderson encouraged my research and intellectual growth. Wayne Francis and Michael Martinez never ducked my endless questions. Dennis Galvan challenged me to always dig deeper for ideas; and he spent hours critiquing my various writings. Numerous fellow graduate students helped me sharpen my analyses in lively seminar discussions. Africanist librarians Peter Malanchuk and Dan Reboussin enthusiastically helped me locate good source materials. Program Assistants Debbie Wallen and Sue Lawless-Yanchisin cheerfully helped me as a commuter student meet paperwork deadlines.

At Stetson University, in DeLand, Florida, where I previously taught, political scientists Wayne Bailey, my mentor there, along with Anne Hallum, Bill Nylen, Gene Huskey, Gary Maris, economist Ranjini Thaver, and Dean Grady Ballenger encouraged my pursuit of a doctorate through their friendship and scholarly advice. At Principia College, where I taught a term, political scientist Jerry Collester, George Moffett and others set examples of good scholarship and high principles.

At the University of Southern Mississippi, political scientist Joe Parker, my mentor, and Allan McBride, went out of their way to encourage me to complete this research. Graduate assistants Diandra Hosey and Kathryn Thompson gave me needed extra time by assisting with grading for my classes.

Africa scholars Nelson Kasfir and Jackie Kloop read and commented on early drafts of the theory chapter. Robert Dahl and several other senior scholars answered my queries and encouraged me in my examination of the role of individuals in political change.

Robert and Patricia Drabik, President and Secretary/Treasurer of The John J. and Lucille C. Madigan Charitable Foundation, Inc., provided a grant that covered my travel and research costs in Kenya for this project. Members of The Christian Science church of DeLand, Florida gave me moral encouragement. Alys Solar, Martha Moffett, and especially Agnes Lamme, gave me their prayerful support and inspiration.

My late mother and father, John and Maxine Press, encouraged me to explore the world and instilled in me a sense of fairness and respect for others. Finally, and most important of all, my wife, Betty Press, a professional photographer, was my partner in our reporter-photographer team in East and West Africa from 1987-1995, when I was employed by *The Christian Science Monitor* and based in Kenya. During the writing of this book, she also carried more than her share of our household chores, gave up many social events, and listened to far too many comments on political theories. Her reactions and keen insight always helped. She never doubted the value of this project or the importance of completing it.

Introduction

> The brightest lights at the end of the tunnel in Africa must be those held aloft by ordinary citizens. Africans' resilience and stubborn refusal to cave in to despair against the odds of despotism at home and an increasingly hostile environment can be ignored only at great cost by those seriously concerned with the recovery of the region.
>
> *Michael Chege*[1]

At first only a few individuals stepped dangerously across the line of anonymity to demand human rights and democratic freedoms in Kenya, a country whose leader used prison and torture to silence critics. Risking their own safety and careers, they openly demanded freedom of speech, the right of assembly, and the ability to elect their leaders.

Later, some local organizations joined the growing demands for reforms; and some Western governments added pressure on the regime. Ordinary people joined peaceful protests – protests that often were met by riot police and paramilitary troops swinging clubs, throwing tear gas and sometimes using guns. Still the protests continued. The regime, fearful of losing control, reluctantly granted more freedom. This is the story of how human rights and democracy activists can help stir the human spirit as well as political opposition and establish a *culture of resistance* in an undemocratic country. It also highlights a seldom-recognized feature of such resistance: *individual activism*. Individual activists in Kenya helped get the resistance movement started.

Activism has played a key role in the transformation of many authoritarian regimes – from the Philippines to South Korea, in parts of the former Soviet Union, across much of sub-Saharan Africa and in Latin America. But little is known about how such activism actually starts, what tactics initial activists use to get attention and gain more public support. This is the story of how activists can trigger the establishment of a resistance movement that can push a regime to make political advances in human rights and democratic freedoms.

Contrary to a major social movement theory that suggests such movements are largely dependent on political, economic or international conditions beyond the control of activists, this book shows how activists, especially initially, forged ahead on their own initiative despite unfavorable conditions.

Activism in an authoritarian state can be dangerous work. Although some activists may have had selfish motives, many, especially in the risky early stages of the resistance, had far more to lose than to gain by their participation. Most modern scholars deny that people can act on principle and not strictly self interest. Why

---

1   Chege, Michael. 1994. "What's Right with Africa?" In *Current History*, May, 194.

should we be so surprised at the possibility that people can act out of something other than self-interest? The view that self-interest is the only motive is not only a cynical view about mankind, it is one that vastly underestimates the human spirit and the human potential.

Principled ideas (e.g., justice, freedom) were found to offer a better explanation of motivations than self-interest for many, but not all, of the early activists. Other "pro-social" motivations such as "duty, love," are just as real, even in politics, as scholars such as Jane Mansbridge note.[2] This does not mean that self-interest played no role in the motivation of activists, however. After the initial, most dangerous phases of resistance, after individual activists helped wrest some concessions from the regime, organizational activists, including political opposition party leaders, put added pressure on the regime. In this later phase, motivations based on self-interest were more evident as activism for some meant jobs, or a chance at political power. A follow-up study to this one based on what early activists did when in power may well conclude that some of the early activists' original motivations were much more self-serving than was apparent when they took considerable risks during initial stages of resistance.

There is no guarantee of success. If a regime responds with massive repression, it can force the resistance underground, but at the risk of starting a civil war and earning international condemnation. If the regime is reluctant to use massive force and at least pretends to abide by the rule of law, open resistance can grow and reforms are possible.

This study is evidence that at a time when people living in half the world's countries (56 percent of the global population) still lack basic political freedoms,[3] people are not helpless victims of circumstances but can stand up, speak out, and force an authoritarian regime to improve human rights and democratic freedoms. The findings support a much more optimistic assessment of the ability of people to shape their own destinies than described in most of the literature on democratic transitions and social movements.

This book is a case study that focuses on individual and group initiatives. The author is fully aware of – and uses in this book – other ways to focus on political change, including a structural or institutional approach, as well as paying close attention to international factors. But this is one of the few studies to examine from the ground up the dynamics of political activism or resistance in an African country: how it starts; how it can grow; how at times it can also falter; how people can risk much for principles they believe in, and how a reform movement is sometimes used for personal gain or power.

This is also one of the few studies to apply social movement theory to an African country. Building in part on theories of social movements (in this case the term

---

2 Mansbridge, Jane J., ed. 1990. *Beyond Self-Interest*. Chicago: University of Chicago Press, ix.

3 Freedom House. 2005. *Freedom in the World 2005: The Annual Survey of Political Rights and Civil Liberties*. New York: Freedom House.

resistance movement is used), the present investigation builds on previous work but also differs.[4] Social movement analyses usually focus on organizations; and they generally assume such organizations already exist. This book takes a different approach and includes the important, though largely undetected in other studies, role of individual activists, people who challenge a regime early on without the benefit and protection of an organization. It shows how this, in turn, can help encourage organizational activism.

Moving beyond a static model of social movements and resistance, this book provides the kind of dynamic research that newer thinking about the study of resistance politics calls for involving many participants from different parts of society. The methodology used suggests an alternative research focus in regions where formal institutions are not strong, as often is the case in the developing world. Instead of concentrating on institutions of varying quality, the focus for an investigation of democratization and a human rights struggle can gain fresh insights from assessing the political process of resistance – and the tactics of people leading it.

As already mentioned, this is not a book based only on one theory or focus, that of agency, or activism. Institutional factors are also carefully considered and their effects are noted. Someone who examines political change through an institutional focus might argue that institutional and so-called structural factors were the main determinants of what happened in Kenya. They might point to the levels of government repression as limiting the amount of activism that can take place in an authoritarian regime. They might also point to Kenya as less repressive than some other African nations because it eventually allowed protests; then they might conclude that this 'institutional' factor, not activism, was the key to any ground that a resistance movement gained.

This book suggests a different view: that without the activism that took place, reforms would have come much slower. The research finds a clear relation between repression and activism, but the relation is not as straightforward as it may at first seem. Instead of blocking resistance, state repression led to more resistance, a feature noted in some earlier literature. As will be noted, a regime bent on destroying an opposition activist movement can probably do so, but only at risk to their eventual hold on power. Extreme repression can drive a movement underground but probably will not destroy it; and it can re-emerge in armed rebellion and possibly civil war. This is an institutional argument used in this book.

Activism, on the contrary, can push a strong authoritarian regime to make some concessions. It can encourage widening participation in the resistance even in the face of repression. This is an agency argument. The emphasis of this study is on the role of agency or personal initiatives in the face of institutional barriers.

Others may look at this book and disagree with another finding: that domestic activism played a greater role in regime concessions than international pressures.

---

4   A number of terms are used in the literature to explain protest politics, including social movements, contentious politics, and sometimes people power. Definitions will be clarified in chapter 1.

Many excellent studies of international relations are made from afar and not on the ground. Such archival or statistical studies add richly to our understanding of factors involved in political change. Other studies, including this one, are based primarily on field research and add closer perspectives.

The resistance movement in Kenya is examined in the context of both domestic and international politics, including the ending of the Cold War, the role of diplomats, donors and international watchdog agencies in affecting human rights and democracy in Kenya. Both bi-lateral donors and multi-national ones, including the International Monetary Fund and the World Bank played a role in shaping Kenya's human rights and democracy. On several occasions, donors withheld new funding pending reforms; and international agencies such as Amnesty International and Human Rights Watch publicized abuses and brought world attention to the plight of key activists when they were threatened or arrested by the regime. On balance, however, the research shows that in Kenya domestic pressure posed a greater threat to the regime than inconsistent pressures from the diplomatic and donor community and thus provided the primary reason the regime made concessions.

In summary, both institutional and agency factors are considered in this book. But the emphasis is on the role of agency or initiatives by people in the face of institutional barriers. The book points to the need for a greater appreciation of what people can do in the face of difficult and dangerous barriers, or institutional obstacles.

Chapter 1 presents the main theoretical arguments of the book and includes a model that helps explain the findings in Kenya and which can be tested in other authoritarian settings, past or present. Chapter 2 examines Kenya's history of repression and resistance up to 1987, when overt resistance became more evident again in response to state repression. The next four chapters are empirical chapters, examining the work of individual activists (chapter 3), organizational activists (chapters 4 and 5) and mass participation and the shift of norms for a segment of the population from deference to defiance (chapter 6). Chapter 7 is the conclusion with a summary of the findings and their implications for future research. Chapter 8 is the Appendix, which includes a section on how this research was carried out, as well as further examples of the repression that took place in Kenya.

How much can one generalize from a single case study? Historical, cultural, political and other circumstances will differ from country to country. There is no certainty that the Kenya resistance will be mirrored elsewhere; and the study makes no prediction that such resistance leads to more human rights and democracy, or a regime change as happened in Kenya. The author makes no cause and effect prediction that activism results in more democracy. But the Kenya findings show that a resistance movement can pressure some regimes to make reforms. Some scholars may point to a country like Zimbabwe, however, and ask if activism is so important, then why hasn't it brought more human rights and democracy there? This is a good research question for a subsequent study. Some of the factors worth examining in follow-up studies include: what tactics did activists use; did the regime resort to extreme repression to block an activist resistance?

The methodology and focus used in this study can help researchers analyze activism and document early resistance in other authoritarian states; it can help explain how such movements start and how they help establish a culture of resistance. The study's findings are based on a careful review of news accounts and some 70 in-depth interviews, including with most of the key human rights and democracy activists in Kenya between 1987 and 2002, when Kenya's then ruling party suffered its first defeat. It presents a model based on three major domestic elements involved in the establishment of a culture of resistance: first, individual activism; second, organizational activism building on initial concessions won by individual activists; third, and overlapping both of these to some degree, mass public support expressed in open, usually illegal political rallies.

This study treats activism as an independent variable, not beyond the influence of such factors as regime repression, economic hardships and international issues, but not controlled by them either. Regime repression continued to be a catalyst for activism. Each stage of activism helped open wider the door of opportunity for additional resistance to the regime.

*To Betty Press, my wife and partner, whose love, patience,
and inspiration allowed me to complete this project,
and whose photographs from Africa show that we share
the belief in the dignity of people and their ability
to make a better world.*

*To all those in Kenya and elsewhere who have struggled,
often at great risk, to bring greater freedom to their countries.*

Chapter 1

Establishing a Culture of Resistance: Theoretical Perspectives

"Turn it on now," the prison guard said.

Almost immediately a torrent of water from the fire hose hit the naked body of political prisoner and human rights activist Wanyiri Kihoro. Wherever he moved in the basement cell, the guard aimed the hose at him. He screamed in pain but the hosing continued for some four minutes.

When the torture ended, the cell, with a specially raised doorway designed to trap water, was flooded ankle deep. Then guards slammed the cell door shut and turned off the lights.

On three separate occasions, between July 29 and October 10, 1986, he was forced to stay in the flooded cell, once for ten days, twice for seven days each. At first he was given nothing to eat in an attempt to starve him into submission. Each time he was confined in the flooded cell, he stood as long as he could, shifting his weight from one foot to another to keep one out of the water. But eventually, exhausted, he had to sit in the water despite the corroding effect on his buttocks.

Shortly after his secret detention began earlier that year, he had been stripped and beaten with clubs by government guards. They wanted to know about his activism as a university student and later about his contacts with Kenyan dissidents in London where he went for graduate studies. The confession they sought would be used in a sham trial to imprison him for years. Not satisfied with his answers, they resorted to the water torture to break him.

Like many authoritarian African heads of state in the mid-to-late 1980s trying to stem growing agitation for more human rights and democratic freedoms, Kenyan President Daniel Arap Moi, who had survived a coup attempt in 1982, was cracking down on suspected dissidents. Kihoro, an attorney, was one of many Kenyans detained in this period. By the time a group of mothers of detainees began their protest in 1992 in a public park in downtown Nairobi, there were some 50 known political prisoners.

A 1987 report by Amnesty International detailed torture and other abuses in Kenya, including a distortion of the judicial system in an attempt to give the trials of political prisoners an air of legitimacy.

Most of the confessions those brief trials recorded were obtained by torture according to Amnesty's report, based in part on the secretly-written details of his own torture that Kihoro was able to smuggle out eventually after the water torture ended.

African Resistance

Against such repression, a resistance movement was gathering strength in many African countries in the late 1980s and early 1990s. Across much of sub-Saharan Africa the twin pinchers of deteriorating economies and harsh political rule stirred human rights and democracy activists to action. In the next few years, well into the 1990s, lawyers, clergy, students, mothers, opposition politicians and others would take great risks in challenging authoritarian regimes determined to hold onto power. They and the crowds that supported them would face riot police armed with guns, clubs and tear gas. Political opponents faced expulsion from ruling parties and financial ruin; activist leaders faced possible imprisonment and torture.

Yet against these odds, the resistance paid off in many countries. The glacial pace of political reform speeded up; authoritarian, one-party regimes were replaced by multi-party systems. In 1989, only five African states had more than one political party; by 1995, three out of four African states had "competitive party systems." [1]

Though some of the newly elected leaders later became abusive themselves, for the most part they were not as repressive as the old ones. Human rights and democratic freedoms took a major leap forward in the early 1990s in sub-Saharan Africa. The momentum for reform slowed by the mid 1990s, and economies generally continued to languish. And there were exceptions, including Togo and Zimbabwe, whose repressive leaders managed to hold on to power longer than most of their fellow heads of state. But across much of Africa, basic freedoms such as freedom of speech, the right to assemble, and the right to choose one's leaders, are today accepted norms.

How did this happen? What forces or combination of forces led to such changes?

This chapter presents a model or way of explaining how a *culture of resistance* is established, involving individual and organizational activism as well as mass public support at rallies, including illegal rallies. With some modifications, the study uses concepts of social movements to examine the dynamics of human rights and democracy activism, especially in the initial stages of movement formation.

In this book a *culture of resistance* is one in which public challenges to the abuse of power by a regime becomes a norm for activists and a visible segment of the

---

1   Wiseman, John A. 1996. *The New Struggle for Democracy in Africa*. Aldershot, Eng.: Avebury.

general public.[2] The term *social movement* is used to describe the process by which a culture of resistance is established.[3]

---

2   The term resistance, widely used in literature on political change, implies here not just holding firm against repression, but making attempts to advance human rights and democratization. In Kenya the resistance was almost entirely non-violent except for associated rioting; the state, however, consistently used violence to try to stop the resistance.

The term resistance movement is used to depict the various elements of society engaged in seeking greater human rights and democratic freedoms. This term is broad enough to encompass all three categories of activism highlighted in this study: individual, organizational and the general public.

3   There are many definitions of a social movement. In this study, I use a concept identified by Foweraker in theorizing about social movements in Latin America: "...there is some agreement that the social movement must be defined not as a group of any kind but as a process" (Foweraker, Joe. 1995. *Theorizing Social Movements*. London: Pluto Press, 23). That concept is appropriate to Kenya where there was never a formal "movement" to improve human rights and democracy, but there were a small band of individuals, at first, and later, an array of organizations that would meet from time to time to discuss their activism.

Gamson and Meyer suggest that a social movement is a "sustained and self-conscious challenge to authorities or cultural codes by a field of actors" (Gamson, William A., and David S. Meyer. 1996. "Framing Political Opportunity." In *Comparative Perspectives on Social Movements: Political Opportunities, Mobilizing Structures, and Cultural Framings*, eds. Doug McAdam, John D. McCarthy, and Mayer N. Zald. Cambridge: Cambridge University Press, 283).

Tilly defined a social movement as "a sustained interaction between a specific set of authorities and various spokespersons for a given challenge to those authorities." (Tilly, Charles. 1984. "Social Movements and National Politics." In *State Building and Social Movements*. eds, W. Bright and S. Harding. University of Michigan Press: Ann Arbor, 305).

In Kenya, however, the resistance was not "sustained;" there were long lulls between peaks of activism. The resistance was a "self-conscious" challenge to authorities; but there was no "sustained interaction" between authorities and spokespersons for the resistance.

Tarrow's minimum definition of "contentious collective action" comes closer (Tarrow, Sidney. 1998. *Power in Movement: Social Movements and Contentious Politics*. 2nd ed. Cambridge, U. K.: Cambridge University). Those in the resistance movement were engaged in a struggle (one definition of contentious) with the regime, though not always in a "collective" way. The resistance in Kenya began overtly mostly with individual activists. Later there were organizations working together; but opposition political parties were part of the struggle, too, and they were not working together but competing against each other for support. Goodwin and Jasper (Goodwin, Jeff, and James M. Jasper, eds. 2004. *Rethinking Social Movements: Structure, Meaning, and Emotion*. Oxford, U. K.: Rowman & Littlefield, 81) chide political process theorists because they "cannot adequately explain social movements."

The definition of social movement used in this study is not limited to "sustained" challenges or just to some form of "interaction" with authorities in a "contentious" way. The definition used is broad enough to cover a variety of tactics. Though political parties usually are not included in a definition of a social movement, they are in this study, because they represented the main driving force for democratic reforms during much of the study period and were often the main mobilizing force for mass public demonstrations, a key part in the resistance movement.

Despite some excellent statistical studies about events during Africa's move toward greater freedoms, and despite probing studies of the role of civil society in the changing African political climate, few, if any, studies have offered a close-up analysis of the often-dramatic efforts by human rights and democracy activists in the late 1980s and 1990s. One scholar notes a lack of social movement studies focused on activism. "In particular, little attention is given to understanding, and depicting the processes that generate and sustain highly committed activists and that examine systematically the roles such activists play in the movement."[4] In examining how a culture of resistance was established in Kenya, among the findings that come to light is the existence of a pre-organizational phase of activism that this book identifies as individual activism. Though individual activism – unsupported in any significant way by an organization – played a major role in the re-emerging resistance to authoritarian rule in Kenya, it is a concept barely recognized by most of the literature.

This chapter examines various theoretical perspectives regarding the resistance movement that developed in Kenya to authoritarian rule, including a new way of looking at resistance to a regime as a social movement. Social movements normally focus on government policy changes or strengthening particular values in a society. The social movement or resistance movement in Kenya began as a human rights and democratization effort, but it soon focused on a much larger goal: regime change. The concept of resistance movement is used to encompass various elements of political and civil society that are normally analyzed separately.

It should be clearly noted here, as in the preface, that this study does not predict that activism automatically leads to democratic elections. It may or may not. After a period of growing activism, Kenya did have a fair election that saw the ouster of the ruling party. And though this has happened elsewhere, it did not happen everywhere. Regimes using excessive force, for example, can keep an opposition activist movement off balance and even break it up or force it underground.

This book builds on previous studies, adding to an understanding of how a non-violent resistance movement starts, how it operates, how it grows, and the impact it has on human rights and democratic freedoms. Based on extensive interviews in Kenya and a careful search of documents, this book offers a close look at patterns of activism and theoretical explanations that help explain those patterns. Archival research of events and crosschecking the interviews greatly diminished the risk of an interviewee overstating their role in the resistance.

The result is a fresh (and rare) application of social movement theories to an African case. Most social movement studies take as a starting point the existence of such a movement: this one captures the formation phase of a movement. In so doing, it reveals a force almost entirely overlooked in political analyses: individual

---

4   Flacks, Richard. 2004. "Knowledge for What? In *Rethinking Social Movements: Structure, Meaning, and Emotion*, eds. Jeff Goodwin and James M. Jasper. Oxford, U. K.: Rowman & Littlefield, 143; 146.

activism. Though later replaced by organizational activism, individual activism played an important part in resistance in Kenya to authoritarian rule.

This book also provides evidence regarding the importance of domestic resistance in addition to international pressures in bringing about reforms and suggests that sometimes domestic pressure can be more important than international. The combination of domestic and international pressures is seen in what happened to Wanyiri Kihoro, who survived the water torture.

"The physical and mental exertion was traumatic," he later wrote of his ordeal. Somehow Kihoro decided he would not make a confession that would give the government an excuse to imprison him for years. Somehow he resolved to endure the torture and hoped he would survive to be released.

"I was furious at the violation of my legal and human rights in my own country.... The longer they continued to hold me without charge, the more certain I became that they did not have the file which could do the damage. Delay was calling off the police bluff."[5]

At one point in his confinement in a secret basement cell in a government building in downtown Nairobi (Nyayo House), a sympathetic prison guard arranged a brief meeting with Kihoro's wife, Wanjiru, in a car in an adjacent parking lot. There he was able to recount his torture and ask his wife to contact an attorney to represent him. His wife contacted human rights lawyer Gibson Kamau Kuria.

Two other detainees had managed to get word to Kuria asking for representation: Mukaru Ng'ang'a, former university lecturer who died in 1997; and Mirugi Kariuki, another human rights attorney, who, like Kihoro, was later elected to Parliament.

Kuria prepared documents detailing the torture and filed notice February 26, 1987 with the government, as required by the law, that he intended to sue the government to stop the torture and to release the detainees. But the government instead detained Kuria, though they did not torture him.

If the regime thought Kuria's detention would end the matter, it was mistaken. Kuria's law partner, Kiraitu Murungi, refiled the papers.

"I knew that I would be detained on doing it," said Murungi. For the next few days he stayed at home. "Every time a vehicle passed by we thought it was the police and we couldn't sleep for several weeks. But finally nothing happened to me." He attributed this to "the dust which had been kicked up",[6] especially by the international community – more specifically The American Bar Association, The Lawyers Committee for Human Rights and Amnesty International.

And by the *Washington Post*.

Before he filed papers in the case, Kuria briefed *Washington Post* reporter Blain Hardin about the torture in case Kuria, as he anticipated, was detained himself. Hardin wrote the story that his editors published March 13, 1987 with a photo of

---

5   Kihoro, Wanyiri. 1998. *Never Say Die: The Chronicle of a Political Prisoner*. Nairobi, Kenya: East African Educational Publishers, 88–89.

6   Murungi, Kiraitu, in an interview with the author in Nairobi, Kenya, July 2002.

President Moi and US President Ronald Reagan emerging together from the White House. The headline of the story read: "Police Torture is Charged in Kenya."

The President apparently was furious. Hardin was nearly expelled from Kenya. In a rare interview, with Hardin, Moi denied that Kenya practised torture and insisted that any minor incident should not be interpreted as government policy. Amnesty's report makes clear that torture was a regular practise, however.

But the torture of political dissidents soon dropped dramatically. Had Kihoro and the other two detainees not resisted confession; had Kihoro not managed to smuggle out details of his torture; had two attorneys not been willing to take up the case and challenge the government, things might have been different. International pressure certainly helped reduce the torture in Kenya, but the domestic resistance was a critical factor.

Theoretical Perspectives

Human rights and democracy activists can help tame or bring down an authoritarian leader, as they did in Kenya in December 2002. The transition was rapid and peaceful, by way of an election; but the process of resistance leading up to that election took more than a decade. Starting first with individual activism then broadening to include organizational activism, the resistance increasingly attracted domestic public support and some international help.

This chapter examines theoretical perspectives on the overt resistance movement in Kenya from about 1987 to 2002. This case study offers one answer to a puzzle in a world where human rights abuses are increasing and many authoritarian regimes persist: how can people living under a regime that pretends to uphold the principles of human rights and democracy but severely abuses them develop an effective, nonviolent resistance to the regime?

More than a compelling account of political change, the investigation offers insights on a number of current debates in the discipline. For example, it joins a growing debate on a key aspect of political process theory that has been dominant in social movement literature for several decades, one with potentially wide applicability in political science: that "opportunity" for political change depends largely on external structural conditions.[7] This book presents an alternative view:

---

7 The concept of political opportunity structure, part of the political process theory, is credited to a synthesis of the literature by McAdam (McAdam, Doug. 1982. "The Political Process Model." In *Political Process and the Development of Black Insurgency*. Chicago: University of Chicago, Chapter 12.) The structural bias of that process is re-examined in an edited work (Goodwin, Jasper 2004) which includes chapters by McAdam and others credited with advancing the political process theory, including Charles Tilly and Sidney Tarrow, and their critics.

that political change can come primarily as the result of individual initiative in spite of negative external structural conditions.[8]

This work also marks one of the few times that political process theories have been examined in a developing country and not in the usual "context of advanced industrial democracies…. The degree to which these theories are applicable to the rest of the world is not known."[9] And the inductive examination of what happened in Kenya is one of the few to look at activism from the ground up, probing the dynamics of resistance at various points over a period of time.[10]

Structural constraints, or unfavorable background conditions, do play a part, as the literature reminds us.[11] This book does not ignore structural factors such as regime behavior, the economy, international support and geopolitical issues; but it argues that rather than waiting for a change in external factors to provide an opportunity for resistance, activists often create opportunities.

The research for this book led to a model to help explain how a culture of resistance is established in an authoritarian regime and suggests that the concepts it presents offer a way of viewing the role of activists in past or contemporary democratic transitions, whether successful or not, in other countries.[12] Activism is treated primarily as an independent variable, though it is also a dependent variable in terms of regime repression. Regime behavior is treated as both a dependent variable (in terms of concessions to activism and international support for reform) and as an

---

8   The debate over the extent of political process theory being biased toward structural explanations is part of a larger and longer debate over whether structure or agency influences political change more, a debate which has been growing "in recent years" (Hay, Colin. 2002. *Political Analysis: A Critical Introduction*. Houndmills, U. K.: Palgrave, 89).

9   Meyer, David S. 2004. "Tending the Vineyard: Cultivating Political Process Research. In *Rethinking Social Movements: Structure, Meaning, and Emotion*, eds. Jeff Goodwin and James M. Jasper. Oxford, U. K.: Rowman & Littlefield, 57.

10   In an extensive literature review, the author has found no similar study in Africa or Latin America, though there are some studies (cited later in this chapter) of activists in Latin America, including a political-psychological analysis of activists. Many studies take as a starting point the existence of a social movement of some kind. Zamosc (1994), for example, in his study of agrarian protests by Indians in the Ecuadorian Highlands cites as the key to their efforts the existence of an umbrella organization that represented them in their demands. One study that does document formation of a more spontaneous resistance group is Schneider's (1999) study of shantytown resistance in authoritarian Chile.

11   Among scholars making this point are:
Andrain, Charles F., and David E. Apter. 1995. *Political Protest and Social Change: Analyzing Politics*. New York: New York University Press; Tarrow, 1998; Hyden, Goran. 2002 "Development and Democracy: An Overview." In *Development and Democracy: What have we learned and how?* eds. Ole Elgström and Goran Hyden. London: Routledge.

12   In any society, there are some historical roots of resistance, as there was in Kenya (chapter 2). This study focuses on a relatively brief time period, however, starting when there were few overt signs of a culture of resistance, when the norm for almost everyone was deference to a regime abusing human rights and democratic principles.

independent variable (in terms of repression). Both regime repression and activism are the driving forces in the model.

The study argues that rational choice fails to offer an adequate explanation of motives of activists in the early stages of resistance whose risks far outweigh potential benefits. In later stages of resistance when there was less danger and more employment and political opportunities related to human rights and democratization, self-interest may be a more likely explanation for some activists. But rational choice also fails to explain why some members of the general public and not others stepped forward to join public protests, given that most Kenyans had roughly the same knowledge of the political nature of the regime and the risks in challenging it.

There was much working against the activists, particularly regime repression, that one might assume would have discouraged resistance. But as the model of resistance presented below suggests, and as the empirical evidence will show, resistance often was carried out in the face of repression. At times resistance seemed to be stimulated by repression, a phenomenon some scholars have documented[13] and which will be discussed.

This study argues for a consideration of the power of ideas, as well as idealism, in analyzing why activists, especially in the most dangerous, early phase, and members of the general public, took the risks they did. Yet ideas often are not part of our analyses of political change, as one scholar of human rights notes: "It is a paradox that scholars whose entire existence is centered on the production and understanding of ideas, would grant ideas so little significance for explaining political life."[14]

Though it is beyond the scope of this research to provide a thorough examination of the question of prediction in political science, the empirical evidence will show that in this case, at least, and possibly in similar social movements, if one examines the initial stages of resistance, there is little predictable about it. The work of early activists often depends on the intervention and help of minor actors who are not even aware of the important role they play. For this and other reasons that will be presented, this work makes no prediction that a culture of resistance leads inevitably to reforms, much less regime change. But the study makes one modest prediction: that if the methodology and analytical approach applied to the Kenya case are applied in roughly similar settings, similar patterns of resistance are likely to be discovered. Where a culture of resistance is established, reforms are more likely to occur unless the regime fights back with massive repression.

In focusing on activism, the author pursues a question generally given little attention in the social movement literature: how does a movement actually start? Many studies focus on how one is attracted to an ongoing social movement, or how, when structural conditions are favorable, a movement advances, but not how one

---

13 Piven, Frances Fox, and Richard Cloward. 1977. *Poor People's Movements*. New York: Vintage.

14 Sikkink, Kathryn. 1991. *Ideas and Institutions: Developmentalism in Argentina and Brazil*. Ithaca, NY.: Cornell University Press, 3.

begins. In a contribution to our knowledge of social movements, this study focuses in some depth on the very first steps of how a movement is started, building on Tarrow's concept of "early risers." Tarrow introduces the concept but does not develop it or provide empirical evidence of how it can work as this book does.[15] To distinguish between Tarrow's limited use of the idea and the broader development of the role of initial instigators in resistance movement, this study uses the term "early resisters".

By focusing on the role of human rights activists and how human rights are used as a way of advancing democratization, the research also adds to our knowledge of democratic transitions. It suggests a new analytical concept that brings together the various elements of society seeking democratization and/or greater respect for human rights, including: formal civil society organizations; informal networks; individual activists; social movements; and opposition political parties (see below).

The preponderance of literature on transitions focuses on the role of elites inside or outside of a regime and specifically on negotiations and pact making.[16] O'Donnell and Schmitter's 1986 work is an often-cited example of this kind of transition explanation.[17] But pact making does "not resemble the African experience in the 1990s" in democratic transitions.[18] In the case of Kenya the transition was not a matter of elite negotiating or pact-making but involved confrontations between elites and the regime. It also involved an important role by civil society organizations, political society (opposition parties) and the general public. Even though these actors are usually cited in the literature, it is normally not with much attention on how the process of resistance begins.

Research Design

The research design (see Appendix A for details) included the following: an archival review of major political resistance events to note the events and key participants and leaders; approximately 70 interviews, almost all in person and about half of them with Kenyan human rights/democracy activists identified by the archival review and a snowball technique of asking the well-known activists to help identify other key

---

15 Tarrow, *Power in Movement*, 145. Tarrow mentions briefly the "demonstration effect' of a group of early risers that "triggers a variety of processes of diffusion, extension, imitation, and reaction among groups that are normally more quiescent and have fewer resources to engage in collective action." But he does not carry the concept further.

16 South Africa's transition is a notable exception and involved several years of negotiations and pact making between leaders of the black majority and the white minority government.

17 O'Donnell, Guillermo, and Philippe C. Schmitter. 1986. *Transitions from Authoritarian Rule: Tentative Conclusions about Uncertain Democracies*. Baltimore: Johns Hopkins University Press.

18 Lindberg, Staffan. 2002. "Problems of measuring democracy: Illustrations from Africa. In *Development and Democracy: What have we learned and how?* eds. Ole Elgström and Goran Hyden. London: Routledge, 135.

activists; and a review of international donor assistance levels. The interviews, many of them lasting more than one hour, were taped and the transcriptions combed for connecting themes and patterns.

Coming at a time of mostly pessimistic assessments of Africa's political circumstances and the slowing down of democratization after a surge in the early 1990s, the Kenya findings are much more positive than continental conditions would seem to warrant. They show how people can take steps to reduce repression and advance democratic governance. The "principled ideas" that Keck and Sikkink write about[19] that drive human rights movements were evident in Kenya, especially among the early resisters who took big risks.[20] In extensive interviews with key activists, corroborated by archival accounts and an assessment of the dangers involved, the study finds that courage, principle, and idealism played an important part in the process, especially among early resisters.

But the author also takes notice of more negative aspects of resistance, including self-serving motives of some activists, strategies of repression by the regime, and notes the possibility that having achieved their immediate goal of regime change, activists have no guarantees that the momentum for democratization will not stall under a new regime.

It is important to note that the author does not claim or predict that a culture of resistance leads inevitably to regime change or even major reforms. Extreme repression can push such resistance underground, though this risks turning a nonviolent movement into a violent one, something authoritarian leaders have to calculate. The study does suggest that political change is more likely in a society where a culture of resistance has been established and is active.

Study Questions

The Kenya research began with a question: why did a reluctant authoritarian regime make some key concessions in terms of greater practice of human rights and democracy? This led to another question: how do individuals and organizations in civil society resist an authoritarian government and try to force it to make concessions on an issue such as human rights? In Kenya, individual and organizational human rights activists, sometimes with support from international organizations, pressured an authoritarian government for concessions and won some.

Several subsequent questions arise in such cases: under what conditions do elements of civil society win concessions in human rights and democratization; what conditions prevent further gains? What are the main characteristics of the domestic

---

19 Keck, Margaret E. and Kathryn Sikkink. 1998. *Activists Beyond Borders: Advocacy Networks in International Politics*. Ithaca: Cornell University Press, 119.

20 Political scientists are often hesitant to consider courage, idealism, principle and other non-material motives in assessing political issues. In a recent work re-assessing the dominant paradigms in social movement theory (Goodwin and Jasper 2004), one author (Gould) argues that passion and emotion should be brought back into the study of movements.

activists (both individual and organizational) and what motivates them to take risks? How do the changing domestic and international political dynamics affect what these actors can do and how the state responds? What role do mass participation and support of activists, international agencies and donors play in the advancement of human rights and democracy in an authoritarian state?

Varied Literature on the Dynamics of Resistance

There is no one body of literature that describes the process of resistance that took place in Kenya. One has to draw on a variety of literature and themes such as social movements; the debate over agency vs. structure in political protests and mobilization; democratization and civil society; motivational explanations; and the concept of political learning.

Constraint and Opportunity Theories Re-examined

Because the resistance model developed contrasts with the structure of political opportunity[21] concept of the political process theory, it is worth briefly examining what that theory is and how others, including some of its main proponents, have begun reassessing it. The structural emphasis in explaining social movements has been "dominant now for thirty years." [22]

The political process model is credited to a synthesis of the literature by sociologist Doug McAdam.[23] It is an advance over the resource mobilization model, which focused on necessary resources but without analyzing the political circumstances that could help explain why some groups were more successful than others having the same resources. Rather than looking inward at the resources of a movement, as the earlier theory suggested, political process theorists examined both internal and external factors that affect a social movement.

For more than two decades, many social movement theorists, including Tarrow, have accepted the political process model.[24] Social insurgency, McAdam argued, was dependent on "the confluence of expanding political opportunities, indigenous organizational strength... the presence of certain shared cognitions within the minority community ... (and) the shifting control response of other groups to the movement."[25] The ebb and flow of social movement activity depends, McAdam

---

21 The term political opportunity derives from Peter Eisinger (1973).

22 Goodwin and Jasper, vii.

23 McAdam, Doug. 1982. "The Political Process Model." In *Political Process and the Development of Black Insurgency*. Doug McAdam. Chicago: University of Chicago.

24 The term "political process" was popularized by Doug McAdam's 1982 book on black protest movements in the US, but as he acknowledged, he took the term from an article by Rule and Tilly (Rule, James, and Charles Tilly. 1975. "Political Process in Revolutionary France, 1830–1832." In *1830 in France*. ed., John M. Merriman. New York: New Viewpoints).

25 McAdam, *Political Process*, 190.

argued, on shifts in the structure of political opportunities. And what causes those shifts? The likely events and processes that cause such shifts, he stated, include "wars, industrialization, international political realignments, prolonged unemployment, and widespread demographic changes." These are "broad social processes" that operate over a long time.[26]

But at what point does such a condition in society spark the start of resistance? The answer is not clear. And much of the work of the "process paradigm has been theoretical, with less empirical testing than practitioners of the paradigm tend to admit," Goodwin and Jasper note.[27] Table 1.1, though a static representation, illustrates the basics of the opportunities and constraints concept.

Table 1.1   Domestic and global constraints and opportunities[28]

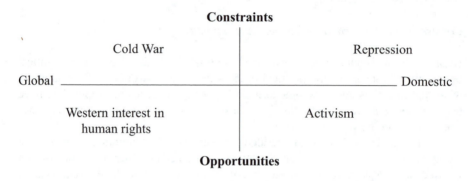

Political process theory, while addressing the political and economic opportunities and constraints in which a movement operates, is incomplete. It analyzes the big pieces of a puzzle but does not provide an adequate explanation of how the little pieces come together, how individuals and groups actually take advantage of the opportunities and constraints.

The political process leaves people largely dependent for opportunities arising from external events. But as the Kenya case shows, activists are capable of resisting and working with others to launch a movement in the face of discouraging structural challenges. The political process approach misses much of the creativity of man, the stubbornness, the daring and courage, which, even if for self-interest, defies easy analysis.

---

26 McAdam, *Political Process*, 176; 177.

27 Goodwin and Jasper, *viii*.

28 Suggested by University of Florida Professor of Political Science Goran Hyden, the author or editor of numerous books on human rights, in a conversation with the author in 2003.

Individual initiative is not necessarily dependent on large-scale societal conditions. Activists need not wait for major disruptions in the political status quo to begin to try to change things themselves through use of pressure tactics and overt criticism of a regime. Political process theory leaves individual initiative in launching a resistance movement dependent on large-scale, often long-lasting structural circumstances in society. Tarrow's theory of contentious politics, for example, pays little heed as to how activist organizations that are supposed to take advantage of new opportunities are formed in the first place. Instead of waiting for changes in political opportunities and constraints, as Tarrow and others suggest, individual activists may, as in the case of Kenya, plunge forward into the messy and unpredictable waters of resistance in the face of unfavorable structural constraints.

Some scholars, including McAdam, Sidney Tarrow, and Charles Tilly, have been rethinking their earlier structural explanations.[29] They have begun paying more attention to cultural factors and initiatives by activists. McAdam notes: "Movements are held to arise as a result of the fortuitous confluence of external political opportunities and internal organization and framing processes. At root this is a structuralist account of movement emergence (similar to the one he introduced in 1982) … I am increasingly aware of the limits of the framework and the often wooden manner in which it has been applied by movement scholars…. I have now come to regard this singular preoccupation with opportunity as excessively narrow." [30] Tarrow, writing in the same edited book, notes: "Our hope is to challenge our own political process models by confronting them with new and more demanding contexts and different theoretical traditions."[31]

In a jointly-authored book, *Dynamics of Contention* (2001), McAdam, Tarrow, and Tilly go beyond the more static model of social movements they helped create to a dynamic model with the primary focus no longer aimed just on the state and those challenging it. Instead, a more fluid analysis is offered that examines relationships between the various groups and forces in society involved in challenging the status quo or defending it, including relations between various challenging groups. They zoom their lens out for a wider focus on contention in politics, including historical

---

29 McAdam says he now would pay more attention to international and transnational factors (McAdam, Doug. 2004. "Revisiting the US Civil Rights Movement: Toward a More Synthetic Understanding of the Origins of Contention. In *Rethinking Social Movements: Structure, Meaning, and Emotion.* Oxford, U. K.: Rowman & Littlefield.)

Goodwin and Jasper examine McAdam's revised version of political process, however (McAdam, Doug, John D. McCarthy, and Mayer N. Zald. eds. 1996. *Comparative Perspectives on Social Movements: Political Opportunities, Mobilizing Structures, and Cultural Framings.* Cambridge: Cambridge University Press.) Goodwin and Jasper argue that McAdam's revision retains "a structural bias … people's intentions, choices, and discretion disappear in a mechanical play of structures" (Goodwin, Jasper, 9).

30 McAdam in Jasper and Goodwin, *Rethinking Social Movements*, 204–205.

31 Tarrow, Sidney. 2004. "Tending the vineyard: cultivating political process research. In Goodwin, Jeff, and James M. Jasper, eds. 2004. *Rethinking Social Movements: Structure, Meaning, and Emotion.* Oxford, U. K.: Rowman & Littlefield, 45.

context, but also zoom it in for a closer look at often over-looked relationships among the principal actors.[32]

They call for more case research using a dynamic model of contention, which is what the Kenya case does with its multiple-focus, use of historical context, and probing of how one group's actions affected another in the contentious struggle for greater human rights and democracy. At the same time, the Kenya research found a greater ability of activists to shape their own future than most scholars have detected in studying social or resistance movements.

But Goodwin and Jasper argue that political process theory minimizes the role of activists. "[A]ctivists can sometimes create their own opportunities and mobilizing structures. Strategic decisions depend heavily on interaction among movements and other players (especially, but not exclusively, their opponents and the state), and this interaction is strongly shaped by the expectations that each side has of the other."[33]

The Kenya study argues that this is similar to what happened in Kenya, where early resisters created their own opportunities by forging ahead with activism despite unfavorable conditions in society. By setting an example and winning some concessions, their activism in turn provided opportunities or openings for organizational activists who in turn organized activities that provided an opportunity for a portion of the general public to express their dissent, shifting from deference to the regime to open defiance.

The structural constraints activists may be operating under can include the strength of a state's security apparatus (police, military, paramilitary forces, intelligence system); the willingness of a regime to use force to overcome opposition; geopolitical realities (e.g., Cold War-era support from the West for authoritarian regimes because they were not Communist); ethnic rivalries that tend to divide people and thus weaken reform efforts; poor economies that might render some too busy making a living to join protests; or a tenuous middle class that is too vulnerable to losing material possessions to take risks. As we will see, activism in Kenya took place in the face of such constraints. And the concessions that followed energized activists to push for more reforms. They interpreted such initial reforms – sincere or not – as a sign of vulnerability of the regime, a willingness to change when pressured enough. As Alexis de Tocqueville noted, "The most perilous moment

---

32 McAdam, Doug, Sidney Tarrow, Charles Tilly. 2001. *Dynamics of Contention.* Cambridge: Cambridge University Press. In an email to the author in November 2005, Tarrow noted that political process theory was "overly structural and eluding agency," but that its "major failing was that it was NOT a theory of process but was entirely static ... [T]he goal of the revised political process theory in *Dynamics of Contention* and related work by McAdam, Tilly and myself, is a serious attempt to transcend the sterile division between agency and structure by a REAL focus on process, and particularly on the social mechanisms that bring about change ... [W]hat we intended the book to show [was] that attention to mechanism and processes can overcome the distortions of excessive voluntarism and excessive structuralism...

33 Goodwin and Jasper, *Rethinking Social Movements*, 28.

for a bad government is one when it seeks to mend its ways."[34] Most literature on social movements begins with the existence of a social movement. It does not deal with resistance at the level of the individual.[35] If there are already organizations of resistance, they can take advantage of new "opportunities," such as the breakdown of a state's "administrative and military power," which may lead to a revolution;[36] or a negotiated "pact" between reformists and outgoing military rulers.[37] But what happens when there are no preexisting organizations of resistance; and where there are no negotiations or pact making?

I ask how the spark is lit in a resistance movement; what starts the resistance? Who starts it? What tactics do activists use? The in-depth interviews with 70 Kenyan activists and other analysts plus archival records provide some answers.[38] The details and patterns that emerge offer a nuanced and revealing insight on resistance not easily detectable through archival works or those based on a theory of personal grievance or deprivation as a motive for joining a movement,[39] or works that focus heavily on international influences.[40]

A Different Approach to Cycles

Tarrow suggests that contention occurs in cycles, with increasingly active social movements responding to "opportunities and constraints" but eventually declining in force and likely evolving into institutionalized protest, becoming a part of the system.[41] His focus on cycles of contention helped bridge a gap in the literature among three groups of scholars, as Tarrow points out, who studied cycles of entire systems: (1) cultural theorists who see culture as the cause of change; (2) political historians; and (3) historical economists. "The first group of scholars emphasizes the globality of cycles, the second their regularity, and the third their derivation from

---

34 Tocqueville, A. de. 1955. *The Old Regime and the French Revolution.* Translated by S. Gilbert. Garden City, N.J.: Doubleday, 176–7.

35 Keck and Sikkink; Tarrow, Sidney. 1998. *Power in Movement: Social Movements and Contentious Politics.* 2nd ed. Cambridge, U. K.: Cambridge University; Risse, Thomas, Stephen C. Ropp, and Kathryn Sikkink, eds. 1999. *The Power of Human Rights: International Norms and Domestic Change.* Cambridge: Cambridge University Press.

36 Skocpol, Theda. 1979. *States and Social Revolutions: A Comparative Analysis of France, Russia, and China.* Cambridge: Cambridge University Press, 285.

37 O'Donnell and Schmitter, 1986.

38 There are some works based on in-depth interviews with activists, but they tend to take a political psychology approach toward the motivations of the actors. This provides valuable insights but does not shed much light on the process by which such commitment is actually carried out and it tends to minimize the difference between organizational and individual activism.

39 An example of this kind of literature is: Gurr, Ted Robert. 1970. *Why Men Rebel.* Princeton: Princeton University Press.

40 An example of this kind of literature is: Risse, Ropp, and Sikkink.

41 Tarrow, *Power in Movement*, 71 and chapter 9.

configurations of structural change." Tarrow adds that while all three are useful, they examine "the progression *between* waves of contention [emphasis in original]" and seldom examine the dynamic of the cycle itself.[42] Tarrow provides a critical advance in the analysis of social movements with his attention to the dynamics of cycles.

The Kenya study builds on Tarrow's foundational conceptualization of cycles but has empirical findings, uses a different model to explain resistance, and differs with some of his arguments. Tarrow's 1998 book is mostly a theoretical analysis, while a book by Meyer and Tarrow the same year includes case studies that test the cycles theory.[43] But the studies in both works take as a starting point the existence of a social movement that then has a cycle of rise and decline. Tarrow's theorizing on contention envisions an organized and forward-moving progression from start to climax to decline. The initial phase of resistance in Kenya was a much more fragile process than Tarrow envisions, as the empirical evidence will show.

The Kenya research found different dynamics and, for the relatively brief period examined (approximately 16 years), a different pattern of cycles.[44] The pattern in the Kenya case was much more uneven, more a series of mini-cycles of resistance with activism increasing in election years. Activism faded considerably when opposition political parties and non governmental organizations did not have an election issue to stir up excitement. The process resembles the term developed in biology and applied to political science by Stephen D. Krasner: "punctuated equilibrium."[45] As applied in political analysis it refers to a "discontinuous conception of political time in which periods of comparatively modest institutional change are interrupted by more rapid and intense moments of transformations." But an even more accurate term is "punctuated evolution ... which draws attention to the cumulative nature of often incremental change." [46]

"Punctuated evolution" is also a better description of the accumulation effect of activism in Kenya that encouraged further activism. Even after a pause, or lull of several years, renewed and more intense activism emerged, building on previous resistance. Those challenging the regime did not slip back to previous levels of engagement after each lull; they applied lessons learned in earlier confrontations and moved ahead. This evolution was a process of learning, which is discussed below. The concept of evolution here is not to be confused with a Whig-like, inevitable march toward greater and greater resistance or success. There was no inevitability to it; and success was never guaranteed. The cycles could repeat if, for example, concessions were followed by sharply increased repression.

---

42 Tarrow, *Power in Movement*, 143.

43 Meyer, David S., and Sidney Tarrow. 1998. *The Social Movement Society: Contentious Politics for a New Century*. Lanham, MD.: Rowman & Littlefield.

44 It is possible that over a longer period the cycles detected in Kenya may more closely resemble the long-term rise and decline pattern Tarrow describes in his 1998 work (*Power in Movement*).

45 Krasner, Stephen. 1984 "Approaches to the State: Alternative Conceptions and Historical Dynamics." *Comparative Politics* (16):223–246.

46 Hay, 161; 163.

At the same time, the Kenya study suggests, the accumulated effect of the acts of resistance first by individuals and later organizations drew a significant segment of the public into open protest in defiance of the still very authoritarian regime, one that did not hesitate to use force to block protests. The organizational phase is also much more uncertain than implied in the almost deterministic accounts by Tarrow and some others. There is no curvilinear progression from start to climax to decline. The process has mini-cycles within cycles, with an uncertain outcome.

Civil Society and a Conceptual Framework: "Resistance Movement"

Civil society has often played "a crucial role if not the leading role, in producing a transition to democracy." It was the outpouring of hundreds of thousands of citizens in Manila "to reclaim their stolen [1986] election that enabled the rebellion of military reformers to survive in the Philippines" and force Ferdinand Marcos from power.[47] A year later in South Korea, a coalition of students, workers, and middle class business and professional groups, along with opposition politicians, forced the authoritarian regime to agree to direct election of the President.[48]

There have been numerous studies of democratization in Africa since the Cold War ended in 1989 that include analyses of the strengths and weaknesses of civil society.[49] But in comparison to Latin America, there are few studies of social movements in sub-Saharan Africa and even fewer on informal, presocial movement forms of resistance. Bratton and van de Walle's 1997 study is one of the few to examine transitions to democracy in sub-Saharan Africa.[50] But while their archival research does quantify variables associated with political protests and transitions, they do not examine the dynamics of a resistance movement itself nor how one starts, which this book does.

In highlighting the resistance of informal networks and individual resistance outside the usual group-focused concept of civil society, the Kenya investigation

---

47 Diamond, Larry. 1999. *Developing Democracy: Toward Consolidation*. Baltimore. Johns Hopkins University Press, 99 and 235.

48 Hsin-Huang, Michael Hsiao, and Hagen Koo. 1997. "The Middle Classes and Democratization." In *Consolidating the Third Wave Democracies: Themes and Perspectives*, eds. Larry Diamond, Marc F. Plattner, Yun-han Chu, and Hung-mao Tien. Baltimore: Johns Hopkins University Press, 312–333.

49 Examples of this literature include the following: Chazan, Naomi, Robert Mortimer, John Ravenhill, and Donald Rothchild. 1992. *Politics and Society in Contemporary Africa*, 2nd ed. Boulder, CO.: Lynne Rienner; Harbeson, John W., Donald Rothchild, and Naomi Chazan, eds. 1994. *Civil Society and the State in Africa*. Boulder, CO.: Lynne Rienner; Ottaway Marina, ed. 1997. *Democracy in Africa: The Hard Road Ahead*. Boulder, CO.: Lynne Rienner; Hyden, Goran. 2000. "The Governance Challenge in Africa." In *African Perspectives on Governance*, eds. Goran Hyden, Dele Olowu, Hastings W. O. Okoth Ogendo. Trenton, N. J.: Africa World Press, 2000.

50 Bratton, Michael, and Nicolas van de Walle. 1997. *Democratic Experiments in Africa: Regime Transitions in Comparative Perspective*. Cambridge: Cambridge University Press.

questions whether too much emphasis has been placed on the role of formal elements of civil society, the organizations, in pushing for human rights and democracy. This work suggests that formal civil society in the initial stages of public resistance to an authoritarian regime is not strong enough to challenge the regime effectively. Instead, individuals only very loosely a part of informal networks of activists may begin the process. Too often researchers apply Western concepts of a strong civil society to Africa, as Kasfir warns, which doesn't always work.[51]

Putnam takes a very broad approach, including a wide variety of associational life that he sees as an important cultural basis for democracy. He writes: "Networks of civic engagement, like the neighborhood associations, choral societies, cooperatives, sports clubs, mass-based parties, and the like ... represent intense horizontal interaction. Networks of civic engagement are an essential form of social capital..."[52] But while such associations may provide a backdrop that enhances democracy, at least according to Putnam, many such groupings have little to do with the striving for improvement in human rights and democracy, the actual day-to-day strategizing and resistance in an authoritarian regime.

Diamond offers this definition of civil society: "...the realm of organized social life that is open, voluntary, self-generating, at least partially self-supporting, autonomous from the state, and bound by a legal order or set of shared rules." He goes on to point out that civil society is distinct from society in general in several ways: "...it involves citizens acting collectively in a public sphere to express their interests, passions, preferences, and ideas, to exchange information, to achieve collective goals, to make demands on the state, to improve the structure and functioning of the state, and to hold state officials accountable."[53]

In other words, it is political, seeking political change, making demands on the state, which, in an authoritarian state, is likely to put them in confrontation with the state. This is a much narrower definition than Putnam uses, but it brings us closer to the process by which change occurs, not the cultural setting (a historically-based, deterministic setting) that enhances democracy, Putnam's focus.

Civil Society, a "Troublesome Concept"

Despite the volume of literature that has been written on civil society, one scholar finds it a "troublesome concept" in the study of democratization because it tends

---

51 Kasfir argues that too often academics and donors "import into Africa their notion of how civil society works in Western Democracies." They should beware of putting too much emphasis on a strong civil society in the democratization process, he adds. If civil society organizations are too strong, they can pose a problem "by making it more difficult for African states to reconcile competing social interests." Kasfir, Nelson, ed. 1998. *Civil Society and Democracy in Africa: Critical Perspectives*. London: Frank Cass.

52 Putnam, Robert D. 1993. *Making Democracy Work: Civic Traditions in Modern Italy*. Princeton: Princeton University Press, 173.

53 Diamond, Larry. 1999. *Developing Democracy: Toward Consolidation*. Baltimore. Johns Hopkins University Press, 221.

to lump together associations seeking political change with those that are not.[54] Building on this observation, one can see several other theoretical problems in the way the literature tends to separate elements of society working for democratization and human rights:

Formal vs. informal associations. Many Africans are likely to pay more attention to informal associations than formal ones. "In Africa [m]uch associational life and all unorganized protest or demands must occur outside civil society."[55] If one counts only formal associations as playing a critical role in democratization, many people will be missed. Also, a narrow concept focusing just on groups misses the important contribution of early resisters who are individual activists operating with little or no help from organizations or formal associations.

Social movements. They are "typically more concerned with realizing specific values than putting a particular regime in place."[56] But the resistance in Kenya had the markings of a social movement and they were focused on democratization – and regime change. Social movements in Africa in authoritarian settings often focus on democratization and regime change. Most Kenyans felt the only way to reach democracy was to have a change of regime. Here the typical Western concept of a social movement limited to influencing government rather than taking it over does not work.

Opposition political parties. Often political parties are not counted as part of civil society but are considered in a separate category. Yet in authoritarian settings, opposition political parties often take the lead in democratization. Even when they win seats in a national legislature, they still try to take control. Winning the presidency in an authoritarian setting involves more than a change of parties; it may involve a dramatic shift away from authoritarian rule to democratic.

In authoritarian settings, there is a need for an analytical concept that combines these forces: civil society democratization-focused groups; informal networks; individual activists; social movements aimed at democratization; and opposition political parties. Findings from Kenya suggest a unifying concept may be more helpful in analyzing the push for human rights and democratization in an authoritarian setting.

This book suggests that these forces comprise a *resistance movement*, not in the formal sense of a movement with membership and elected leaders, but in the informal sense of various elements of society that focus on democratization and/or human rights by way of public challenges to the regime.

By focusing less on the formal positions of various elements of society and more on their goals, one can begin to analyze the effectiveness of the resistance as a whole

---

54 Hyden, *Development and Democracy*, 16.
55 Kasfir, 127.
56 Hyden, *Development and Democracy*, 18.

instead of in pieces. Using a unifying concept such as a *resistance movement*, the analysis is more complete by considering various elements of the movement. This focus on purpose rather than place in society helps overcome some of the artificial and unhelpful analytical boundaries that have hindered analysis of human rights and democratization efforts.

Human Rights and Transition

The Kenya study adds to the general knowledge of how human rights activism is used to advance a transition to democracy. One scholar notes that "the literature on the human rights situation in East Africa or Nigeria is relatively scant."[57] Most of the Kenyans who were individual human rights activists in the early stages of the resistance of the late 1980s and early 1990s became democracy advocates as organizational activists. Some activists sought democracy and regime change all along, while a few continued to focus on human rights the entire period. This study suggests that human rights and democracy should be examined together in democratic transition analyses as some scholars of Kenya have done.[58] In looking at how human rights and democracy are connected, it may be instructive to start by asking whether it would be possible to have a non democratic State that promotes human rights or, in the reverse, whether a State structured in such a way that it is involved in systematic denials and violations of human rights can be regarded as democratic.[59]

Most analyses of democracy and transitions fall into one of two main categories: (1) studies that assume "structural" conditions in society are the key – including the economy or political institutions; (2) studies that assume human initiative (agency) is the key in combination with either the economy or political institutions.[60] The focus on activism and human rights in a democratic transition falls into an agency/institutions category. But it differs from most such studies. Most transitions in Africa, including Kenya, did not involve negotiations among elites in the outgoing regime and elites in a reform movement that Rustow, and O'Donnell and Schmitter

---

57 Kakwenzire, Joan. 2000. "Human Rights and Governance." In *African Perspectives on Governance*, eds. Goran Hyden, Dele Olowu, Hastings W. O. Okoth Ogendo. Trenton, N. J.: Africa World Press, 65.

58 Examples of this literature include: Barkan, Joel D. 2001. "US Human Rights Policy and Democratization in Kenya." Manuscript; Gutto, Shadrack B. O. 1993. *Human and People's Rights for the Oppressed: Critical Essays on Theory and Practice from Sociology of Law Perspectives*. Lund, Sweden: Lund University Press.

59 Gutto, 134.

60 One can identify certain studies with each category. For example: (1) structure/economy (e.g., Geddes 1999; Lipset 1959; Moore [1966] 1993; Przeworski, et al. 1996; Rueschemeyer, Stephens and Stephens 1992); (2) structure/institutions (e.g., Dahl 1971; Putnam 1993; Steinmo et al 1992); (3) Agency/economy (e.g., Bates 1981; Ingelhart 1977; 1988; 1990; Przeworski 1991); (4) agency/institutions (e.g., Almond, Verba 1963; Downs 1957; Huntington 1991; O'Donnell, Schmitter 1986; Rustow 1970; Tocqueville 1955).

write about.[61] Huntington, too, argues that transitions normally begin at the top, specifically within the authoritarian regime itself. He identifies several dynamics that may operate during a transition, including the dynamic between the regime and opponents (though he does not go into detail); the dynamics between reformers and "standpatters" in government; and the dynamic between moderates and extremists in the opposition.[62] Huntington reminds us, as does the categorization of literature above, that there are numerous ways to analyze a transition to democracy. The current study is only one of those ways.

Mobilization and Political Protests

An important element in the establishment of a culture of resistance is the shift of norms from deference to defiance that a portion of the public experiences, giving added weight to the activists" claims to be representing many people. The most common demonstration of this mental shift on the part of some Kenyans was participation in a public protest for better human rights or democratization, including attending an opposition rally. Many theoretical works have included arguments about a change of political consciousness that leads someone to join a public protest.[63] Some other works, especially on Latin America, examine indigenous protest movements.[64]

Piven and Cloward argued that social movements entail "a transformation both of consciousness and of behavior," in other words a change of ideas and a change of actions. The change in consciousness, they described, involves three aspects, all of which were seen in Kenya: (1) a loss of "legitimacy" of the rulers; (2) people previously "fatalistic" begin to assert their rights and demand change; (3) people shift from feeling helpless to believing that they can "alter their lot."[65] McAdam

---

61 Rustow, Dankwart. 1970. "Transitions to Democracy: Toward a Dynamic Model." *Comparative Politics* 2(3):337–363; O'Donnell, Guillermo, and Philippe C. Schmitter. 1986. *Transitions from Authoritarian Rule: Tentative Conclusions about Uncertain Democracies.* Baltimore: Johns Hopkins University Press.

62 Huntington, Samuel P. 1991. *The Third Wave: Democratization in the Late Twentieth Century.* Norman, OK.: University of Oklahoma, 127; 123.

63 Examples of this literature include: Piven, and Cloward, 1977 ; Melucci, Alberto, 1994. "A Strange Kind of Newness: What's 'New' in New Social Movements?" In *New Social Movements: From Ideology to Identity,* eds. Laraña, Enrique, Hank Johnston, and Joseph R. Gusfield. Philadelphia: Temple University Press; Foweraker, Joe. 1995. *Theorizing Social Movements.* London: Pluto Press.

64 Examples of this literature include: Salman, Ton. 1994. "The Different Movement: Generation and Gender in the Vicissitudes of the Chilean Shantytown Organizations, 1973–1990. *Latin American Perspectives* 21(3):8–31; Zamosc, Leon. 1994. "Agrarian Protest and the Indian Movement in the Ecuadorian Highlands." *Latin American Research Review* 29(3):237–252; Crain, Mary. 1990. "The Social Construction of National Identity in Highland Ecuador," *Anthropological Quarterly* 63:43–59, January; Schneider, Cathy. 1999. "Mobilization at the Grassroots: Shantytowns and Resistance in Authoritarian Chile. *Latin American Perspectives* 18(1):92–112.

65 Piven and Cloward, 3–4.

argued that the emergence of a social movement requires that people must feel their situation is "unjust and subject to change through group action." He referred to this shift of norms as a "transformation of consciousness within a significant segment of the aggrieved population."[66]

Melucci (1994, 127) comes the closest to suggesting that something other than a formal social movement is involved in the mobilization for public protests, which was the case in Kenya, especially in the early resistance. When potential protesters are drawn out "into the open, they do so in order to confront political authority on specific grounds …. Visible action strengthens the hidden networks, boosts solidarity, creates further groups, and recruits new militants who, attracted by the movement's public action, join its hidden networks." The Kenya study shows the importance of this kind of "visible action" in attracting a widening support for reforms as an essential phase of establishing a culture of resistance. But it does not agree with the result Melucci foresaw: a "pact" between the resistance and the regime leading to improved institutions, which was not present in Kenya.[67]

One of the most evident signs of support for a culture of resistance in Kenya was participation by the public in protests. In their quantitative analysis of 31 African countries from 1985–1994, Bratton and van de Walle found that the frequency of political protests was one of the more reliable predictors of democratization.[68] They provided an often-cited source of information on regime change that, despite a critique of their data, holds up pretty well.[69] Both of these studies advance our way

---

66 McAdam, Political Process, 184.

67 Melucci, Alberto.1994. "A Strange Kind of Newness: What's "New" in New Social Movements?" In *New Social Movements*: , eds. Laraña, Enrique, Hank Johnston, and Joseph R. Gusfield. Philadelphia: Temple University Press, 127–128.

68 Bratton and van de Walle, chapter 4.

69 In a re-examination of their data, Lindberg (2002) agreed that protests and the three other main variables the two authors used for that period (the role of the military, the level of official development aid, and the degree of cohesion among the domestic political opposition) were valid predictors of democratization (Lindberg, Staffan. 2002. "Problems of measuring democracy: Illustrations from Africa. In *Development and Democracy: What have we learned and how?* eds. Ole Elgström and Goran Hyden. London: Routledge).

Bratton and van de Walle had eliminated five countries already democratic by 1988, plus 11 more for lack of data on international assistance for their study period of 1988 through 1994. Lindberg added back 10 of the 11 countries, using alternative data on foreign assistance; and he extended the study period. Looking at a different time period, from 1988–1998, Lindberg argued that Bratton and van de Walle gave an inaccurate portrait of what caused some African nations to democratize in the 1990s. He argued that when the study period was extended to 1998 and the number of countries increased to 41, the original findings become irrelevant.

Based on the new data set, Lindberg dismissed Bratton's and van de Walle's model, arguing that it "*does not account adequately for the extent of democratization in Africa either over a shorter time-span or over a longer time-span*" (emphasis in original). For example, Lindberg found with his new data set that: "Political protests as such did not cause states in Africa to democratize." He added that protests were statistically relevant only in 1992 and 1994 (125–126).

of looking at the process of democratization in Africa and provide building blocks for future research even as they remind us of the importance of combining research methods.

Like most archival-based works, theirs misses the close up feel of a case study such as this one on Kenya. What the Kenya probe found that is not easily detectable from an archival investigation is not just what political protests were held or which factors correlate with them on a statistical basis but insights on a whole range of activism and resistance events that evoked public support. Lindberg as well as Bratton and van de Walle are limited in their findings by the nature of quantitative studies in general and further by the uncertain nature of much of the data coming out of Africa. Both these studies of democratization in Africa are supported by sophisticated data analysis. Yet official data is often not collected in Africa as

---

With so few attempts at broad analysis of democratization available, Lindberg's work has stirred attention. Hyden, for example, commented that: "Lindberg, in examining Bratton and van de Walle, has already dismissed 'political protests' as a variable that has played a significant role in promoting democratization on the continent." He added that Lindberg's study "convinces us that further qualitative studies are needed to strengthen the basis for quantitative analysis in the future' (Hyden, *Development and Democracy*, 152).

While Lindberg does make a useful contribution to the still under-studied issue of why some countries in Africa have democratized and others have not, a close look at his thesis, choice of data and interpretation of that data raises some questions. His conclusions should neither be accepted nor dismissed as a valid dismissal of the Bratton and van de Walle's study of democratization factors in Africa. Rather, they should be qualified.

Lindberg, for example, argues that political protests had occurred throughout the 1960s and 1970s and 1980s without much change in terms of democracy. van de Walle, however, in a later study (2001, 239–240) noted that in contrast to earlier protests, in the 1990s, many governments were no longer able to "repress or accommodate" the protestors. In the post-Cold War world, key Western donors were paying more attention to human rights; and in an era of economic crisis, regimes had less money and other benefits to use to "placate" dissenters according to van de Walle.

Lindberg divides sub-Saharan democratization into two periods: 1988–1992 and 1993–1998. (It is worth noting that Bratton and van de Walle's book was completed by January 1997.) But he then combines the two periods to make several generalizations. In doing so, however, the value of the protest explanations in the shorter period studied by Bratton and van de Walle (1988–1994) disappears. The shorter span was the most rapid period of political change in post-independent Africa. It had a particular set of dynamics worth analyzing rather than diluting them by combining them with additional years. The two periods Lindberg identifies are distinct in a number of ways. Lumping the two periods together in his critique of Bratton and van de Walle tends to smooth out the important changes that occurred in the shorter span and substitute an observation that, while it may be statistically accurate, loses much of the flavor and relevance of the shorter, highly charged period.

For example, donor strategies changed during the 1990s; so did the strategies of incumbents. The importance of these factors changed over the ten-year period; they were not static. Behind the statistics or data lay an undisclosed story of process and changing dynamics, reminding us once again that correlation cannot be assumed to equal causation.

precisely as in other regions. "Getting a handle on what is really happening in the field of African democratisation, therefore, is difficult."[70]

The Kenya research is both qualitative and quantitative. While quantitative studies provide a degree of generalization, they lack the nuances and local relevance a qualitative case study provides. The two approaches are complementary.

There are obvious problems with relying just on statistical assessments. Bratton and van de Walle and Lindberg's studies, for example, use a numerical count of political protests. The assumption is that the greater the number of protests, the more relevant that indicator is. Missing is an explanation of the importance of any particular protests in the context of the country in which it occurs. In Kenya there were only a few national protests, but each one was considered very important locally and had its own set of dynamics. If one were to analyze only the few, big public rallies or riots in Kenya that show up in archival records, they alone would not explain how a culture of resistance was established. It was not the number of protests that was important but who planned them, the credibility of the organizers, how the state responded, and what impression the protest had on public awareness of abuses.

Institutional Learning: a Chess Game of Resistance Politics

The concept of institutional learning is important in explaining how resistance develops against an authoritarian regime. It is a concept a few scholars of American politics have developed with regard to Congress. Polsby, for example, suggests that members of the House, over time, learned as a body, to make changes, which helped Congress adjust to the changing and growing needs and demands of society.[71] Dodd develops this concept further, applying it not just to Congress but to American society as a whole and uses it to counter rational choice arguments of regularity in behavior.[72]

"It is not simply that assumptions of substantive rationality and general substantive theories of politics are wrong. It is that they are dangerous. They imply regularity to history that is not true but that political actors might take seriously... What scholars can attempt to do is to decipher the substantive logic of particular eras and thereby understand the political dynamics of a time and place, including, let us hope, our

---

70 Hyden, *Development and Democracy*, 139.

71 Polsby, Nelson. 1968. "The Institutionalization of the US House of Representatives." *American Political Science Review* 62(1):144–168, March.

72 Dodd, Lawrence. 1991. "Congress, the Presidency and the American Experience: A Transformational Perspective." In *Divided Democracy*. James Thurber. Washington: Congressional Quarterly; Dodd, Lawrence C. 1994. "Political Learning and Political Change: Understanding Development Across Time," In *The Dynamics of American Politics: Approaches & Interpretations*, eds. Lawrence C. Dodd and Calvin Jillson. Boulder, CO.: Westview Press.

own." In other words, Dodd suggests, the world is not static and neither should our theories be static.[73]

Dodd looks at the gap between "formalists, who emphasize the search for general laws that identify and predict the regularities of politics" and "interpretivists, who emphasize the unique and open-ended nature of politics across distinctive contexts and historical eras." He opts for a synthesis of the two through a focus on "evolutionary learning" that shows that "both of these schools have important contributions to make" in political inquiry.[74]

Dodd"s epistemology is one of shifting paradigms, of evolving ideas and learning in which individuals – and institutions – adapt based on what has gone before. Dodd calls for a synthesis of hard (predictive) science and soft (interpretive) science methods of inquiry in order to appreciate the use of history and the learning process individuals in politics go through individually and in institutional settings. He calls this process institutional learning. It involves learning in which people "create, implement, rigidify, dissolve, and recreate a collective epistemology appropriate to a changing world."[75] In this sense institutions can be either formal (e.g., Congress) or patterns of behavior. Weaver, and Rockman focus on the formal institutions of government,[76] while Rothstein defines them as "rules of the game," then breaks that into formal political institutions and informal ones including "routines, customs, compliance procedures, habits, decision styles, social norms and culture."[77]

In the Kenya study, institutions include the state, primarily the Executive Branch and often specifically the President. They also include patterns of resistance. Activists tried various tactics against the regime. As the empirical chapters will show, activists and the regime engaged in a process of institutional learning, adjusting their tactics to try to match the previous moves of the other side.

Motivation and Ideas

In examining any resistance movement, one is led to ask why participants did what they did, not just under what circumstances and with what effect. Here the economic man or rational choice model does not fully explain what happened in Kenya, especially in the early phases of resistance, as will be illustrated in chapter 3. The early phases of this resistance movement were quite dangerous; activists faced possible imprisonment and torture, or financial ruin.

There is no need to try to force all human actions into one pigeonhole or another, or to try to label human motivation either self-serving or altruistic. In the volume

---

73 Dodd, "Political Learning and Political Change,' 298.

74 Dodd, "Political Learning and Political Change," 355; 360.

75 Dodd, "Political Learning and Political Change," 355.

76 Weaver, R. Kent, and Bert A. Rockman, eds. 1993. Do Institutions Matter? *Government Capabilities in the United States and Abroad*. Washington: Brookings Institution.

77 Rothstein, Bo. 1996. "Political Institutions: An Overview." In *A New Handbook of Political Science*, eds. Robert E. Goodin and Hans-Dieter Klingemann. Oxford: Oxford University Press, 145.

she edits, Mansbridge[78] argues that she and the contributors are not rallying against rational choice but against an insistence that human motivation be limited to either for or against self-interest. "Rather, it is a sustained argument in favor of the idea that people often take account of both other individuals" interest and the common good when they decide what constitutes a "benefit" that they want to maximize."[79] Kenyan activists in the early stages of resistance, had little to gain personally then and much to lose, in stepping forward against a belligerent government bent on staying in power. In subsequent stages, activism was still dangerous but offered benefits to some in the form of jobs, notoriety, or political power, as well as a chance to improve one's community.

The community man model or normative/affirmative model of Etzioni (1988) helps explain why some activists were attracted primarily to the later option, of advancing the good of their community.[80] Motivational issues of early resisters will be examined in chapter 3 and of organizational activists in chapter 4.

This book also suggests that ideas matter and that the idea of a less abusive, more democratic society was a driving force behind the resistance. As one political analysis scholar put it: "If we are prepared to concede that what differentiates social and political systems from their counterparts in the natural sciences is the presence of reflexive actors capable of shaping the environment in which they find themselves, then it is no large step to acknowledge that the ideas actors hold – both normative and descriptive – about that environment must be accorded an independent role in political analysis"[81]

Rational choice straddles several epistemological issues that show up in the Kenya findings, including prediction and the structure/context vs. agency/conduct debate. "If actors can be assumed rational and there is only one way in a given context to behave rationally in pursuit of a particular preference set, then an analysis of the context alone will provide us with all we need to predict political behaviour and hence political outcomes."[82]

But such a one-theory-fits-all doesn't work in Kenya or anywhere else. If one assumes rationality means self-interest, how rational were activists or their supporters to face high risks with no immediate or long-term benefits worth the possibility of being killed or receiving a life sentence in prison? Why did anyone resist the regime? Given that most Kenyans knew the general abusive ways of the regime and the risks involved in challenging it, why did some Kenyans act and not others in the early stages of resistance? If rationality is not a sufficient explanation, then what is?

Interviews with and about key activists in the early phases of resistance in Kenya pointed to idealism, courage and principle as motivating ideas for their activism, as

---

78 Mansbridge, Jane J., editor. 1990. *Beyond Self-Interest*. Chicago: University of Chicago Press.

79 Mansbridge, x.

80 Etzioni, Amitai. 1988. *The Moral Dimension: Toward A New Economics*. New York. Free Press/Macmillan.

81 Hay, 257.

82 Hay, 206.

the empirical evidence will show. Keck and Sikkink also point to the importance of "principled ideas" in human rights activism.[83] Another scholar points out that "political scientists prefer to study things that they can see, measure and count and ideas seem to be the opposite – vague, amorphous and constantly evolving."[84] But that leads one back to the debate on context vs. conduct. Why should one side in the debate exclude the other entirely? Marx argued context; Weber, in his book on the Protestant work ethic, a rebuttal to Marx, took the other side and was "a contribution to the understanding of the manner in which ideas become effective forces in history."[85]

International Advocacy

The impact of international human rights and other networks has been addressed by Keck and Sikkink,[86] along with the impact of international norms on human rights in authoritarian countries by Risse, Ropp, and Sikkink.[87] These important works provide greater understanding of the links between the developed and the developing world in an age of expanding communication networks. The Kenya research builds on such scholarship by taking a closer look at the domestic human rights and democracy networks.

Risse, Ropp and Sikkink point to the importance of both international and domestic human rights networks but argue that of the two, transnational human rights advocacy networks are the "primary instigators of human rights change."[88] In contrast, the Kenya study argues that while international advocacy networks did help provide some measure of protection through publicity for leading human rights activists and important help to human rights organizations, the primary instigators of human rights change were Kenyans themselves, as the empirical chapters will show. Their model suggests a process through which international human rights norms may come to be adopted by a resistant regime through pressure from domestic and international networks. In the case of Kenya, except for strategic reforms, ones made to stave off more reforms, the incumbent regime never adopted these universal human rights norms. The empirical chapters will also examine the inconsistency of donors in using aid as leverage, with only one key exception. Even then the regime made no rush to get funds restored, dragging out negotiations, weakening the argument that the donor freeze on new funds, not domestic resistance, was the main reason for the regime's agreement to adopt a multiparty system of politics.

---

83 Keck, and Sikkink, *Activists Beyond Borders*, 119.

84 Berman, Sheri. 1998. T*he Social Democratic Movement: Ideas and Politics in the Making of Interwar Europe*. Cambridge, MA: Harvard University Press, 116.

85 Weber, Max. [1930] 1992. *The Protestant Ethic and the Spirit of Capitalism*. London: Routledge, 90.

86 Keck and Sikkink.

87 Risse, Ropp, and Sikkink.

88 Risse, Ropp, and Sikkink, 277.

A Model of Resistance

This book presents a model of nonviolent resistance to explain the findings in Kenya; the model encompasses elements of structure and agency in a process explanation stemming from the rich literature on social movements. The model, which may prove useful in analyzing resistance in other authoritarian settings, considers structural factors and recognizes that activists were bounded somewhat by them. Activists, on the whole, as noted earlier, did not wait for supportive structural conditions to begin or expand their resistance. Often the opportunity that enabled further resistance came as the result of previous activism. For example, individual activists by their high-risk actions opened the way to organizational activists by winning some concessions that reduced repression and made resistance easier. Organizational activists helped attract mass participation, which further legitimized the claims of activists to be representing demands for change from more than just themselves.

The model of resistance puts more emphasis on agency or individual initiative (sometimes referred to as conduct). It has three, somewhat overlapping elements. For example, although the first three empirical chapters (3–5) cover distinct periods with activism peaking in election years, mass support of activism (chapter 6) occurred, in varying extent, throughout the study period. And although chapters are identified by the dominant type of resistance (i.e., first individual, then organizational), there was some organizational activism early on.

The dynamics of resistance as depicted in the model are important. Repression triggers the initial resistance by individuals; the resulting activism, especially if it is able to gain some concessions, encourages organizational activism when it is safer to emerge into the open. Both types of activism encourage mass demonstrations of support for political change. Where political process theorists such as McAdam [89]saw "opportunity" as exogenous or something outside a movement that enabled activists to proceed, this model of resistance recognizes opportunities as endogenous, created largely within the movement by activism itself.[90]

The resistance movement model is also much more fluid than the word "movement" normally suggests. Started by individuals, and joined by organizational activists, the movement in Kenya was never a formal one but a loose coalition that also included rival political opposition parties. The parties shared the same goal – regime change – but only managed to come together in late 2002 to defeat the President's hand-picked, intended successor and offer the ruling party its first electoral loss since

---

89 McAdam, *Political Process*, 1982.

90 This endogenous element of the dynamics of resistance is not to be confused with the earlier resource mobilization theory, which the synthesis of political process theory by McAdam challenged. In the Kenya study, the kinds of resources the earlier theory pointed to often were not available to activists. The inward dynamic of the political process of resistance seen in Kenya refers to activism not material resources.

independence, forty years earlier. Sometimes they cooperated with civil society activist groups and sometimes not.

There are different levels of risk-taking involved in establishing a culture of resistance: (1) high risk takers: early resisters, unprotected by organizations, operating without the benefit of initial reforms that make activism easier; (2) medium risk takers: organizational activists who have at least some help from an organization and who attempt to institutionalize resistance rather acting as pioneers; (3) low risk takers: people in crowds who turn out for a political rally or other protest against an incumbent regime.

Everyone involved in resistance faced risks and it was not always at an anticipated level. While there is some truth about the adage of safety in numbers, a regime bent on stopping demonstrations can strike at anyone and in Kenya did, targeting leaders or anyone else within reach of a police baton. Many demonstrators were injured; some were killed. The risk gets lower in the later stages of resistance when resistance becomes the norm for a segment of the population.

The model of Kenyan resistance has three main elements. Each is distinctive, but each is linked to the others and at times overlaps another element; and they may be repeated if a new cycle of repression occurs.

1. *Individual Activism.* Repression by the state leads some individuals, whose background, tactics, and apparent motivations can be analyzed, to make some of the first challenges to an authoritarian regime. Through interviews and archival research, one can glean insights into (a) the circumstances under which individuals resist a regime; (b) the variety of tactics they use; (c) their personal characteristics. Their actions are not supported, or only minimally, by an organization. Most organizations at the initial stage of resistance have either not formed or consider it too dangerous to take a bold stand in favor of human rights or democracy. The norm for most potential activists and members of the general public at this time is deference to the regime, not defiance.

Any concessions early on send a strong signal to others in civil society and nascent political opposition parties that there are some openings, some opportunities for further change. Lack of success toward change at this point is likely to slow down the resistance process, especially if the regime steps up the repression. A regime can block the resistance at any point with enough repression, but that becomes less and less likely because of potential reactions, both international and domestic. Instead, the regime is faced with other options including full or partial concessions, selective repression, or a combination of repression and concessions.

Individual activists develop informal mechanisms for support. They may meet clandestinely to map out strategy. These sessions amount to fire-fighting tactics to avoid arrest and, perhaps, pursue a few critical cases in courts staffed by proregime judges. Activists are unable to obtain from an organization – even if they are a member – the kind of practical help that would expand their activism in the early stages, such as clerical, publicity, legal, financial aid. Most activist organizations are not yet formed. Those that already exist at this point are either are considered safe such as churches, or are reluctant to speak out. It is only later, after individual activism has made the first cracks in the wall of authoritarianism that organizations begin joining the resistance.

2. *Organizational Activism.* Initial acts of resistance, primarily by individuals and safe organizations reveal a vulnerability of the regime to criticism and regime willingness to make some concessions. This encourages the formation of activist organizations with leaders who join the still-dangerous work of pressing the regime for political reform. In the early phase of this second stage, only a few organizations are likely to follow up the initial resistance from stage one. Most still consider activism too dangerous.

Later, in this second stage, one sees a variety of organizations taking up resistance, including various human rights groups, more churches, student groups, and opposition political parties. Some of these organizations have contacts with counterparts in the developed world and are able to attract donor funding from abroad. Some of the activists have been educated abroad and maintain supportive contacts. Some groups get indirect support in their work, as Keck and Sikkink point out, through the lobbying efforts of groups abroad contacting their own governments, or by sending funds and advice directly to the resisting organizations.[91] Concessions are most likely to come when there is a convergence of domestic and international forces on the regime. In the later stages of resistance, however, when massive demonstrations are common, the necessity of international support diminishes and is largely supplanted by a culture of resistance.

In the organizational phase of resistance, when the role and necessity of individual activism has faded, key activists within organizations are able to muster more formal support for their work. Donors are more easily attracted from within the country and abroad because there is some progress toward change, seen in the concessions by the regime.

In this phase, when a demonstration is planned, instead of a last-minute notice in sympathetic newspapers, the planning is more thorough. Young volunteers fan out across urban neighborhoods, relying on nuclear groups (or cells) to contact people in the immediate areas where they live. Word of the upcoming demonstration is also spread by teams using microphones atop vehicles which pass quickly through crowded neighborhoods, still aware of the danger of being arrested, but knowing the risks are far lower than in the individual activism stage when the targets were fewer and the repression greater. Some international donors may begin helping finance the organizations, many of which are nongovernmental organizations (NGOs). Churches, some of which were supportive of resistance or involved in it through sermons by activist clergy in the first phase of resistance, are now regularly publicizing examples of repression and calling for reforms or regime change.

---

91 Keck and Sikkink, 1998.

3. *Mass Participation.* This element overlaps the other two. As individuals and then organizational activists challenge the regime, especially, if concessions are won, a shift in public norms begins to take place. The old norm of deference shifts to a new norm of resistance. Repression the public once considered normal now is considered intolerable. Resistance becomes the norm for such members of the public because the first two stages of resistance have shown the vulnerability of the regime and how it can be pressured to makes concessions. Protest once considered unthinkable because it was so dangerous is still seen as dangerous but no longer unthinkable. The regime is still authoritarian, may still torture and arbitrarily arrest dissenters, but a few concessions have shown that change is no longer impossible and the public hunger for more is strong. International help continues during this stage but may be uneven due to shifting global priorities.

It does not take an entire population to shift norms, only enough to make a public show of resistance that encourages more such acts. The emergence of a movement, as McAdam notes "implies a transformation of consciousness within a significant segment of the aggrieved population."[92] Public participation in the resistance process sends a major signal to the regime that resistance has now gone beyond a few brave individuals and some initial organizations and is appealing to a widening segment of the public. It is likely that only the bravest of the public come forward to join protests; those who show up, therefore, signal to the regime that there is an even broader opposition to its continued rule. This adds more pressure on the regime for concessions.

Explanation, Uncertainty, Prediction and Causation

The Kenya study involves more explanation and uncertainty than prediction and causation. Whether the model holds up in other settings or not remains to be seen, but the logic of its implications suggest that it will help explain political change in other countries in Africa and beyond which lack a history of strong formal political institutions and whose democratic record is relatively weak, as was the case in Kenya. The model for explaining what happened in Kenya may work in other settings but only in a general way. There will always be "idiosyncratic" features of each setting and a need to take note of nuances. But starting with such a model is better than starting with nothing; at least it gives the researcher points of reference against which to measure what she or he finds elsewhere.

The resistance model recognizes human inventiveness and also incorporates the concept of uncertainty. There is nothing deterministic about the establishment of a culture of resistance. Important steps in the process involve unpredictable events, as well as thought-out plans and execution of those plans.

For example, when Kenyan detainee Kihoro sued the government to stop torture of political detainees, a sympathetic guard played an important role. If the

---

92 McAdam, *Political Process*, 184.

guard had not arranged a secret meeting between the detainee and his wife during the period he was being tortured, Kihoro might not have had the chance to ask his wife to find an attorney willing to take up the case. And the timing of the publicity about the torture in a major US newspaper – the day after the Kenyan President visited President Reagan at the White House – caught the Kenyan head of State off guard. After a brief period of denial that torture was being used, its use declined dramatically.

The role of minor actors was frequently part of a chain of events leading to acts of resistance in the phase of individual activism. They do not play a major role in resistance during the organizational activism phase. By then, even if some activists are stymied because there is no minor actor to help them, there are numerous other activists who can carry on.

Further, the model of resistance offers no prediction that it will lead to concessions from an authoritarian regime. An intransigent regime could simply respond with the kind of overwhelming repression that effectively stifles the resistance or makes it so dangerous that only a few individuals or groups dare proceed with it. Such a response, however, in an age of global communications can not go unnoticed and would likely incur the condemnation of human rights groups and donors. Even so, if the repression is swift and comprehensive, even an alert international community may fail to respond in time, as happened in Rwanda in 1994 when more than 800,000 people were killed in three months.

Details of how a culture of resistance is established are, to a large degree, unpredictable, especially in the individual activism stage. Since activism is a process that involves learning, the process is not as predictable as one might assume by simply counting up the number of incidents of resistance and the conditions under which they occur with an expectation that things are likely to occur that way again under similar circumstances.

Convergence of Forces. When a convergence of forces is brought to bear upon an authoritarian regime such as Kenya's, there is a greater likelihood of the regime being obliged to make concessions than in the face of separate pressures. Such a convergence usually involves a variety of domestic forces and international support, though at times domestic forces are strong enough alone.

Global politics play a role as a backdrop to the convergence of such forces and, indeed, appear to have been a factor in the bringing of at least one force, the use of international financing as leverage for reform. The exact global circumstances are not likely to be replicated the same way in the future: the Berlin Wall can only come down once. So a prediction built on the reappearance or recreation of the exact convergence of forces seen in this study is not very useful. But it is not necessary for the exact circumstances in a case to be duplicated to make the model useful in other settings. Weber's explanation of the emergence of modern capitalism deals with circumstances never again replicated in history but has proven useful in many ways.

This book highlights a political process that is not dependent on specific historical circumstances repeating themselves. The forces or pressures involved in the establishment of a culture of resistance, in a generalized way, are likely to involve domestic and international actors and to be set against some international backdrop of the time. The details of both conduct and context will vary, but the process and the patterns described in the resistance model can be tested in many settings.

Multiple Causes. This leads us to consider another theoretical perspective: the danger of monocausation or too narrow a focus. This work avoids the trap of single cause explanations. For example, regime concessions appear to be the result of a convergence of forces or pressures and not due to any single cause. The study notes who was bringing the pressure (activists, donors), what they were doing in terms of tactics and strategies, when they brought this pressure, and why. With regard to causation, the author emphasizes the importance of ideas and norms developing from those ideas as an essential ingredient in the establishment of a culture of resistance. But the argument stops well short of presenting these factors as a deterministic explanation of resistance or regime concessions or specific results.

Weber pointed to ideas as causative, but he was cautious about using a single explanation of change. In response to Marx's emphasis on economic causation, Weber closes his most renowned and controversial work with the statement that it is not his aim "to substitute for a one-sided materialistic an equally one-sided spiritualistic causal interpretation of culture and of history."[93]

Hirschman warned that over adherence to theory or a paradigm can be a hindrance "[T]he quick theoretical fix has taken its place in our culture alongside the quick technical fix" He saw a "compulsion to theorize,"[94] often too hastily. He argued that reliance on paradigms, especially gloomy ones, tends to "blind" us to alternative explanations and theories. It is not that paradigms are not useful, but that the style with which we use them and the kind we adopt are potential problems. Hirschman argues that we tend to think that things are somehow simpler in developing nations and thus adopt simplifying paradigms that are unrealistic. "I believe that the countries of the Third World have become fair game for the model builders and paradigm molders, to an intolerable degree."[95] The Kenya study encompasses complexity while still looking for general patterns. It rejects the idea that politics in the developing world are either simple or too complex to understand.

---

93 Weber, 183.

94 Hirschman uses this phrase as a rough translation of Flaubert's comment on the nineteenth century trend Flaubert perceived involving *la rage de voluoir conclure* (Hirschman, Albert O. 1970. "The Search for Paradigms as a Hindrance to Understanding." *World Politics* 22 (3), 170).

95 Hirschman, 163; 170.

In his effort to explain why Western theorists should move cautiously in assessing political issues in developing countries, Hirschman presents two contrasting styles of analysis in Latin America. One by Womack tells the story of the Mexican Revolution without "pretense at full understanding ... without the shadow of a paradigm."[96] The other by Payne suffers from over reliance on a paradigm and its tedious production of some 34 hypotheses with which he presents readers.[97] Hirschman's point: don't be overly impressed with one's methodology, theories or paradigms. Womack's model, according to Hirschman, abstains from being highly precise and is multicausal, yet it delivers a much richer explanation than the overly precise and attempted prediction of Payne's model.

The conclusions from Kenya have a wider applicability that remains to be tested. And though the study looks at a number of what seem to be critical variables, another scholar could well decide that additional or alternative variables are more appropriate. It builds on known theories, especially social movement theories, but it makes no pretense of offering a complete understanding of the topic. It does attempt, however, to be as precise as the facts allow, in analyzing the circumstances under which individuals and organizations resisted the regime and the circumstances surrounding the regime's decisions to make concessions.

Human Spirit. The book takes note of an element hard to measure, the human spirit. Writer, human rights advocate and former President of Czechoslovakia, Vaclav Havel notes this element in political change: "Communism was not defeated by military force, but by life, by the human spirit, by conscience, by the resistance of Being and man to manipulation." Havel points to qualities not usually included in political science research but ones that seem appropriate to include in an examination of a dangerous process of resistance against an authoritarian regime, a process that involved not just political opposition leaders but a variety of professionals and organizations and, significantly, many ordinary people who were drawn into the resistance.

Havel hints at new paradigms yet unformed that may guide politics in the future: "Sooner or later politics will be faced with the task of finding a new, postmodern face...Soul, individual spirituality, firsthand personal insight into things; the courage to be himself and go the way his conscience points, humility in the face of mysterious order of Being, confidence in its natural direction and, above all, trust in his own subjectivity of the world – these are the qualities that politicians of the future should cultivate."[98] It might be added that these are some of the qualities that political scientists should consider today. They are qualities seen in some of the Kenyan activists, especially in the early, most dangerous stages of resistance.

---

96 Womack, John. 1969. *Zapata and the Mexican Revolution*. New York: Knopf.

97 Payne, James L. 1968. *Patterns of Conflict in Columbia*. New Haven: Yale University Press.

98 Havel, Vaclav. "The End of the Modern Era," *New York Times*, 1 March 1992.

Implications

The debate over whether social movements are more the result of structural circumstances or agency is an important one. For at the heart of the debate is a serious question about the nature of man. Is man (generically speaking, of course) basically at the mercy of larger forces surrounding him such as the economy, international relations, class structure, etc. Or is man able to rise up against the immediate repression he sees and challenge it in some way, either as an individual or as part of a group?

In Kenya there certainly was no sign that the incumbent authoritarian head of state wanted to share or give up any powers at all. He tried various ruses and arguments to justify holding on to power. In the long run, it may be shown that he was right in fending off multiparty elections because they could lead to divisions in society and eventually civil unrest. But that aside, and there is a good chance it won't happen, people in Kenya were able to pressure their President into some reforms, reluctantly accepted for various strategic reasons (e.g., small reforms could buy time and avoid larger ones), but reforms nevertheless.

Kenya went in just sixteen years from authoritarian rule involving systematic use of torture for leading dissidents and little freedom of speech or assembly to a change of regime in an election in December 2002. The resistance to the defeated regime had grown to the point where the election that saw its defeat was conducted under conditions of much greater freedom of expression and assembly than previously allowed. By then, although police torture of common criminals continued, mistreatment of leading political dissidents had practically ceased and people were free to speak openly about the regime.

A culture of resistance is greater than the sum of the acts of resistance. A culture of resistance involves a change of thinking, a new conscious awareness of the power of people to change their circumstances. Resistance is not simply a matter of attending a political rally or rioting; it involves a decision to no longer accept authoritarian rule in daily life, not just at the top with regard to a one party vs. a multiparty system, but at all levels. It includes challenging police, once feared as arms of a repressive regime, demanding accountability from them.

Chapter 2

Repression and Resistance in Kenya: Historical Perspectives

Mekatalili was not a traditional ruler, but she was a good listener and a charismatic speaker. In the early 1900s the British colonial administrators in Kenya forced the Giriama, a coastal group, to pay taxes and to supply ivory. In 1912 when they demanded free labor for British plantations and government projects, Mekatalili passionately appealed to her people to resist. As a result, the Giriama refused to supply more labor, which led to a devastating chain of events explored in this chapter.

In another case, in 1938, some 2,000 angry Kamba farmers from one of Kenya's many dry farming areas marched to the capitol, Nairobi. They camped there three weeks in protest of British policies of limiting the number of cattle allowed on their lands. In a rare example of success in Kenyans' long history of resistance to authoritarian rule, the Governor agreed to their demands.

In the 1950s, as part of a revolt known as Mau Mau, not all the leaders were men. Esther Njeri Mugunyi organized the escape of a group of imprisoned freedom fighters. Though later captured and tortured, she refused to reveal the identities of her fellow fighters.

Repression and resistance in Kenya have long roots, as these accounts, explored further in this chapter, show. After independence, Presidents not only inherited the harsh laws used by the British that suppressed human rights but strengthened them to repress opponents. Much of the early and contemporary resistance was carried out against overwhelming force and at great risk. It defied arguments of scholars who claim such activity is mostly limited by conditions outside the control of the challengers, so-called structural or societal conditions, including the state's use of repression.

Tracing some of the history of both repression and resistance reveals the long roots of a culture of resistance in Kenya. It also reveals that, contrary to the usual assessment of such resistance, much of it was a result of human initiative, not structural conditions, which for the most part were extremely negative.

The most noted example of early resistance in Kenya, the Mau Mau rebellion, is a prime example of this argument, as John Lonsdale notes, "[m]ost studies of Mau Mau have analyzed the structural conditions of African resistance to colonial rule... But real people in their own time seldom have the same sense of structural oppression as academics ... without fired-up human intention there can be no structural outcome..."[1]

The human rights activists of the 1980s and 1990s in Kenya were pursuing peaceful resistance, unlike Mau Mau fighters. In that respect they are quite different. These more modern activists have more in common with middle-class, anti-colonialists than with Mau Mau fighters; but they do have something in common: both the fighters and the more modern day resistance participants faced tremendous, negative structural or societal barriers; and both attempted to overcome them rather than wait till circumstances changed in their favor.

This chapter highlights some of the main historical examples of resistance, including the early 1900s revolt by the coastal Giriama to colonial repression, the path to the Mau Mau rebellion and an overview of its campaigns, including the role of women and of one of its most prominent leaders. Next the chapter briefly examines the authoritarian aspects of rule by Kenya's first President, Jomo Kenyatta and the emergence of a climate of fear. Finally the chapter points to early examples of resistance in the Moi era by academics and others and how such resistance was driven underground before reemerging in the late 1980s, where the current study picks up.

There are important differences between the earlier resistance and that in the current study. Most of it took place when the enemy was foreign, not domestic, and when there was little in the way of international norms of human rights. Unlike the resistance starting in the late 1980s, the resistance to colonial rule in the extreme cases was a violent one. What international attention focused on Africa before the late 1980s concerned nationalism not democracy and later the Cold War struggle over influence on the continent. In the period leading up to independence in 1963, the focus of those in the resistance was the "allocation or distribution of resources; in the 1980s, it was more a matter of what rules were seen as legitimate in carrying out political economy."[2]

There were also important similarities between the early resistance and that featured in the current study. The Giriama revolt was an example of an earlier establishment of a culture of resistance. It began on the individual level, led by a woman, drew in organizational resistance (informal networks of women and men; and the headmen by way of co-opting them); and led to a general resistance of most of the people (a shift of norms from deference to defiance).

Later, pre-Mau Mau resistance shows the role of a few key individuals, though they turned more promptly to formation of organizations than activists in the late 1980s. British repression in the pre-Mau Mau period, like repression by the regime

---

1   Lonsdale, John. 1997. "Foreword" In *Mau Mau from Below*. Greet Kershaw. Oxford: James Currey, xvii–xviii. In this Foreword, Lonsdale, a noted scholar on Kenya, offered strong praise for Kershaw's book for the methodology and for capturing motives of Mau Mau participants.

2   Goran Hyden of the University of Florida, in a personal communication with the author, May 2003.

of Kenya's second President, Daniel arap Moi, drove the resistance underground. Some of the women leaders in the Mau Mau offer explanations of motivation similar to those offered by women in the current study.

Repression and resistance, one could argue, are intertwined in African history as far back as one may wish to follow the trail. African slavery, for example, was not an invention of the white man from Europe or of the Arabs. African slavery long predates the arrival of such outsiders. When the outsiders came seeking labor in Arab countries and later for sugar plantations in Brazil or cotton farms in the United States, it was Africans who captured and enslaved their fellow Africans, transported them in a rough manner to the coasts, and sold them for guns and other attractive items from the so-called civilized world. "If there is one consistent theme in the history of Kenya over the last four hundred years or so...it is surely one of the Kenyan people's struggles against foreign domination. At various times and places, they have fought against the Arab, Portuguese and British invaders..."[3]

As the historical culture of resistance began to reemerge in the late 1980s, the domination activists challenged was domestic. Under Moi, especially after the aborted coup of 1982, which apparently left him somewhat paranoid and more determined than ever to remain in power, there was repression. And there was resistance, mostly covert because of the increasingly high price to be paid for open dissent, a price that culminated in a series of arrests of suspected members of the underground movement Mwakenya in the mid to late 1980s and the confession-by-torture routine that was finally challenged openly in 1987 by a Kenyan attorney and by Amnesty International's hard-hitting expose of the practices of Moi's agents.

Thus 1987 is a good starting point for a study of open resistance in Kenya to a repressive regime, but it is not a sufficient starting point to trace the roots of a culture of resistance. Most of the authoritarian powers the Moi regime exercised were inherited from the Kenyatta regime, which in turn were carry-over powers from the colonial period that sparked earlier resistance.

The Giriama: Coastal Resistance with Echoes in the 1990s

The struggle by the Giriama, a coastal Kenyan people, against British colonial oppression in the early 1900s, offers insights into the nature of early Kenyan resistance as well as the severe nature of British colonial rule. And as in the later Moi years, the Giriama resistance began with individuals, then drew in more organizations and finally led to a popular upsurge against the British.

The initial resistance was led by a woman, not an elite member of the society, but an ordinary woman frustrated by the demands of the British on her people. The leaders of her society were, in fact, more inclined to try to meet the demands of the British for local labor. Resistance by the Giriama became, for a while, a test of

---

3   Thiong'o, Ngugi wa. 1987. "Foreward." In *Kenya's Freedom Struggle: The Dedan Kimathi Papers*. ed., Maina wa Kinyatti. London: Zed Books, xviii–xiv.

early British authoritarian rule in Kenya. In the eyes of the British, the Giriama had gone too far in refusing to meet British demands; the British were concerned that the example of this relatively small coastal group might inspire similar resistance elsewhere in the colony. The case of the Giriama also offers the only early instance in Kenya of a local society functioning successfully but forced to bow to the destructive demands of the colonial power for labor.[4]

In 1912 there was a labor shortage throughout Kenya, including on coastal plantations and government projects in Mombassa. At the end of 1912, the first British officer, Arthur Champion, was assigned to the Giriama interior. Charles W. Hobley had just been appointed provincial commissioner in November 1912. Champion was told to "press for taxes, and to send all the young men who could not pay to work outside their area, on estates or for public works." The headmen the British worked through (indirect rule) were aging and had lost much credibility in the face of younger men who "had legitimate rights to power" but who were "dependent on the retiring elders to install them." Against this tension, the British tried to impose an unpopular hut tax, which even Champion argued would "throw more onto the already heavily laden shoulders of the women."[5]

The spark for resistance occurred in June 1913, when Hobley visited the Giriama area. By then the Giriama were complaining about taxation, the presence of government stations, demands for labor, and demands for half of their valuable ivory trade. Hobley did not listen to such grievances. In August 1913, Champion detained nine young men who had refused to work to earn money to pay their taxes (The system of imposing taxes on farmers in order to get them to work to earn the tax is a scheme that was used in South Africa to get workers for gold mines.) They were forced to carry stones to build a government outpost. When some Giriama attacked the outpost, colonial police officers shot and killed one of them.[6]

Finally, Mekatalili, a Giriama woman, led a revolt. In retrospect, her strategy was effective in rousing what today one might call a sense of civic consciousness. She gathered women and listened to their complaints. Then she accused the headmen of taking bribes from the British to capture their men for slavery. She called for restoration of the traditional government, including use of the Kaya, a term which referred both to the fortified clearing where homes were built and to a political system.[7] At a mass meeting she helped organize, there were more calls for a return to traditional government. Oaths were taken against the headmen in case they didn't stop cooperating with the British; this tended to neutralize them, much to the dismay of the colonial rulers.[8]

---

4   Brantley, Cynthia.1981. *The Giriama and Colonial Resistance in Kenya, 1800–1920.* Berkeley: University of California Press, 151.

5   Brantley, 77–81.

6   Brantley, 83–84.

7   In the traditional Giriama Kaya political system, a council of elders representing all six clans oversaw such functions as the Giriama's role as middlemen in trade between Mombassa and the interior (Brantley, 8).

8   Brantley, 86.

Mekatalili's authority came mostly from a sense of "charisma," not any rank or position in the group. It was her anguish over the growing disintegration of Giriama society that led her to try to convince others to do something about it ... "She was an effective and emotional public speaker, and as she began to publicize the injustices she felt, she found many Giriama who agreed with her. Although her legitimacy was nontraditional, her plea appealed to tradition." She wanted rejection of British labor demands. "[H]er impact was immense: this was the beginning of a formal attempt by Giriama to retain their political independence." She was "able to provide a sense of unity of purpose the Giriama had not had for over a century, in a form that was not threatening" as it might have been if a clan elder had called for a return to the restrictions of traditional government.[9]

The result of her pleas was that the Giriama simply refused to provide volunteer labor for the British. But by 1914, as the standoff continued, the British had switched their goals from getting labor from the Giriama to getting control so the Giriama would not set a bad example of disobedience in the rest of the country.[10] The British burned the Kaya. Then one of Champion's men raped a local woman and was killed by an arrow shot from the bush. For the Giriama, the score had been settled; but Champion reported the killing to the DC without explaining the provocation.

It was the British, not the Giriama, who pushed things into open conflict in 1914 after the colonial administration demanded 1,000 Giriama laborers be sent to Mombassa for military purposes . The Giriama threatened to kill the headmen if they continued to cooperate with the British. World War I had begun about the time fighting broke out between the Giriama and the British. In the Kenya conflict, which lasted only a month, the British prevailed.

After the conflict, the British withdrew from the interior areas of the Giriama territory and reduced the demands for labor. But the Giriama were forced off the fertile coastal strip, left mostly on their own in the hinterland, with few trade links. As "the colonial economy passed them by...The Giriama were relegated to the backwater, both economically and politically, from 1920 onward."[11]

Ironically, those punished for the war were not the ones who had resisted the British. The British extracted a heavy fine and 1,000 laborers, but they were drawn largely from those who had opposed conflict, not the dissidents. By the time the conflict had broken out, Mekatalili had been captured (for a second time) and sent into internal exile in Kissi, so she had no direct part in the Giriama rebellion of 1914. In 1920 she went to live in the revived Kaya and became head of a women's "kambi" or council of elders, though it had limited influence.[12]

What the Giriama conflict shows is the lack of understanding the British had at the time with the nature of domestic resistance. The British assumed that "removal of leaders who urged rebellion would destroy the basis for resistance," thus the

---

9 Brantley, 87–88.
10 Brantley, 110.
11 Brantley, 152–153.
12 Brantley, 139–140.

arrest and exile of Mekatalili. But Mekatalili had not caused the resistance, merely articulated the grievances. The conflict also highlighted the tactics of resistance used by the Giriama, tactics that would be echoed to some degree in the Mau Mau and postcolonial struggles for freedom and human rights.[13]

Oath taking, used to win support of the Giriama headmen in opposing British demands, would be a key feature of Mau Mau resistance. The Giriama men had fought without defined strategies or long-term goals, and leadership was spontaneous and short-lived. In the resistance in the late 1980s and early 1990s, there was often an element of spontaneity and lack of overall strategy among many of the human rights activists, though those pushing for multiparty politics had a clear goal they pursued.

The Giriama women had incited the elders to support the demand of the young men to not be pressed to work. In Moi's Kenya, women would stage a public strike to gain the freedom of their sons who were being held as political prisoners – and they would win. The striking mothers of the prisoners also forced opposition politicians to pay attention to the issues of detention and political imprisonment.

The Path to Mau Mau

In the early part of the 20th century, elders among the Kikuyu took the lead in resisting colonial oppression, especially land grabbing. (By the time Mau Mau emerged, there were other causes of discontent, including denial of education, poor wages, and lack of political participation.) Their tactics were based on a strategy of cooperation on the assumption that the British were doing more damage to those opposing them. So the elders decided to provide the white settlers with labor, food and peace, even paying the British taxes. They hoped that in return the settlers might not seek to take more of their land away and might allow Kenyans' cattle to graze on lands the settlers had seized. By making available labor for the colonial administration, they also hoped to gain information useful to the Kikuyu community. But there were divisions even then between those who still owned considerable land and those who had lost much of their land; and there were divisions between older Kikuyu whose main concern was land and the younger ones who were concerned more with productivity of the land, urban affairs and colonial policies.[14]

One of the younger generation, Harry Thuku, a former government telephone operator, formed the Young Kikuyu Association (YKA) in 1921 that soon became the East African Association (EAA), focusing on taxes, low wages, poor urban conditions, and the *kipande* or registration of males. As opposed to the Kikuyu Association (KA), formed around 1920 as primarily a council of elders, the EAA was based on paid membership pledging loyalty to a leader whose program they endorsed. But Thuku's organization ran into trouble when a hierarchical pattern

---

13 Brantley, 150.
14 Kershaw, Greet. 1997. *Mau Mau from Below*. Oxford: James Currey, 177–179.

grew within it, with Thuku gradually relying more and more on an inner circle of associates to carry out his plans. Then the group ran into conflict with Kikuyu moral and ritual codes, features of the community that would later provide the basis for splits over the correctness of Mau Mau.[15] Thuku "allowed his associates to threaten the wives of those who refused to become members with the curse of barrenness." That and the membership fees, equal to a week's income of a rural common laborer, undermined the credibility of the organization.[16]

But in 1922, after traveling to Kisumu and persuading a small number of Luo to form a political association, Thuku's arrest on sedition charges by colonial authorities sparked what became known as "Kenya's first political riot." Supporters gathered at the Nairobi central police station and were fired upon but refused to disperse. In 1925 Thuku's YKA was succeeded by the Kikuyu Central Association (KCA). Three years later, Johnstone (later Jomo) Kenyatta became its general secretary. "From this point until his death fifty years later, Kenyatta was the most important actor in Kenya's colonial and immediately postcolonial history."[17]

As younger members began taking over the KA, they brought in a new strategy of resistance: instead of cooperation in hopes of favors from the colonial government, they would seek economic strength "to make Europeans listen." But the KCA challenged the supremacy of the KA and began pressing claims on the colonial government not in the name of individuals but in the name of the Kikuyu community.[18]

Hopes for a major return of lands to the Kikuyu[19] were dashed by the colonial report of the Kenya Land Commission in 1932 (also known as the Carter Commission). It did lead to the return of several large tracts of land to Africans but did not recommend abolition of the so-called native reserves, large tracts of land that Africans were

---

15 When younger men began assuming leadership roles in early Kikuyu resistance in the early 1900s, they challenged the elders for a greater voice in pressing demands on the British. But as they became guardians of their land, they recognized that it "was their obligation to see to it that the land, the ancestors and the living were protected from *thahu* (Kikuyu for a state of ritual uncleanliness). "Resistance, however justified, which defiled the land and the people, would bring doom rather than freedom" (Kershaw 187, xii).

16 Kershaw, 181; 183.

17 Miller, Norman, and Rodger Yeager. 1994. *Kenya: The Quest for Prosperity*. Boulder, CO.: Westview Press, 20–21.

18 Kershaw, 186; 185.

19 In 1888, a private trading company, the Imperial British East Africa Company was awarded a royal charter from Britain to develop commerce. The British claimed Kenya as its East Africa Protectorate in 1895 and in 1920 annexed all but a coastal strip as Kenya Colony. In 1899, Britain declared that "wastelands and other unoccupied land and that occupied by savage tribes" should come under the control of the Crown to be used as the Crown saw fit. Like the Dutch settlers in South Africa, the British in Kenya often ignored the fact that Africans occupied many of the lands they claimed. Between 1895 and 1915, white settlers flooded into the Kenya highlands. Missionaries built schools, clinics, and churches; Asian and European traders set up businesses (Miller, Yeager 1994, 11; 15).

allowed to occupy if not held by Europeans, but on which they were not granted land titles.[20] In a country where less than 20 percent of the land is considered suitable for producing crops,[21] the sizeable land grabbing by colonial settlers had a major impact and left grievances simmering, especially among the Kikuyu, who were the main, though not the only occupants of the highlands areas most favored by the settlers.

Settlers were supposed to pay the government for lands they occupied, presumably paying less for "unused" lands. And government inspectors were supposed to protect Kikuyu land Kenyans had cleared and used. But settlers developed ways to fool the inspectors into thinking the land was unused by chasing away the local occupants' livestock, demolishing the Kenyans' homes and uprooting their crops. Those Kenyans who stayed on land the settlers occupied often were obliged to provide long hours of labor clearing land in exchange for the right to stay and graze their own livestock. The settlers also began imposing increasingly stringent limits on the amount of livestock the Kenyans could keep. Some Kikuyu ended up working for the settler who had evicted them from their land.[22]

The worldwide economic depression of the 1930s reduced demand for primary commodities from producing countries such as Kenya. This in turn, cut into employment in Kenya, forcing many workers back to the land, often to the overcrowded reserves. By 1939, the KCA had become the main African protest organization in Kenya, but it was banned in 1940, along with many interest organizations representing other ethnic groups. In 1946, just after WW II, Kenyatta returned from an extended stay in England and was soon elected president of the recently organized Kenya African Union (KAU).

There were several kinds of pressures driving a segment of the Kikuyu community toward militancy after WWII. In the White Highlands, wages for laborers remained very low after the war and a growing number of families were forced off European farms; the reserves were becoming crowded, causing soil erosion and lower farm productivity and landlessness; in the cities, especially Nairobi and Mombassa, the predominant Kikuyu labor force was hit by rising inflation and bad living conditions. "The deterioration of socioeconomic conditions came on top of existing grievances relating to the [appropriation] of land to European settlers, attacks on Kikuyu traditions by missionaries (i.e., the female circumcision crisis of 1928–31), internal conflicts over the role of appointed chiefs, the increasing accumulation of land and wealth by the chiefs and other members of the tribe's colonial elite, and the harassment and repression of Kikuyu political activity in the 1930s by the colonial authorities."[23]

---

20 Miller and Yeager, 22.

21 Miller and Yeager, 187, fn 16; Nelson, Harold D. 1984. *Kenya: A Country Study.* Washington: American University/Department of the Army, xxvii.

22 Kershaw, 88.

23 Berman, Bruce. 1992. "Bureaucracy & Incumbent Violence: Colonial Administration & the Origins of the 'Mau Mau' Emergency. In *Unhappy Valley: Conflict in Kenya & Africa; Book Two: Violence and Ethnicity*, Bruce Berman and John Lonsdale. London: James Currey, 228–229.

Kamba resistance. The Giriama and Kikuyus, of course, were not the only people to resist British rule in the years before the Mau Mau. In 1938, the Kambas, for example, were upset with a colonial policy of trying to reduce the number of their livestock to reduce soil erosion in their dry farming area. The Ukamba Members Association (UMA) was formed and sent petitions and memoranda to representatives of the colonial government. They got no response. So in July 1938, "UMA organized about 2,000 Kamba men, women and children for a march to Nairobi... The protest camp lasted three weeks at the end of which the Governor revoked forced destocking." But such success "was rare." [24]

Mau Mau Resistance

There are many explanations for the term Mau Mau. Some Kikuyu said it describes children and ill-mannered adults who "take food which is not theirs, or eat it noisily." But if they had been denied food by their mothers or not taught manners, then it was the mothers who were the "real culprits." In the context of resistance to colonial oppression, the Europeans and the colonial government were the "guilty party" since they had "taken the land; the people were Mau Mau because they were poor."[25] Historian John Lonsdale describes Mau Mau as "the greedy eaters."[26]

But what exactly was Mau Mau; why did it happen, and who made it happen? It is beyond the scope of this study to dig deeply into the answers to these questions, but we have this cautionary note from one scholar: "It would be impossible for any student of history to understand the history of nationalism in Kenya without examining the Mau Mau liberation struggle."[27] So in a very brief way, with no pretense at in-depth analysis or presentation of the many conflicting views on the phenomenon of Mau Mau, the following section touches on some of the highlights.

We can start with one rather sparse description of Mau Mau by Miller and Yeager to get an overview. Under the subtitle "Kikuyu Revolt," the authors describe Mau Mau as a violent uprising by several Kikuyu political forces between 1952 and 1956 against the colonial British, motivated by loss of land in the central highlands that dated back some 30 years. They estimate there were some 16,000 Mau Mau fighters who fell back into the heavy bamboo forests of Mt. Kenya and the Aberdares. At its peak, some 100,000 Kenyans were in detention. Over a four-year period, Mau Mau guerrillas attacked police posts and isolated farms as British troops responded. In a major sweep against the Mau Mau, some 27,000 Kikuyu, Embu and Meru residents in Nairobi were rounded up; many ended up in detention centers because of their supposed Mau Mau activities. About one million Kikuyu were forced into stockaded

---

24 Kanogo, Tabitha. 1992. *Dedan Kimathi: A Biography.* Nairobi, Kenya: East African Educational Publishers, 5.

25 Kershaw, 208.

26 Lonsdale, Mau Mau from Below, xix.

27 Kanogo, 27.

villages; thousands of homes and many small villages were destroyed to prevent their use as Mau Mau bases. The British at first thought the uprising was just the work of a "fanatical religious current..." Mau Mau violence "began with sporadic arson and cattle killing targeted at European and loyalist African farms."[28]

Then on October 7, 1952, Senior Chief Kungu Waruhiu, one of the colonial government's strongest supporters in the Kiambu region of central Kenya, was assassinated by Mau Mau rebels. After consulting with London, local British officials on October 20, 1952, declared a state of emergency, which amounted to a "preemptive attack...against a significant segment of the African political leadership in Kenya and its supporters...[It was] a powerful weapon of bureaucratic politics with which administrators could attempt to reverse the decline of their prestige and authority in relation to the technical departments" [of the central offices in Nairobi]. With virtually all of their educated and experienced leaders in detention, the resistance fell to "local leaders and the rank and file." It was not until early 1953 that the bands in the forests had organized enough to resist the colonial security forces.[29]

Grassroots View of Resistance.

In the foreword to anthropologist Greet Kershaw's book *Mau Mau From Below* (1997), John Lonsdale writes that the Mau Mau uprising of the early 1950s involved "tens of thousands of Kikuyu people [who] felt impelled for reasons which remain hotly disputed, to organize and bind together their loyalties in order to undertake possible civil disobedience and even political murder."[30] He praised the study by Kershaw, who was also a former aid worker in Kenya during the Mau Mau "Emergency," as the British termed it, as solid research on two counts because she knew Kikuyu, the language of those involved in the resistance; and she offered "deep insight" into the motivation of rebels. "Explanations of rebellious action based on intimate, culturally sensitive understandings of human decision, as here provided by Kershaw, can look utterly different from those inferred from the structural situation."[31]

Lonsdale's point is similar to an important argument in the current study of resistance to authoritarian rule in Kenya in the late 1980s and 1990s, that it is a combination of structural and individual responsibility (e.g. initiative or activism) that provides an explanation for the dynamics of political change or attempts at

---

28 Miller and Yeager, 24–25.

29 Berman, 253.

30 Lonsdale, Mau Mau from Below, xvi.

31 Lonsdale, Mau Mau from Below, xvii–xix. Berman, in *Unhappy Valley*, 229, argues that analyses of Mau Mau that look only at the reasons why people rebelled are insufficient. He cites Ted Gurr's *Why Men Rebel* (1970) and Eric R. Wolf's *Peasant Wars of the Twentieth Century* (1969). "They can explain the factors that brought the Kikuyu into conflict with the colonial authorities and made them mobilizable for mass action, but not those that shaped the response of the authorities to Kikuyu demands." (The current study of resistance to the Moi regime argues that part of what shaped the response of the state was the resistance from activists as well as such structural factors as shifting global politics.)

change - attempts to bring more human rights and democracy to Kenya. Looking just at structural factors, such as the poor economy or global politics, including the ebbs and flow of Western interest in reform in Kenya, or on the other hand just at activism, is not sufficient to explain the resistance that occurred in Kenya. Both are important. But activism gets much less attention from scholars.

Lonsdale points out that Kershaw's data suggest, as other scholars have also accepted, "that there never was a single Mau Mau movement and that none of its members, even those who supposed themselves to be its leaders, ever saw it as a whole, not because they did not have political aims, but because that agenda was contested within different political circles over which they had no control and of which they may scarcely have had any knowledge. This, in the end, is one of the most important things that Greet Kershaw has to tell us." Kershaw's study is based on interviews with residents of four villages in Kiambu, in 1957 and 1962. "...[N]obody – not Kikuyu participants, neither Kenyan nor European scholar – has provided such startlingly authoritative ethnographic insights into the values, fears and expectations of Kikuyu society and thus of the motivation of Kikuyu action...," according to Lonsdale.[32]

In 1948 and 1949 oath-taking among the Kikuyu was underway but "the questions of whether, why and how they became Mau Mau oaths is difficult to answer."[33] Kershaw[34] and Lonsdale point out that there was more than one origin of Mau Mau. It was not a united movement, as the British argued. Lonsdale argues that "[o]ut of class conflict Mau Mau became an internal ethnic war. Its thought was more moral than political, about personal reputation rather than structural relations." [35] Those taking a second oath in Nairobi, for example, pledging not just support for the resistance but a willingness to perform unspecified tasks assigned by unnamed leaders, were "more or less aware that they had joined 'Nairobi Mau Mau,' though the name would not be part of the oath."[36]

Nevertheless there was a great deal of fear surrounding the movement in its various parts, fear of reprisals from the British, fear of reprisals from Kenyans for those opposed to Mau Mau. Many were hesitant to join. But the arrest of Kenyatta, who was charged with heading Mau Mau, prompted many more Kenyans to join it, according to Kershaw and Lonsdale. Kershaw notes that the arrest "changed fear and anger to hope" for those who had not been overly impressed with Kenyatta's lack of success in winning political concessions but now felt that as the acknowledged head of a resistance movement he was able to lead Kenya to freedom.[37]

---

32 Lonsdale, Mau Mau from Below, xix; xviii.

33 Kershaw, 119–120.

34 Kershaw, 220.

35 Lonsdale, John. 1992. "The Moral Economy of Mau Mau: Wealth, Poverty & Civic Virtue in Kikuyu Political Thought." In *Unhappy Valley: Conflict in Kenya & Africa; Book Two: Violence and Ethnicity*, Bruce Berman and John Lonsdale. London: James Currey, 426.

36 Kershaw, 223–224.

37 Kershaw, 248.

The British assumed the arrest of Kenyatta and others leaders would thwart the resistance; instead it increased it. The British colonial officials of the 1950s had learned nothing from the mistakes of the British in the early 1900s dealing with the Giriama. There, too, officials had assumed that by arresting the leaders, things would cool down. Instead they heated up. Presidents Kenyatta and then Moi would make a similar misjudgment, assuming that the removal of leading opposition figures would somehow eliminate resistance to their regimes. It took President Moi quite a while to learn that he had more to lose than gain in seeking to silence his most outspoken foes.

Courageous Women in Mau Mau Resistance

Just as they would in the 1990s, women played key roles, if not as prominent as the men, in the resistance to colonial rule leading up to and through the period known as Mau Mau. They used a variety of tactics. Rahab Wabici was one of them. Elected by the Independent Schools Committee as a Secretary to the Church Committee of Kiambu District in 1935, she noted that by then active politics had taken root among women all over the country. In her post, she traveled all over the country, spreading her message that "we want land and freedom." She encouraged donations for building local schools for girls.

Wabici later became a freedom fighter and a member and Secretary to the Women's wing of the Kenya African Union (KAU). She took numerous secret oaths pledging her resistance. She was arrested and had to do hard labor and suffered beatings by the police. She was freed, by her account, with the help of a local earthquake that convinced the warden to set the prisoners free. She witnessed a number of executions of women while she was in prison. Women "bought it [independence] with our blood," she said.[38]

The tactics such women used showed imagination and courage. They used to carry bullets to Mau Mau freedom fighters in the forests. They helped organize secret harambees, which Haugerud (1993, 46) describes as "self help development projects," and which were also political fund raisers. When forced by the home guards, Kenyans recruited by the British to oppose the Mau Mau, to search the forest for freedom fighters, "would cut leaves and cover the fighters and the whites would never know." And they would place themselves in different locations in the forest and light torches to confuse the loyalists and British about which direction to chase them.[39]

They communicated among women freedom fighters by songs and idioms. For example, if someone suspected of being loyal to the colonial government visited a Mau Mau home, someone might say "your place is inhabited by fleas and they are

---

38 Kabira, Wanjiku Mukabi, and Patricia Ngurukie, eds. 1997. *Our Mothers' Footsteps: Stories of Women in the Struggle for Freedom.* Nairobi, Kenya: The Collaborative Centre for Gender and Development, 4; 12.

39 Kabira and Ngurukie, 17; 27.

biting me…" If the newcomer was a known Mau Mau supporter, the response would be "I sprayed the other day and all the fleas are dead." Then people would feel free to talk. But if it was a colonial loyalist, the response might be, "Oh, yes, despite my spraying them with hot water, those fleas are still not dead."

Wabici explained her motives for getting involved in such dangerous pursuits this way: "Our country had been blanketed by the Whiteman's darkness, and he never wanted us to see the light anymore. Something had to be done and by us to remove this blanket of darkness, by brave people who would never betray their people's trust. That is why we took the oath – for our country and for our children…so that you could live freely after our suffering."[40]

In 1992 when she was interviewed, she was as straightforward in her criticism of the Moi government and the Kenya African National Union (KANU) ruling party. "KANU leaders, like hyenas, are greedily feeding themselves" on the fat of the land, causing the state to collapse by their "greed, greed, greed." She lamented that there was no dialogue between the government and the opposition; and she felt that people had lost the freedom she and others before independence had fought to win. She urged women to "guard their freedom and "wake up this country" to the abuses going on.[41]

One more example of a woman activist in the pre-independence years helps show the resourcefulness, bravery, and determination of such Kenyans. Esther Njeri Mugunyi was also active in the Mau Mau uprising. She both took an oath and administered oaths, for which she was forced to relocate and her house was burned down. "Our main task was to scout on home guards, entice them and steal their guns and bullets and pass them on to Mau Mau." She was caught, jailed and beaten. Released, she became known as a "Kaana ka Itungati" (Freedom Fighter's Child). Some other members of her family were also involved in the resistance.[42]

Messages about meetings in the forest were written and hidden under stones by particular trees. The group she joined faced hunger in the forest and the danger of being discovered. They made guns and got ammunition from a sympathetic policeman. They would move from place to place to escape detection.

One of her assignments was to free freedom fighters from the Naivasha Prison. It was a well-organized operation. The prisoners got out regularly to work on a prison farm and left letters on prison details hid inside maize cobs. The intended rescuers would get the messages at night and leave an answer. Women on the outside sewed civilian clothes for the prisoners to slip into once they were freed. Nevertheless, the rescue would be a bold and risky move, though Mugunyi was apparently unfazed by the potential danger. "It did not matter whether anyone of us was killed or not – death was nothing to us as freedom fighters." They were successful and freed the prisoners. She was later captured and beaten, then thrown inside a big hole with brown (biting) safari ants. But she refused to reveal information about where other

---

40 Kabira and Ngurukie, 18; 20.

41 Kabira and Ngurukie, 35.

42 Kabira and Ngurukie, 40.

freedom fighters were hiding. "No amount of beating or torture would make us betray our fellow freedom fighters...none!"[43]

Echoes of Mau Mau Women in the 1990s

In the resistance in Kenya in the 1990s, women would play a key role. But in contrast to the British government, the Moi regime was hesitant to torture women dissidents, though it showed no hesitation in using police to attack them in public demonstrations. The difference appears to be that the British at the time of the Mau Mau rebellion considered themselves to be in the midst of a war and showed little concern for abuse of human rights by their agents, whereas the Moi regime was being challenged by a growing culture of resistance in an era in which it nominally subscribed to near-universally accepted standards on basic political human rights.

Esther Njeri Mugunyi, like Wabici, was interviewed in 1992 and showed the same concerns over the state of freedom in her country. "What are you doing to the independence we fought for? Do you young people stop and think what we went through that you may be free? Do you know the cost of freedom?" She wept quietly as she recalled the hard past.

During the Mau Mau period, when a young British District Officer had asked Mugunyi why she was a Mau Mau, she roared back that she was fighting for her country's freedom from the white man who had invaded it and made the people slaves. "We want to liberate ourselves from you [British] – you have to go back to your country where you came from – you have milked our country enough – we want our land back."[44] Her spirit of defiance was echoed in the actions of the group of mothers in 1992 who staged a public hunger strike in downtown Nairobi to win release of their sons being held as political prisoners.

Dedan Kimathi: Controversial Mau Mau Leader

This study makes no attempt to dig deeper into the complexities of the Mau Mau resistance beyond what has already been presented except for taking a brief look at one of its most famous leaders, Dedan Kimathi, as seen through the work of Kenyan historian Maina wa Kenyatti, a lecturer at Kenyatta University when he was arrested in the 1980s. Kenyatti, according to Ngugi wa Thiong'o, traveled widely in Kenya and "spent many an evening and weekends in the homes of those who had fought the British and who were now condemned to living in hovels, and on the edges of starvation. He recorded their stories. They in turn came to trust him. They started giving him documents they had hidden for years."[45]

Ngugi, giving a Marxist interpretation to the Mau Mau, described it as a movement that brought together the "new working class[that] joined hands with peasants and

---

43 Kabira and Ngurukie, 45–55.
44 Kabira and Ngurukie, 56; 58.
45 Thiong'o, xv.

tried to forge links with the workers and peasants of all the nationalities to overcome the divide-and-rule tactics of British colonialism."[46] Kenyan historian Kinyatti, too, tended to give a Marxist interpretation to events. He was, for example, disappointed that neither in Kenya nor anywhere else in the world, in his view, had a "nationalist ideology succeeded in consolidating working class power by overthrowing the forces of imperialism and establishing a socialist government."[47] It must have been disappointing to him that the independent regimes in Kenya were capitalistic.

But leaving aside the question of the accuracy of the Marxist interpretation of Mau Mau, one Lonsdale disagrees with,[48] one finds in the documents Kinyatti pulls together in a slim volume on Dedan Kimathi some insights into the enormous administrative as well as political challenges Kimathi faced as a leader of the resistance. And one finds in Kimathi an individual responding to oppression differently than many of those who went before him and most of those who came after him. His reliance on violence stands in stark contrast to the methods of most Kenyans resisting the British before Mau Mau and, with few exceptions, in contrast to the methods of most of those resisting the post-colonial regimes of Kenyatta and Moi.

"What we have to do is to unite and organize ourselves for a long struggle until we drive them from our country," Kimathi wrote. "My grandfather would have definitely hated and opposed this slave system; my father would have bitterly hated, but tolerated, it. But I march with the times and I have decided to use violence to crush it. War is a natural game for nations of the world and death is a true friend who will never fail you."[49]

No Option but Violence?

Would Kimathi have been so determined to use violence to "crush" the British rule if he had been exposed to Ghandi's nonviolence techniques which were used to great effect in the campaign against British imperialism in India leading to the independence of India and Pakistan in 1947 within the Commonwealth, just a few years before the outbreak of Mau Mau in Kenya? Or were the circumstances of British rule in Kenya so different that such nonviolent tactics would have had little chance of succeeding? One can look around Africa and notice that some of the most violent struggles for freedom from colonial rule came where white settler populations were located, populations intent on holding onto farmable land, as in the Kenyan

---

46 Thiong'o, xiv.

47 Kinyatti, Main wa, ed. 1987. *Kenya's Freedom Struggle: The Dedan Kimathi Papers*. London: Zed Books, 12.

48 Lonsdale, in Unhappy Valley, 298, characterizes Kinyatti as a radical. "In Maina wa Kinyatti's hands 'the people' have become 'revolutionary masses' while Kenyatta has lost his name and been multiplied into 'our national heroes'. . . My own response would be to ask the radicals to enquire more closely into the ethnic languages of class. . . Without such enquiry the dead will remain just that, lifeless bearers of abstract class forces, not engaged in the moral uncertainties of once living, historically conscious, individually ambitious, human beings."

49 Kinyatti, 111–112.

highlands, Zimbabwe, and South Africa. In India it was a matter of holding onto an empire whose motherland sold manufactured goods to its subjects. In Kenya it was land and the products that land produced, not land farmed by natives but by settlers. It was against such an entrenched presence that Kimathi and others in the Mau Mau found themselves facing the British. Nonviolence had been tried by Kenyans in the early 1900s; it had not gotten them back their land nor achieved their freedom.

Kimathi was not going to try an option that already had failed. His resistance and that of the other Mau Mau fighters was a violent one, expressed through organization. Some years later, under the Moi regime, resistance would be nonviolent and begin with individuals, later expanding to organizations and mass participation. There are several reasons for the different approaches. The British in Kenya, unlike in India, showed few signs of susceptibility to world opinion in response to their oppression against the local population. Some colonial officials saw Mau Mau as part of an internal conflict among Kikuyu, while white settlers in Kenya tended to see it as a "sinister challenge of 'them or us'." But both groups were agreed that "Mau Mau had to be suppressed; political negotiations were totally inconceivable."[50]

Moi showed a similar reluctance for negotiations with the opposition and a determination to suppress the Mwakenya dissidents of the mid-1980s. But by the end of the Cold War, which also brought an end to the practically unquestioning Western support for Kenya, Moi began showing signs of susceptibility to nonviolent tactics because of his nominal acceptance of universal standards of human rights and democracy, though he practiced neither one. He did not resort to the kinds of massacres and wholesale use of violence that the British used at times during the Mau Mau rebellion, often in response to raw violence by the Kenyan fighters.[51] Individuals in the late 1980s and early 1990s stood a chance of surviving in their resistance against Moi; individuals resisting British rule had much less freedom, and once the rebellion broke out stood little chance at all without the limited support of organized resistance.

The glue that held the resistance in Mau Mau together was the taking of secret oaths which bound the oath-taker to sacrifice and violence against colonial authorities. Kinyatti points out that from the beginning, "Mau Mau leaders used oathing as a major political weapon in politicizing, educating and mobilizing the Kenyan masses against the British occupiers." The first oath bound recruits to "never reveal the secrets of this organization," and to "obey without question all the rules and regulations of this organization" on penalty of death. The oath bound its takers to fight for the "total liberation of Kenya from British colonialism sacrificing even my own and my family's lives." Another pledge was to kill if necessary and to "surrender all one's wealth to the movement."[52]

---

50 Clayton, Anthony. 1976. *Counter-Insurgency in Kenya: A study of military operations against Mau Mau.* Nairobi, Kenya: Transafrica Publishers, 1.

51 Kershaw, chapter 8.

52 Kinyatti, 2–3.

Although the British colonial government accused and convicted Jomo Kenyatta as the mastermind of the Mau Mau movement, "it was Kimathi who became the Commander-in-Chief of the nationalist guerrilla movement." He sought to coordinate the Mau Mau forces that were scattered across vast areas, acted as a political educator of the freedom fighters and took the position of an administrator as well as a guerrilla leader.[53]

Making of a Resistance Leader

Keen on getting an education, Kimathi earned school fees selling tree seeds to the Forest Department and operating a night school in his home where he taught writing and reading. After a brief stint in the army during WW II in 1941, he dropped out of school in 1944 for lack of funds. He later worked as a field hand in a piggery. He began helping organize meetings for the Kenya African Union (KAU), Kenya's first multi-regional nationalist party, formed in 1944. It was in this period that one saw "the beginnings of territorial nationalism" in Kenya, including the roots of Mau Mau liberation.[54]

"Significantly, Kimathi was very careful to emphasize that the freedom fighters did not see themselves as Mau Mau. To Kimathi, and the forest guerrillas, they were the Kenya Land and Freedom Army (KLFA), an army that was fighting for the return of African lands and the attainment of independence from their colonial masters." Soon he became the "acknowledged leader of all the forest forces." He was made the Field Marshal of all the Mau Mau or KLFA forces as they were known. "The majority of the forest guerrillas were Kikuyu."[55] Kimathi was captured October 21, 1956, sentenced to death and on Feb. 18, 1957 executed.

But there is another interpretation of Kimathi, one that portrays him as an "usurper" of the leadership of Mau Mau, someone without previous military experience who may have caused a split in the Mau Mau leadership that helped lead to their defeat. "The educated Kimathi had usurped the overall leadership of the unlettered [Stanley] Mathenge, who, unlike Kimathi, had military experience. Their rivalry became generalized…," causing a "fatal" division in the Mau Mau. The rival camp in Mau Mau loyal to Mathenge viewed Kimathi's leadership as a "dictatorship."[56]

Regardless of which version of Kimathi one is inclined to accept, there was little debate over the difficult conditions under which Mau Mau fighters operated, but according to Lonsdale, motivations for joining varied. One former Mau Mau guerrilla, a farm worker, gave historian Kinyatti this account of his personal and clandestine service, which revealed not only the determination of such fighters but

---

53 Kanogo, 8–9.

54 Ogot, B.A., and W. R. Ochieng'. 1995. *Decolonialization & Independence in Kenya 1940–93.*London. James Currey, xii.

55 Kanogo, 13–15; 25.

56 Lonsdale, Unhappy Valley, 456.

also the conditions they fought under and the type of weapons they used. He said he fought "for our stolen land and freedom. In fact, our aim was to drive the white man out of the country so that we could rule ourselves." Asked if he fought for the liberation of Gikuyu [often written Kikuyu], Embu and Meru, or Kenyans in general, this ex-guerrilla fighter responded that "We fought for Kenya liberation."

This former fighter added, "[w]e used to get food from the people and we also stole cattle from white settlers.[Later they] had to rely more on wild game, wild honey, wild fruits and the like for food.It was…the responsibility of our men to steal guns and ammunition. Besides, we made our own guns. Also, don't forget that each one of us had a panga [machete] which proved to be an indispensable weapon in this struggle."

This same ex-guerilla fighter said he was disappointed with the outcome of the war. He had expected the independent government to grant Mau Mau fighters land for their sacrifice in the forest; instead they had to buy it "from the same thieves who had stolen it from us, as if the price of blood we had paid was not enough…As you can see, we are still very poor; if anything, our situation has worsened. I lost my entire family, my small piece of land and now, after independence, I have to be contented with being a farm labourer – earning [Shillings] 120 a month [a small amount]. The person who owns this farm was a home guard, a killer of our people. So I am not satisfied at all. To be more frank, I am very bitter." Kimathi wrote in his diary: "This war has robbed us of our best compatriots, but we shall never forget them." And yet one of the complaints against President Kenyatta was that he forgot the sacrifices the Mau Mau fighters made. [57]

An Impact of Mau Mau: Legacy of Repression

By the time hostilities waned in 1956, official estimates indicated 95 European, 29 Asian, and 1,920 loyalist African civilians and soldiers had been killed. And a reported 11,503 Mau Mau fighters had been killed, 1,035 wounded and captured, and 1,550 captured unwounded.[58] Lonsdale estimates the number of "insurgent" dead was close to double the approximately 4,500 killed in the northern districts.[59]

There were several outcomes of the resistance. Among other things, Mau Mau "triggered major policy changes concerning African land rights and representation in government."[60] It also left Kenya with a colonial legacy of repression that would carry through the first forty years of independence. But it was not Mau Mau that caused such a legacy. Well before the outbreak of Mau Mau in the early 1950s, the

---

57 Kinyatti, 121–122.

58 Rosberg, Carl G., Jr., and John Nottingham. 1966. *The Myth of Mau Mau:. Nationalism in Kenya*. London: Stanford Praeger, 303.

59 Lonsdale, Unhappy Valley, 453. "By the end of 1956 the Kikuyu Guard were reckoned to have killed 4,500 Mau Mau, not far off half the total insurgent dead, and to have lost 730 men of their own."

60 Miller and Yeager, 26.

colonial administration "was already an effective and highly authoritarian instrument of control."[61]

Mau Mau may also have changed Kenya's geopolitical position in the world of British colonialism. "Until Mau Mau, a view that, irrespective of what might be happening in Asia or West Africa, East Africa was different, was commonly held in Britain. There were British settler interests and defense needs, it was argued, and no apparent nationalist demands."[62] Much of what colonial rule in Kenya did was to protect the white settlers "as part of the colonial so-called civilizing mission...Both racism and a premodern notion of authority merged in a system where those deemed too uncivilized to have rights were ruled by those who had deemed themselves the right to judge...There was little notion in Kenya that subjects had formal rights to free speech and association; both were periodically suppressed for Africans." The colonial system in Kenya was a system with little concept of individual freedom. It was based on "the rights to power, and the moral duties of such power, implicit in the reciprocal authority structure of feudal social relations."[63] As one District Officer said, "[w]e were an elite corps of an elite system, created for the benevolent exercise of paternal power."[64]

That arrogant perspective began to change once the State of Emergency began. Within the Conservative Party in Britain, questions were raised about the costs of supporting "a European property-owning minority regime" that was not considering the wishes of the native population. It was part of a general questioning about the whole issue of imperial rule.[65] Lonsdale goes further in his interpretation of the outcome of Mau Mau. Although the Mau Mau was defeated militarily by the British by 1956, "...the British accepted that the huge political and financial costs of quelling the rising made African majority rule the only possible future for Kenya."[66] One scholar links Mau Mau to the early granting by the British of majority rule in Tanganyika (which later became Tanzania), Kenya's southern neighbor. "Further, Mau Mau came slowly to show Kenya's Europeans that Rhodesian-style white supremacy, or even 'multi-racial' solutions ignoring majorities, were beyond their local resources to impose or maintain..."[67]

The State of Emergency was finally lifted in January 1960, though the main campaign of violence took place between 1952 and 1956. A transitional constitution was drafted in January and February 1960 which allowed African Kenyans a large majority in the legislative council and also allowed political parties. The Kenya

---

61 Mueller, Susanne D. 1984. "Government and Opposition in Kenya, 1966–9." *The Journal of Modern African Studies* 29(3), 403.

62 Clayton, 60–61.

63 Murphy, John F. 1986 "Legitimation and Paternalism: The Colonial State in Kenya. *African Studies Review* 29(3):September, 61–62.

64 Kirk-Greene, A.H.M., ed. 1979. *Africa In the Colonial Period. III. The Transfer of Power*. Oxford: University of Oxford Inter-Faculty Committee for African Studies, .126

65 Clayton, 61.

66 Lonsdale, Mau Mau from Below, xvii.

67 Clayton, 61.

African Union (KAU) became the Kenya African National Union (KANU), which was to become the ruling party in Kenya until December 2002 when it was defeated in an election. KANU won a decisive victory in the general election of May 1963 and Kenyatta became prime minister. In December 1964 he became Kenya's first President.[68]

A Repressive Colonial Legacy

After resistance, both violent and nonviolent, to its foreign occupiers, culminating in the Mau Mau conflict known in the 1950s, Kenyans inherited from the British colonial administration a repressive legacy. Not only did the newly independent government adopt most of the repressive laws the British had used to maintain control of dissent, it inherited a mind set among its new leaders that such laws were not only appropriate but at times needed strengthening. To blame repressive behavior by the independent state entirely on a colonial legacy is to overlook the ways the independent state used the British control measures and even made them stronger as the years went by.

"It appears that many of the tools of repression which were articulated under colonialism, and then refined by a new ruling class following independence, are still being used to consolidate the state against its detractors," one scholar wrote in 1984. Clearly the deck was stacked in favor of repression because of the colonial experience. And the roots of the repressive nature of the colonial state in Kenya were long ones. "It is sometimes argued that 'Mau Mau' was the catalyst which ensured the creation of a more political, more authoritarian civil service which could effectively control opposition on a country-wide basis..." But several political opposition groups had been forced underground due to colonial repression before Mau Mau hostilities broke out. "The period after 1952 simply elaborated methods which had been used earlier to blunt political opposition."[69]

Following the banning of the East Africa Association in the 1920s, political organizations were allowed to form, providing that they limited their membership to a single tribe. Only in 1944, after the first African representative to the Legislative Council had been appointed, was a country-wide political group allowed to be organized. Even so, the colonial administration had powers that could easily control dissent. "The legalistic tools to control political opposition were in effect prior to Mau Mau."[70] Such tools of control included requiring permits to move from one

---

68 Kenyan historian Macharia Munene notes (e-mail to the author, November 2005): In 1960, after the First Lancaster Conference, there had been an attempt to revive KAU but the colonial government blocked the idea. Kenyans then settled on KANU which was acceptable to the government.

69 Mueller, 399, 403.

70 Mueller, 403.

District to another, and the power to ban political meetings, powers the independent regimes of Kenyatta and Moi would inherit and use.

The colonial government in Kenya "...developed a highly authoritarian set of institutions, laws and tactics designed to administer the country and to repress emerging African associations opposed to its rule. It was this "common authority"[71] and this "centralized authoritarian apparatus that was transferred from whites to black at independence."[72] In Kenya, as across much of Africa, colonial regimes created an imbalance of power: "institutions of governance with a near monopoly of authority" and an "absence of countervailing institutions."[73]

There was no pretense in the British colonial rule in Kenya of representative government, of democracy. The colonial state was based on a "pre-modern, non-democratic model... Kenya colony was a political tabula rasa upon which the colonial administration could write with substantial freedom. The fact what was written there contained so few features of a modern state had much to do with the peculiar dilemmas of administering an untenable colonial system."[74] Control was the issue.

The colonial administration in Kenya, despite its weak legitimacy, had methods of extending its control or presence and exerting its power throughout the territory, methods in place well before the most powerful test of its control, the Mau Mau period. The Outlying Districts Ordinance, for example, came into effect in 1902, requiring permits for people to move from one District to another, a control aimed at making it virtually impossible for people to organize resistance. Such laws, later augmented by the British before independence, gave the colonial administration the means to "control African politics on a country-wide basis down to each small locality."

The state also used patronage and other economic tools to suppress dissent and reward supporters throughout the country, including forcing people out of private sector jobs through intimidation of their employers and by blocking businesses by labeling them dissidents. Employing these and other measures of control, the post-colonial Kenyatta and Moi regimes were able to extend their control throughout most rural areas, with the exception of Northeast Kenya along the Somali border where militants attacked even some Kenyan army convoys during the 1990s. Under the colonial administration and later the independent regimes of Kenyatta and Moi, "a vast array of officials, including provincial and district commissioners, district officers, and locational chiefs, effectively penetrated the rural areas, and indeed they finally forced underground most organized political groups opposed to the colonial government during the 1940s and 1950s." By the time Mau Mau broke out, "the

---

71 Wallerstein, Immanuel, ed. 1966. *Social Change: The Colonial Situation*. New York: Wiley, 2.

72 Mueller, 401.

73 Burke, Fred G. 1969. "Public Administration in Africa: the Legacy of Inherited Colonial Institutions." In *Journal of Comparative Administration* 1(3), 356.

74 Murphy, 58.

colonial administration was already an effective and highly authoritarian instrument of control. The period after 1952 simply elaborated methods which had been used earlier to blunt political opposition."[75]

Inheriting and Using Repressive Colonial Laws and Practices

One scholar sums up the colonial political legacy at Kenya's independence this way: "African nationalists were bequeathed a legacy designed to provide the government with a monopoly of coercive sanctions and resources that could be used to maintain law and order, to repress opponents, and ultimately to discourage dissent or politics itself."[76] But they not only inherited such coercive measures – they used them.

After independence, Kenya's first two Presidents accepted and took advantage of what amounts to a massive, country-wide spy system developed by the British in which officials from the lowest village chiefs to the Vice President were all under the control of the President, who appointed them. The task of this administrative machinery was not only to keep the country running but to inform the President and his key aides of any dissident activity anywhere in the country.

In many ways, independent Kenya looked a lot like colonial Kenya. White faces were no longer in charge; black faces were at the helm, but independent Kenya, as one scholar noted in the mid-1980s, "...adheres as little as its colonial predecessor to bourgeois political norms of the rule of law, freedom of the press, and rights to speech and democratic participation."[77] And "...certain groups found that colonial ways of doing things were admirably suited to the retention of political power... many of [the] preindependence laws and institutions were used to the same ends as they had been during the colonial period....In both pre-and post-independence Kenya, patronage as well as coercion was monopolized by the state."[78]

The disproportionate powers of the President that Moi enjoyed and used, or rather misused, were inherited from the Kenyatta regime, which he took over suddenly when Kenyatta died in office in 1978. Most of those powers, including an Administrative structure that amounted to a formal police state, with government officials from the State House all the way to the chiefs in the villages appointed by the President and subject to him, provided a sitting President with an apparatus of power that made it practically impossible for open dissent to take root and grow very long undetected and unreported. Near the top of the political structure, prominent politicians who spoke out against the regime, or even ones who got too popular, were seen as a threat to the regime and were in danger. There were a number of assassinations under Kenyatta that were blamed on the regime or its supporters. In spite of the dangers, however, there was resistance, even in Parliament where one group of outspoken

---

75 Mueller, 402–403; 407.
76 Mueller, 401.
77 Murphy, 55.
78 Mueller, 405.

legislators dubbed "the seven bearded sisters," risked the consequences by doing what they could to obstruct the lopsided powers and measures of the majority in a single party system.[79]

Kenyatta Regime

The Kenyatta regime was marked by pseudo-democracy, a veneer of freedom that shone brightly enough and with enough economic progress – capitalistic progress – to give Kenya a deceptive international reputation as a bastion of democracy and capitalism. The West was happy with Kenya, especially during the long years of the Cold War when both the Soviet Union and the West, especially the United States, welcomed political and economic states that appeared to emulate their own systems. The Cold War chess game that endured until 1989, the symbolic year of its end with the tumbling of the Berlin Wall and the demise of Communism as it was then known, meant that there was very little attention paid to abuses of human rights in places like Kenya. It was enough to appear democratic, and especially nice (to the West) to be capitalistic, and stable.

On the day of Kenya's independence in 1963, President Jomo Kenyatta told the nation that his government would build a democratic African socialist state.[80] But Kenyatta and his associates "preserved what they most needed from the colonial state, and particularly the law-and-order aspect. Institutions such as the provincial administration, police and army were taken over intact."[81]

Almost immediately there was the start of an accumulation of power by the Executive through a series of constitutional amendments that by the end of Kenyatta's rule numbered thirteen. Critics charged they were rushed through Parliament too quickly and made the President too strong. The regime not only kept in place the colonial era Preservation of Public Security Act, which allowed detention, but in 1966, strengthened it to allow preventive detention as well. The new Act gave the President power to detain individuals without recourse to the courts.

Destroying an Early Opposition Party

In 1963, a Cabinet decision was made to continue the colonial practice of licensing public meetings as a way of preventing meetings that were not in support of the government. "Similar decisions were taken in the years that followed to retain

---

79 The seven "Bearded Sisters" included: Abuya Abuya, Onyano Midika, Moshengu wa Mwachofi, James Orengo, Lawrence Sifuna, Dr. Chibule wa Tsuma, and Koigi wa Wamwere, though one account (Schmidt, Kibara 2002, 10) includes George Anyona instead of Abuya Abuya .

80 Some Kenyans noted that in his speech he had not made reference to those who had given their lives in the Mau Mau struggle for freedom. They feared Kenyatta "had already forgotten the freedom fighters of the forests and detention camps…" (Ochieng' 1995, 92).

81 Ochieng' W. R., ed. 1989. *A Modern History of Kenya.* London: Evans Brothers, 91–93.

the Societies Ordinance which governed the registration of political parties and their branches, the Public Order Ordinance, which governed the holding of public meetings and gatherings, and laws having to do with sedition, detention, and many other restrictions.[82]

In 1966, less than three years after independence, a faction of the ruling party, the Kenya African National Union (KANU), broke away, led by Oginga Odinga, the country's first Vice President. Twenty-nine members of Parliament formed the Kenya People's Union (KPU). Kenyatta, on a Kenyatta Day rally in 1967, called the defectors "snakes in the grass," and said they had nothing to do with winning Kenya's freedom.[83] The Kenyatta-controlled Parliament passed a constitutional amendment forcing all Members of Parliament (MPs) who had crossed over to join the new party to stand for new elections.[84] Laws were passed making it "impossible for independents or individuals who were not nominated by local party organs to run," and the regime had already blocked formation of many of those local party organs of KPU. Only nine of the defectors won reelection, including Odinga.[85]

The government refused to register about half of the KPU branches, blocked their public meetings, and put some of their leaders in detention. KANU won the 1968 local elections when, "allegedly on instructions from the President, District Commissioners...disqualified all of the KPU's 1,800 candidates from nomination on the grounds that their papers were incorrectly filled out."[86] In 1969, the regime banned the KPU altogether. Nine KPU MPs were detained.

Establishing a "Climate of Fear"

Outside of Nairobi, especially, individuals supporting KPU were subjected to economic intimidation and violence. This made supporters fearful. "At first, before the intimidation, it was easy to get people to come forward and then with intimidation they would not like their names to appear on the application forms, although they were willing to do the donkey work for the party." Up country it was harder to support the rival party, where everything one did was noticed; in Nairobi there was a degree of anonymity and dissent was less noticed. "I was under constant surveillance and was being harassed in my job and given warnings that I should behave..." one KPU member said. There were many reports of physical violence against Kikuyus who supported the KPU. But police harassment was only one tool the new government was using to squelch opposition; they also used economic repression, as the same KPU member noted. "Then I started an advertising firm. I got my company going

---

82 Mueller, 406.

83 Ochieng', 98.

84 Kenyan historian Macharia Munene notes (e-mail to the author November 2005) that subsequently, many would-be defectors returned to or stayed in KANU.

85 Mueller, 416.

86 Mueller, 407–408; 417.

and wanted to retain fees for the people I was working for. The Government would ring people up and tell them to forget it...They really harassed me..."[87]

The regime also dismissed opposition party members from government statutory boards. "Conversely, opposition politicians and MPs who rejoined KANU were often rewarded with statutory appointments, or were nominated in by-elections that followed their return." One recipient of a government reward noted, "[t]hey don't give you this for nothing, but give it so that you will keep locked up, talk no more, and feel that you belong." Those who did not give up their KPU membership suddenly found their personal loans being called in by banks under government influence, unable to find employment "in either the public or private sectors" because they had been labeled as "dissidents."[88]

A "climate of fear...was evident throughout the countryside by mid-1968." In June 1968, a survey was published that showed that 66 percent of those interviewed claimed that "on at least one occasion they had been afraid to express their opinions, or to criticize the regime, because they would suffer as a result of adverse reports by secret police and informers.[89]

Murder of Political Opposition Figures

In the span of a few short years after independence, President Jomo Kenyatta had become "authoritarian."[90] He regarded political competition as anathema. One "thorn in Kenyatta's side" was Vice President Oginga Odinga's Asian-born ally, Pio da Gama Pinto, who was murdered in early 1965, a murder widely believed to have been the work of "Kenyatta's inner circle."[91]

In 1969, the year Kenyatta banned the rival KPU party and threw its leaders into detention, Tom Mboya, the popular Luo labor leader, was gunned down in daylight in downtown Nairobi. At one point it had seemed that Mboya might succeed Kenyatta and Kenyatta had "begun to fear Mboya." Mboya was murdered by a Kikuyu who was later charged and hanged. But the Luo community blamed Kenyatta as the man behind the assassination. Three months later, when Kenyatta was visiting the predominantly Luo city of Kisumu, his caravan was pelted with stones and some 43 people were shot dead by the President's bodyguards in the ensuing chaos. In the months after Mboya's murder, Kenyatta concentrated even more power in his hands. "Increasingly relying on provincial administration, the police and the Kikuyu-dominated army, Kenya after 1969 became a one-man show." The level of freedom had fallen dramatically since independence. "Whereas Kenya

---

87 Mueller, 412; 420; 425.

88 Mueller 421–422.

89 Mueller, 417. Mueller cites the Kenya Constitutional Changes, Succession to President, Public Opinion Poll, 18; Nairobi; Kenya Research Services, June 1968, p. 14.

90 Ochieng', 94.

91 Throup, David, and Charles Hornsby. 1998. *Multiparty Politics in Kenya: The Kenyatta and Moi States & the Triumph of the System in the 1992 Election*. Oxford: James Currey, 58.

had emerged into Uhuru [freedom or independence] with a lively multiparty system, a vociferous parliament and an independent press, by 1970, freedom of speech was virtually a thing of the past and government critics were in detention." Kenya's repressive colonial heritage "remained largely unchanged and unsympathetic to and remote from popular wishes."[92]

But now a new potential opponent emerged from KANU's backbenches, populist member J.M. Kariuki. He championed "the people's right to free medical services, education and land," criticizing a political elite who had "steadily but surely monopolized the fruits of independence to the exclusion of the majority of people." Said Kariuki: "We do not want a Kenya of ten millionaires and ten million beggars." By early 1975, Kariuki "knew that a few people around President Kenyatta were plotting to harm him."[93] He was found murdered on Ngong' Hills outside Nairobi in March 1975.

The murder of J. M. Kariuki did more than eliminate a rival to Kenyatta. "Kariuki's death instill[ed] in the minds of the public the fear of dissidence, the fear to criticize, the fear to stand out and take an unconventional public stance."[94] A number of radical politicians and academics were imprisoned or detained by 1977, including George Anyona, Martin Shikuku, and Ngugi wa Thiong'o.

But despite the way Kenyatta's regime "ruthlessly repressed any direct challenge, it was not a system marked by the excesses of personal rule found elsewhere in Africa and later in Kenya itself...While Kenyatta's Kenya was not democratic, it was nonetheless a relatively open and resilient system with multiple secondary centers of power and a measure of real competition – and hence accountability – at the local and regional levels."[95]

Early Resistance to Kenya's Second President

On August 22, 1978, President Kenyatta died in office. Kikuyu power brokers had considered preventing Kalenjin Vice President Daniel arap Moi from succeeding by changing the constitution to have an Executive Prime Minister. But the plan ran into opposition, from Kenyatta himself, from some 98 Members of Parliament who became known as the constitutionalists, and from then Attorney-General Charles Njonjo. In desperation, political foes to Moi's succession organized an armed gang of "would be assassins (the ngorokos)" based in Nakuru with the intent of killing Moi, and several other key leaders upon Kenyatta's death, including Mwai Kibaki and Njonjo. But on the day Kenyatta died, Moi managed to reach Nairobi before the

---

92 Ochieng' 101–102 106.

93 Ochieng', 102–103.

94 Ochieng', 154.

95 Barkan, Joel. 1992. "The Rise and Fall of a Governance Realm in Kenya." In *Governance and Politics in Africa*, eds. Goran Hyden and Michael Bratton. Boulder, CO: Lynne Rienner Publishers, 175.

ngorokos had time to set up roadblocks and was sworn in as Acting President for ninety days until an election was held.[96] In October he was elected unopposed as President of KANU, the only party at the time, and was thus sworn in as President on October 14, 1978.[97]

President Moi faced a formidable political challenge of how a "one-party government that rules over a fragmented and clientelist society [could] …apply corrective politics to redistribute power and resources away from those who have previously most enjoyed them (and who know how to defend them) and toward those least favoured by the previous regime, with the consent of the majority." At first, instead of promising radical change, Moi promised to follow in the footsteps (Nyayo in Swahili) of Kenyatta. Later he would turn the term into a slogan for his own administration and the original concept that Nyayo referred to Kenyatta and not Moi's footsteps would be ignored by the new regime. To be anti-Nyayo was to be anti-government, a "further entrenchment of the political monolithism which had been introduced under Kenyatta."[98]

Initially, Moi practiced reconciliation and forgiveness with his political adversaries. On Kenya's Independence anniversary in 1978, which was also the thirteenth anniversary of the Universal Declaration of Human Rights, Moi launched "a new era of tolerance" in Kenya by releasing all political prisoners."[99] Among those released were Ngugi wa Thiong'o, George Anyona, Martin Shikuku, and Koigi wa Wamwere, all of whom would later become among his most vocal opponents.

The contribution of dissent to the transformation of Kenya from a single party to a multiparty society "deserves serious attention." Two streams of opposition to Kenyatta and Moi's regimes developed: there were political dissidents, and a whole generation of academic scholars. "These two major streams of dissidence were to merge in 1991 to constitute the pro-democracy movement." Among the academic opposition were Katama Mkangi, Mukaru Ng'ang'a, Peter Anyang' Nyong'o, Micere Mugo, Atieno Odhiambo, Shadrack Gutto, Willy Mutunga and Gibson Kamau Kuria. Many were inspired by a Marxist philosophy.[100] In 1978, Ngugi wa Thiong'o, Kenya's leading novelist and Chairman of the Department of Literature at the University of Nairobi, was detained after establishing a community theater group that put on a play he coauthored with Ngugi wa Mirii called Ngahaahika Ndeeda ("I will marry when I want") that was critical of the government.

---

96 Kenyan historian Macharia Munene notes (e-mail to the author November 2005): Kenyatta's health was an issue in 1968 when, anticipating his possible death, what appeared like an anti-Mboya amendment was put into the constitution. With Odinga no longer an issue, the possibility of Mboya swaying other MPs to make him president was the driving fear in the amendment. The new amendment made the sitting vice-president the acting president for 90 days during which a presidential election would be held. It was also in that amendment that independent candidates were disqualified, and the Public Security Act was imposed.

97 Ogot, 189–190.

98 Ogot, 192; 194.

99 Ogot, 193.

100 Ogot, 197–198.

Students at the University of Nairobi had boycotted classes and demonstrated in the streets after the assassination of J.M. Kariuki in 1975. When Moi became President, he was not long in cracking down on them, banning the Nairobi University Students' Organization in 1979 and the following year the Academic Staff Union. As a result of riots that broke out at the University of Nairobi over the barring of outside speakers, passports of twelve lecturers considered critical of the government were seized. Among those affected were Micere Mugo, Ooko Ombaka, Michael Chege, Mukaru Ng'ang'a, Okoth Ogendo, Atieno Odhiambo, Peter Anyang' Nyong'o and Shadrack Gutto. "Throughout the 1980s, various groups opposed the one-party rule, using different strategies. This included academics from the University of Nairobi and Kenyatta University; an attempted coup by junior Air Force officers; and underground movements, such as Mwakenya, Umoja, Kenya Patriotic Front, Kenya Revolutionary Movement and the December Twelve Movement."[101]

The later was a small, underground opposition group that operated in Kenya from about 1975 to 1982, after which it changed its name to Mwakenya, according to Professor Maina wa Kinyatti, a former historian at the University of Nairobi who was imprisoned from 1982–1988 for his alleged underground activities. He was tortured. "I was kept in a small, dark room for so many years and fed food half-cooked," he said.[102]

In June 1982, Parliament passed an amendment making Kenya a one party state de jure; it was already one de facto. The attempted coup came in August that year. The opposition moved underground almost entirely after the attempted coup d'etat and Moi's increasingly repressive response to the attempt. Nearly seventy students were held for about seven months, after which most were granted presidential clemency.

In 1986, delegates at a national conference of KANU, adopted a queue-voting system in which voters would line up in the open behind a placard of the candidate of their choice. This method was seen by analysts as a major mistake by the now clearly-authoritarian Moi regime because so many government-favored KANU candidates won despite having shorter lines, a visible proof of rigging by the regime.

From 1986 to 1988 the government carried out a nation-wide crackdown on Mwakenya. At the same time, the government tightened its already powerful hand on the apparatus of government. In 1986, Parliament passed a constitutional amendment that removed the security of tenure from the office of the Attorney General, Controller, and Auditor-General despite strong vocal opposition from some Christian churches, the Law Society of Kenya and other human rights advocates.

---

101 Ogot, 199; 197.

102 Maina wa Kinyatti, in a telephone interview with the author in the United States, March 2004. "The underground movement was able to go outside the country and expose what was happening in the country," said Kinyatti. "We were able to organize the people within, particularly the youth. I was not an individual; I was part of the collective to oppose dictatorship long before everyone else came out. There were only very few of us who continued to distribute leaflets to encourage people to oppose [the government]."

Charles Rubia, who would later lead the call for a multiparty system, was one of the few members of Parliament to oppose the Amendment.

Resurfacing Resistance.

In 1987, one human rights lawyer, Gibson Kamau Kuria, sued the government in an attempt to get the state to stop torturing one of his clients who was being held as a political prisoner. He was detained himself, although his law partner, Kiraitu Murungi, who after the 2002 election would become the nation's top justice official, took up the same case. The same year, Amnesty International (1987) issued a strong report condemning such torture. The law suit and the Amnesty report together provided one of the most significant public challenges to the authoritarian rule of the Moi regime in years. It marked a coming together of domestic and international pressure on the regime at a time when most opposition had been forced underground.

In 1988 another amendment was passed that removed the security of tenure of office for High Court and Court of Appeal judges and for members of the Public Service Commission. It also extended the power of the police to detain capital offense suspects from twenty-four hours to fourteen days. Attorneys Murungi, Paul K. Muite, and Kuria issued a public statement condemning the Amendment. Then-Minister of Health Mwai Kibaki, who was to win the presidency as an opposition leader in December 2002, moved to reduce the public notification period from fourteen days to five days. It sailed through Parliament in three hours "without even token opposition."[103]

Moi's increasing repression in the mid to late 1980s was a continuation of a long thread of repression in Kenya dating back at least to the start of the British colonial presence. The public resistance that began afresh in the late 1980s likewise was a continuation of a long thread of resistance dating back through the colonial period.

We begin now to examine that resurfacing resistance and learn how at first a relatively few Kenyans, often acting primarily as individuals rather than leaders of organizations, began to speak out against the trend toward increasing authoritarianism. They would later be joined by organizational resistance and public support and participation in the establishment of a culture of resistance.

---

103 Ogot, 212.

Chapter 3

Knocking at the Door:
Individual Activism

Riot police equipped with helmets, shields, wooden batons, and tear gas circled the protesting mothers and slowly began walking toward them. The mothers of political prisoners demanding release of their sons sat singing under an open-sided canopy, protected only by Kenyan volunteers who waited on the grass in a circle around the canopy, arms locked with those next to them in defiance. One of the smallest yet most dramatic and effective human rights protests against the authoritarian regime of President Daniel Arap Moi was coming to a climatic moment.

This was not large, formal organizational activism of a church, nor that of an opposition party, a union, or any other formal, well-established organization. This was individual activism, involving only a few people at most and unsupported by any organization other than a loose network of other individual activists. The mothers, no more than a dozen or so, came mostly from rural areas, were never trained in non-violent resistance and had only minimal educational backgrounds; but they shared a rock-hard determination to win the freedom of their sons. They provided one of the most significant challenges to the authoritarian Kenyan regime, one that caught officials off guard and eventually helped expand the practice of human rights in that country.

Looking back on the protest, some years later, Milcah Wanjiku Kinuthia said she had gotten word that her son, Rumba Kinuthia, might be hanged. She contacted two other mothers of political prisoners, Monica Wamwere, the mother of Koigi Wamwere, and Gladys Kariuki, whose son Mirugi Kariuki had been one of the three prisoners to sue the government to stop torture. Mrs. Kinuthia and the others had no intention of letting their sons be executed or spend years in prison without doing everything they could to stop it.

The three women and a small number of other mothers of prisoners went to Nairobi met with conservationist and human rights activist Dr. Wangari Maathai to plan a protest of some kind. Instead of going to the prison on the outskirts of the city, they decided to make their protest more visible by staging an extended sit-in and daytime hunger strike in *Uhuru* (freedom in Swahili) park in downtown Nairobi.

But that afternoon in March 1992, as riot police began to close in on the mothers protest, located directly across from the high-rise government office building where some of the prisoners had been tortured, prospects of an effective resistance looked dim. The police were serious and about to bash heads. It was a mark of failure on the part of the government – failure in not nipping the protest in the bud the first day when curious and sympathetic members of the public brought them food and stopped by to offer moral support. Opposition politicians began using their protest site as a place to be seen; the number of supporters grew from a trickle to a stream: young couples, angry men, and professionals. The mothers' strike caught the attention of the city, the country, and through the international press their story went abroad.

This chapter examines why individual activism arose and how, in terms of constraints and opportunities which are examined at three levels: structural, institutional and individual. In this study individual activism is defined as someone who engages in open actions challenging the legitimacy and performance of an incumbent regime in terms of human rights or democracy, without the benefit of organizational support. Next the chapter looks at these individual activists, most of whom were professionals – lawyers, journalists, politicians, members of the clergy – including biographical data, what they did and the patterns of resistance that emerged. After considering various motivational issues, the chapter then examines the informal networks activists used and the process of institutional learning involved in their activism. The chapter concludes with implications of the findings regarding individual activism, setting the scene for the next chapter on organizational activism.

Individual activism lacks the clerical, financial, and protective power of solid organizations yet can stir others to action even in dangerous times. In periods when some organizations are too fearful to speak out, and others have not yet formed due to repression, individual activism can fill an important gap in the establishment of a culture of resistance, as this chapter will show. In Kenya, individual activists defied the regime overtly from about 1987 and into 1992. The mothers' protest was one of the last major examples of individual activism in a transitional phase where organizational activism took the lead in the resistance movement.

Individual activism often involves a great deal of courage and raw commitment to an ideal, though the activists themselves are often quick to deny bravery or to see themselves as doing anything more than insisting on basic rights. Others, no less courageous, may be seeking long-term personal benefits, or in the case of the mothers, more immediate benefits – the release of their sons.

"What could I be afraid of when my son had been locked up?" Mrs. Kinuthia recalled some years after she and the other mothers staged their protest. Even when the riot police attacked the crowd, swinging their batons, she recalls not being afraid: "We were expecting that to happen."

That afternoon as the riot police closed in on the mothers, I was standing with them as a correspondent for *The Christian Science Monitor,* based in Nairobi. My wife, Betty, was also there as a freelance photographer. Mrs. Wamwere and some of the other mothers were singing a protest song as the police walked toward them. When the attack began, there were shouts. Mrs. Wamwere alone kept singing. Then there were screams as the police struck would-be protectors seated around the mothers, forcing them to flee, some of them diving on top of the mothers under the canopy.

Wangari Maathai and I were knocked down as people piled on top of us seeking to escape the blows of the batons. I was afraid we might be crushed, but just then a policeman threw a tear gas canister in under the canopy. It bounced off my head and exploded a few feet away. This forced the crowd to get up and run, freeing us and the mothers from the crush.

I ran out of the canopy. Betty was able to duck the tear gas fumes and fleeing people and stayed on the site taking pictures. In further protest, some of the Kenyan mothers stripped to the waist, a traditional defiant curse on the aggressors.

Though ejected from their park protest, the mothers soon reassembled in the basement of the nearby All Saints Cathedral, an Anglican church. There they continued a partial fast and kept some media attention on them and the issue of political prisoners for an entire year.

Eventually, the mothers won. By the end of the year-long protest, all but one of some 50 political prisoners had been released. Unfortunately, within three years, more than that number had been arrested whom an advocacy group, Release Political Prisoners (RPP), described as political prisoners.

Individual Activism: Defying the Odds

By 1987, the state's crackdown on underground dissidents, especially the much–publicized but little-known Mwakenya[1] was at its peak. Amnesty International reported that the crackdown had begun in March 1986. Torture of political prisoners had become a routine tool of repression, often torture of the most brutal kind.[2] The mainstream press was muzzled by self-censorship and fear of being shut down. State repression made it dangerous for small publications to confront the increasingly obvious abuses of power of the regime.

It was against this background that a small number of Kenyan individuals emerged into the open to challenge the regime of President Daniel arap Moi on a variety of issues centering on human rights and democracy.[3] There had been open dissent in earlier years, including from some attorneys and academics in the late 1970s and early 1980s. But after the attempted coup in 1982, the Moi regime had grown increasingly concerned about its security and reacted with a vengeance against any signs of dissent, forcing opponents underground. Around 1987, overt dissent began to appear again in response to the need to save prisoners whose lives were threatened. Part of this timing was chance: a few prisoners were able to send word to

---

1 Swahili acronym for Union of Nationalists to Liberate Kenya.

2 Amnesty International. 1987. "*Kenya: Torture, Political Detention and Unfair Trials.*"

3 This study focuses on a relatively small, prominent group of human rights and democracy activists. There were others, beyond the scope of this research, some of them musicians, some among the poor, who also resisted the regime in various ways.

a human rights lawyer to represent them. Also in 1987, Amnesty International issued a major report highlighting the repression.

For the next five years the resistance in Kenya against repression by the regime would be led, to a significant degree, by individuals not organizations. As will be shown in the next few chapters, the example of individual activism fosters an accumulation effect: organizational activists build on the progress individual activists make in terms of public awareness of human rights abuses and in winning initial concessions from the regime. This in turn attracts growing public support for resistance.[4]

The reason for focusing on individual activism is to better understand the process of political change in a society in which activists push for improvements in human rights and democratization. To begin an analysis of activism with the launching or reemerging of organizations is to miss an important, earlier phase.

Just as most social movement literature begins with an assumption that there is a social movement for individuals to join, most analyses of democratization begin with the assumptions there are organizations in civil society ready to seek change. Yet the experience of Kenya shows there may be an earlier phase, one in which most organizations are not very active, at least not openly, and in which individuals, for various reasons, step forward to get the ball rolling in terms of gaining initial concessions (or trying) and rousing public awareness to the vulnerability of an authoritarian regime to pressure for change.

This section analyzes the constraints and opportunities for individual activism at the structural, institutional, and individual level. It is worth noting again here that activists, for the most part, proceeded despite negative external conditions or constraints, largely creating their own opportunities, or taking advantage of opportunities created within the dynamics of the resistance itself.

Structural Factors

Economy.[5] During the phase of the study period in which individual activism was the most prominent (1987–1991), there were no major fluctuations in the income levels of Kenyans. There was a fairly steady but gradual decline in incomes and gross domestic product, as there was in much of Africa at the time. Therefore the economy is not considered an important variable triggering the rise of individual activism.

---

4   Some individual activists were members of organizations but ones that either offered no support for their activism or, in some cases, opposed it. For example, the leadership of the Law Society of Kenya opposed Gibson Kamau Kuria's early legal actions against the state; and the hierarchy of his Presbyterian Church in Kenya opposed Dr. Reverend Timothy Njoya's activism. Some individual activists operated a family-run publication or were in law partnerships that offered little if any organizational protection for their activism.

5   A more detailed analysis of the economy and the debate on linkages between economic conditions and democratization is found in chapter 6.

Foreign Assistance. Aid to Kenya was increasing during most of this period. Total aid to Kenya increased from $753 million in 1987 to $1,102 million in 1991.[6] This may have made some Kenyans more determined to resist what could be seen as an authoritarian regime with growing international support. Though when asked what spurred them to action, no individual activist mentioned this. And if anything, the increasing aid strengthened the hand of the regime, making resistance more difficult, not easier.

For the most part, donors made little noise about human rights abuses in Kenya or lack of democracy prior to the end of the Cold War in 1989. And only once did donors come together in a dramatic way to freeze new funds, in November 1991, which may have helped push the Moi regime to make a major concession, a constitutional change returning Kenya to the multiparty status for the first time since 1969. But that concession followed domestic resistance that had grown from a few isolated acts by individuals to involve an emerging challenge by a wide array of opponents to the regime, including politicians gathering behind various configurations that would soon emerge as opposition political parties. For this and other reasons that will be explained later, foreign aid, international human rights organizations, and the role of international donors, are not considered critical variables that determined the emergence of individual activism in Kenya.

Class Structure.[7] By 1987 there was a growing middle class in Kenya of professionals, businessmen and women, academics, politicians and others. The largest class by far was still the lower class. Poverty had long been greatest in rural areas,[8] although the urban areas had become ringed with slums where most residents lived in substandard conditions. But these long-term trends showed no major changes in the late 1980s. And many potential activists had been driven into exile by the mid-1980s.

The threat of loss of class/economic status as a result of selective repression for resistance to the regime was a deterrent real enough to discourage most potential activists from emerging into the open. On other hand, one could argue that the prospect of losing a middle class status might give incentive to some to resist. The regime was helping erode the financial status of both the middle and lower class through a combination of misappropriation of funds and by efforts to undermine any perceived economic advantage of the Kikuyus, seen by the regime as mostly opposed to President Moi. There is some indication based on interviews for this study that concerns about the erosion of professional status helped motivate some individual activists to challenge the regime.

---

6   The data comes from a report by T.C. I. Ryan, a Kenyan economist, and Stephen O'Brien, former head of the World Bank delegation to Kenya, which was included in *Aid and Reform in Africa*, a book published by the World Bank in 2001.

7   Joseph (1987) argues against the use of class as a basis of political analysis in Africa because political parties cut across class lines, as they do in Kenya. But in the period before opposition parties were legalized, class analysis is useful.

8   Nelson, Harold D. 1984. *Kenya: A Country Study*. Washington: American University/ Department of the Army, 138–139.

Institutional Factors[9]

Regime behavior. The biggest constraint at the time against the emergence of an open resistance by individual activists was repression by the regime. At the same time, regime repression was the catalyst for activism. The dynamics described in the model of resistance in this study began with regime repression.

As discussed in chapter 2, after the attempted military coup of 1982, President Moi began steadily drawing the reins of power tighter and tighter in his hands and cracking down on opponents, real and suspected. The repression targeted not only educated members of the middle class who were suspected of disloyalty to the regime but also ordinary Kenyans who dared to challenge the power of authorities.

Kenya was not alone, of course, in moving toward increasing authoritarianism after independence. The first wave of post-independence leaders and quite often their successors across most of Africa made "systematic efforts...to overcome the constraints of the colonial legacy by reorganizing public institutions and by concentrating power at the political center." This "process of power consolidation with strong authoritarian and even repressive overtones occurred throughout the continent." The state apparatus, especially the military and the police, became instruments of repression as leaders took measures to prop up their regimes.[10] This is a process Callaghy documented in Zaire under Mobutu Sese Seko.[11] The state was often used for the enrichment of its leaders, something Joseph describes as "prebendal" politics in his study of Nigeria; but it was in no way limited to that country.[12]

Civil Society. By 1987, especially compared to what it would become after 1992, civil society in Kenya was not robust. The regime had tried to co-op whatever looked like an emerging power base outside of government, including a national women's organization that was transformed into a government institution. Kenya by 1987

---

9   This study uses both the formal meaning of institutions (i.e., organizations, either in or outside of government) and the informal meaning (i.e., such as habits, or patterns of behavior by government or society). Numerous scholars use a broad definition, including March and Olson (1989), though these two scholars focus more on the norms of a bureaucracy and how institutional norms help shape the behavior of those who work in them.

10   Chazan, Naomi, Robert Mortimer, John Ravenhill, and Donald Rothchild. 1992. *Politics and Society in Contemporary Africa*, 2nd ed. Boulder, CO.: Lynne Rienner, 46; 57.

11   Callaghy, Thomas M. 1984. *The State-Society Struggle: Zaire in Comparative Perspective*. New York: Columbia University Press.

12   Joseph, Richard A. 1987. *Democracy and Prebendal Politics in Nigeria: The Rise and Fall of the Second Republic*. Cambridge: Cambridge University Press. In Kenya, for example, one of the early steps taken by the new Administration following the 2002 elections that saw the defeat of Moi's ruling party for the first time since independence was to investigate the illegal skimming of funds from state institutions in what became known as the Goldenberg scandal of the early 1990s.

had reached a point where the repression by the state was so severe that only a few organizations were speaking out, including several churches.

Some of the churches continued to issue statements from time to time and several church leaders, discussed in chapter 5, became prominent as critics of the regime. The churches were among the few institutions still able to voice criticism without risking serious reprisals. President Moi, who prided himself on being a church-going Christian, may have felt constrained to fully crack down on outspoken clergy,[13] though he exercised little restraint in his verbal criticism of them when they challenged his actions.

The Law Society of Kenya (LSK) included within its membership a handful of attorneys who had challenged and would increasingly challenge the state on human rights and democracy. But as an organization, there was more silence from LSK than protest during most of this period. Its effectiveness as an organization of dissent would depend on who was chairman, and within its ranks there was a long-standing debate underway as to the proper role of LSK as a professional, nonpolitical organization or one of outspoken criticism. It was not until Paul Muite assumed the chairmanship of LSK in 1991 that the organization became a major part of the resistance movement.

A few groups such as the International Commission of Jurists (Kenya Section) issued statements critical of the government and began speaking out against the abuses in international forums, but they did not imitate the direct challenges to the regime carried forth by individual activists in the form of law suits, alternate publications, and attempted mass rallies.

The proliferation of nongovernmental organizations advocating democratization and human rights in Kenya happened after Kenya adopted a system of multiparty elections again. Thus on the whole, the lack of a strong civil society was a constraint at the time individual activism took place in Kenya. When it became strong, it then switched roles and provided an opportunity for expanded activism by organizations.

Societal Norms. In the face of the authoritarian rule in Kenya, including a police state apparatus of spying and control inherited from colonial rulers (and expanded upon after independence), most Kenyans adopted a norm of deference, not defiance. Especially after the wave of torture of suspected dissidents in the later half of the 1980s, the public norm was one of silence and lack of speaking or acting out against the regime. Thus there was an informal institutional constraint against activism in lack of public support for change. Chapter 6 will examine how those norms shifted for some Kenyans, a shift that became an important part of the culture of resistance.

---

13 Maina Kiai, former head of the private Kenya Human Rights Commission (KHRC), in a telephone interview with the author, September 2003.

Individual Factors

Structural and institutional constraints far outweighed opportunities for the rise of individual activism. Nevertheless, though it involved only a relatively small number of persons, there was a discernable phase of individual activism in Kenya which started the establishment of a culture of resistance.

It is possible to measure and document such a phase. One can begin by examining the archival record for evidence of acts of resistance, noting the names of those most prominently involved.[14] Interviews with those activists and others provide details of the acts, as well as confirmation of whether the acts were carried out with or without organizational support.[15]

Certain individuals were targeted by the regime and thus might be considered more likely to have responded; but to start with their response is to miss the acts that drew the regime's attention to them in the first place. For example, when some individual activist attorneys were detained, it was because of their use of the courts to challenge the power of the state through various suits, including representing political detainees.

Many of the individual activists were educated outside Kenya where they earned advanced degrees. This gave them a certain status in Kenyan society and the expertise, for example, to raise legal challenges to the regime. The experience abroad also put them in touch with an active exile community of dissidents. In some cases, such communities supported campaigns to free activists detained by the regime.

Characteristics of Individual Activists

A few individual activists were quite wealthy; only one was relatively poor. The rest were educated urban elites, members of the middle class. Barrington Moore pointed to the importance of an urban middle class in bringing about democracy: "…we may simply register strong agreement with the Marxist thesis that a vigorous and independent class of town dwellers has been an indispensable element in the growth of parliamentary democracy. No bourgeois, no democracy."[16]

Moore saw democracy coming only at a great cost of human suffering, citing the enclosure of many English fields once farmed but then turned into sheep pastures, a move that sent masses of jobless workers to the cities where living and working conditions proved harsh. Modern day Kenya is not early England. While there were no massive sheep enclosures, however, waves of rural poor were driven to the urban slums by a deteriorating economy which one can attribute in part to an expanding

---

14 For the purpose of this study, *The Weekly Review* was used as a record of major acts of resistance in favor of human rights and democratization.

15 Some 70 interviews were conducted, more than half with activists.

16 Moore, Barrington, Jr. [1966] 1993. *Social Origins of Dictatorship and Democracy: Lord and Peasant in the Making of the Modern World*. Boston: Beacon Press, 418.

rural population, land scarcity, poor international trade patterns, and a patrimonial regime grown accustomed to not only rewarding supporters but to abusing its perceived enemies.

The enemies the Moi regime found itself facing were for the most part intellectuals. These were not revolutionaries, not organizers of battles. Their resistance would be in stark contrast to the Giriama of early 20th century colonial Kenya and far different from the forest tactics of the Mau Mau and its supporters. For one thing, in the first phase of open resistance these enemies of the state would fight with their education, often using the law to challenge a regime that claimed to abide by the rule of law.

Table 3.2 at the end of this chapter provides biographical information about individual activists. If one were to draw a portrait of a typical individual activist in Kenya from 1987–1991, it would look like this: a male, Nairobi resident with a graduate degree; a member of a profession (about half were attorneys); married; probably a Kikuyu (about half were). When opposition political parties were again allowed to start in 1992, he would join one, switching parties at least once. Clearly this was a middle class phenomenon. A few had proven themselves successful in business, but most struggled over finances, using their own resources to resist the regime.

Half of the 20 individual activists documented in this study were attorneys, most with graduate degrees in law, often from the U.K. or the United States. Of the rest, three were academics; two were wealthy businessmen and politicians (Kenneth Matiba, who would run for President in 1992 and 1997; and Charles Rubia); one was an engineer turned activist; one was a renegade member of the clergy; one was a student activist and the other two were politicians. Only one, Rubia, had only a secondary school education, but he had also been an early Mayor of Nairobi.

Those who had been educated abroad had the opportunity to develop contacts with international organizations. Mirugi Kariuki, for example, was active with the International Commission of Jurists (Kenya Section) and attended their international meetings when he could. Information from activists such as attorney Gibson Kamau Kuria regarding allegations of torture by the regime was helpful in the preparation of human rights reports such as those by Amnesty International.

Such contacts also helped protect some individual activists who were extremely vulnerable because they were operating on their own and not as representatives of organizations. When, for example, Gitobu Imanyara was detained for articles published in his magazine *Nairobi Law Monthly*, various human rights organizations abroad issued statements calling for his release, which came fairly quickly. But international publicity alone was unable to win the prompt release of others, including activist Koigi wa Wamwere, a favorite target of the Moi regime for his outspoken criticism who later wrote a book about his long struggle with the regime.[17]

The church was one of the few institutions in Kenya that the Moi regime tolerated in terms of its criticism of the government. Being identified with a church probably

---

17 Wamwere, Koigi wa. 2002. *I Refuse to Die: My Journey for Freedom*. New York: Seven Stories Press.

added to the stature of the activists and may have spurred their own denominations to come to their verbal defense when the activists were detained or under pressure from the regime to keep silent.

Some members of the ruling party, the Kenya African National Union (KANU), did not hesitate to use religious comparisons in berating critics of the regime as unpatriotic in an attempt to create the illusion of widespread public support for the regime.[18] The President spoke out harshly against the few members of the clergy attacking his policies in the mid-1980s and early 1990s. The role of the church resistance will be discussed in chapter 5 where the focus is organizational activism. Rev. Njoya's contributions are noted below because he carried out a resistance without the blessings or support of his Presbyterian Church leaders and in the face of their strong criticism and a reassignment up country in an attempt to silence him.

Unpredictability of Individual Activism: The Role of Minor Actors

In the current study of the establishment of a culture of resistance, there were numerous examples of minor actors playing a crucial role. It was not who these minor actors were but what they did that was important. If they had not offered assistance to the major actors, the major actors might not have been able to continue their activism.

In some cases minor actors such as prison guards helped an activist survive the ordeal of confinement, an important contribution considering that some Kenyans who went to prison died or became incapacitated because of the harsh conditions. In other cases, activists were warned of pending arrests or surveillance that enabled them to escape a trap aimed at silencing them. The fact that minor actors helped activists, sometimes unknowingly, means that at least some of the resistance by individual activists was uncertain.

The contribution of these minor actors is often overlooked in the study of political change. We try to predict outcomes based on known variables; but the variable of chance, of uncertainty, makes prediction less reliable. Minor actors are sometimes invisible links in chains of events that lead to resistance by activists. Take them away, and the chain is broken; the resistance may never have happened, or at least not as soon as it did. It is an argument of this study that often activism is the end result of such chains of events; and that an accumulation of events, or activism can result in increased pressure on a regime.

As stated earlier, there are likely to be setbacks as the regime learns to fend off or limit activism; and the public waxes warm or cold toward activism, depending on the opportunities key players give them to express their discontent. Some examples of the role minor actors played in helping individual activists in Kenya include:

---

18 Haugerud, Angelique 1995. *The Culture of Politics in Modern Kenya*. Cambridge, UK.: Cambridge University Press, 79–81.

Assistance in Legal Challenges. The 1987 example cited in chapter 1 of a prison guard's role in helping an accused dissident, Wanyiri Kihoro, meet secretly with his wife gave him a chance to ask her to get a lawyer, which led to embarrassing publicity that helped bring about a sharp reduction in the regime's use of torture and detention.[19]

Assistance in the Release of Detainees. A prison guard allowed activist George Anyona and his three fellow prisoners to meet for breakfast one day, where they made a plan to fake illness in order to be taken to hospitals in Nairobi. Their bail appeal hearing, they had been tipped off, was coming up and the court would require them to be in Nairobi. Had they not been allowed to make their plan they might have missed the court date and not been released when they were.

Protecting Activists. A taxi driver hired by police to follow activist Martha Karua for several days, tipped her off, avoiding possible harm to her by police. A state security official tipped off activist attorney Rumba Kinuthia that security agents were about to arrest him in a raid on a restaurant where he was eating. He escaped successfully to continue his activism, though he was detained three months later.

A Kenyan businessman helped Rev. Njoya avoid roadblocks aimed at his arrest shortly after security officials interrupted his public, pro-democracy prayer crusade, held in defiance of President Moi's order. On another occasion, several Kenyan journalists threw themselves over Njoya to protect him from what could have been a fatal beating by the government's paramilitary force at All Saints Cathedral in Nairobi in 1997, the day of a major march supporting a new constitution to reduce presidential powers.

What Individual Activists Did

This study argues that the changes that occurred in Kenya in terms of greater recognition of human rights and democratic principles were part of a process, not the result of any dramatic events or conditions. The process, one of resistance, had historical roots but in this study period reemerged through the actions of a small number of individuals. Their efforts won some ground, widening the opportunities for further activism, by reducing the legitimacy of the state and raising public consciousness of and demands for greater freedom. International factors, including help from donors and human rights agencies, were part of this process but not, as some studies argue, the primary or key factors. Table 3.1 categorizes some of the main examples of resistance in Kenya during this period (1987–1991).

From Table 3.1, one can observe that individual activism from 1987–1991 was divided between "formal" challenges using supposedly legal methods of dissent, and "informal" or illegal ones such as unlicensed public rallies

---

19 Kihoro documented his experiences in a book (1998) and discussed them in an interview with the author in Nairobi, Kenya in 2002.

Table 3.1   Individual activism in Kenya 1987–1991
(Activists identified at end of this chapter)

Formal	Activists	Goals
law suits	attorneys	stop torture of detainees
		stop use of detention
public remarks	academics; politicians	curb abuse of power; promote pluralism
published remarks	attorneys; academics	criticism of regime abuses
legal defense	attorneys	overturn charges
Informal	Activists	Goals
political rallies	politicians	promote pluralism
secret meetings	Attorneys; politicians	plan legal defense, rallies
protests	Students; others	release political prisoners

Definitions: Formal: legal under regime laws but often attacked by regime.
Informal: illegal under regime laws.

Formal Resistance

Formal challenges were the most frequent in the early period of individual activism, for very logical reasons. Formal resistance relied on existing state institutions such as the courts, or state-approved publications, although some attorneys were detained and some alternative publications came under heavy criticism and periodically were banned. A few attorneys filing papers in court to challenge the alleged misuse of law offered much less excuse for a harsh response than the informal resistance such as unauthorized public protests. Both kinds of resistance helped usher in the organized activism and mass support that would further weaken the regime's claims of legitimacy.

Activist attorneys tried to use the courts to stop various abuses, challenges usually considered legal though unwanted by the regime. The fact that what was intended as legal resistance under existing laws was often repressed by the Moi regime helped weaken the regime's claims of legitimacy by exposing the hollowness of its supposed support of the rule of law.

Formal resistance also included writing articles critical of regime practices printed in legally-registered publications. On numerous occasions the regime detained the owners and/or editors of the publications on charges of sedition which it interpreted broadly to try to curb political criticism.

Earlier underground activists had issued clandestine publications which the regime interpreted as calling for the overthrow of the government.[20] The regime responded to these alleged enemies of the state with a wave of arrests and confessions often based on torture. A regime that claims to uphold the rule of law could argue that underground enemies of the state justify such a harsh crackdown to maintain order.

Public remarks, especially when published by the mainstream media, were also a part of the formal resistance, trying to take advantage of supposed freedom of speech. In reality, such freedom was severely limited when it came to criticizing the regime. But the state response was uneven. Sometimes individuals would be arrested and charged with sedition, sometimes they would be threatened with it. And sometimes President Moi himself would respond with a vitriolic attack on the speaker.

Informal Resistance

Informal activism involves resistance which the regime considers illegal, such as unlicensed political rallies. Such resistance is more likely to draw public support if it comes after a phase of individual activism that alerts the general population to abuses, especially if concessions are made by the regime. The overt, formal challenges to the regime and any concessions encourage more people to protest to gain further reforms. But informal resistance carries risks of failure. If few people turn up for a rally, the regime can claim there is little support for political change.

A key illegal rally was planned by two individual activists, Kenneth Matiba and Charles Rubia, for July 7 (*Saba Saba* in Swahili) in 1990 to support a change to multiparty politics and was broken up by police. Such informal resistance poses a serious threat to the legitimacy of a regime and is thus likely to be repressed. It defies the regime's orders and calls on the general public, not just a small band of activists, to come out and express their displeasure. The Moi regime went to great trouble to try to prevent, then to break up the intended rally.

The intended rally, the first such public challenge, came after some minor successes won by individual activists using the formal channels of resistance – namely the courts. Those victories, small but symbolically important, not only helped win reforms but signaled to the country that activism could be effective. There is no precise way to measure such a 'signal.' The signal was the example that those challenging the regime lived to tell about it, especially human rights defense attorneys who were able in court to detail their accusations against the regime at a time when most people were afraid to speak them aloud. News of such boldness as rallies or court proceedings spread rapidly through newspapers, sermons, gossip,

---

20 Defendants in such cases later argued that their publications challenged the authoritarian ways of the regime but did not actually call for a revolution or uprising to overthrow it illegally.

and stories, with the help of drivers of long-distance group taxies and buses.[21] Another indication that the signal was received was the fact that more and more people showed up at rallies, legal or illegal ones.

A quantitative analysis of such rallies would serve little purpose. Their importance is not in the frequency. Head counts would be unreliable because of the way crowds ran about dodging attacking police. The importance of such rallies lies in the fact that they received massive newspaper coverage and triggered strong reactions by the President, who obviously saw the importance of such support for change.[22] The suppression of such rallies also brought strong condemnation form a number of donors to Kenya, including the United States and Germany.

Another example of informal resistance was the very public hunger strike by the small group of mothers in 1991 for the release of political prisoners. They claimed the right of assembly but knew it was useless to apply for a permit which the government would not approve. The fact that the protest was violently disrupted by police, drew widespread domestic and international attention to repression in Kenya.

Systemic and Nonsystemic Challenges

One goal of activism was narrowly focused and nonsystemic: to help particular individuals in custody win better conditions or freedom. When they held their public protest in early 1992, the mothers were not seeking a systemic change; they simply wanted to get their sons out of prison. Sometimes attempts to help individual victims of the regime led to wider challenges to a particular practice. The mothers' strike, for example, led to formation of a private organization, Release Political Prisoners, that not only tracked arrests, but also opposed the concept of political prisoners in general.

But one can see from Table 3.1 a much broader, systemic goal of activism: challenging the nature of the regime and the distribution of power. Examples of this include legal attempts to stop the practice of torture and the use of all detention.

---

21 A formal analysis of the content of newspapers and estimations of readership would not help much in a country where poverty blocked most Kenyans from buying them. Instead people often gathered around newsstands or read over someone's shoulders, or passed old copies from hand to hand. But word of mouth was also a major way a 'signal' of resistance was passed through the cities and countryside.

22 There were two kinds of reactions from such events: the public's and the President's. Interviews the author conducted with participants at the time of a second rally, in November 1991, known as the Kamakunji rally for the site where it was held, indicated a depth of anger at the regime and a willingness to face likely police brutality for showing up at the event. As for the President, he gave few interviews during this time; and the ones he gave tended to be public relations events and offered few real insights. His reactions ranged from publicly denouncing individual activists to ignoring them. At times he jailed leaders; at other times he did not. But the concessions he did offer, including a reluctant agreement to allow multi-party elections, followed growing resistance that had increased from a few individuals to many.

Later in this period, the challenges to the system were directed at bringing back multiparty politics to Kenya with the aim of defeating the incumbent regime.[23]

Another pattern that emerges is that activists use the skills with which they are best equipped. Attorney activists tended to use the courts to resist the regime. Politicians tended to turn to the use of public protests. Later many activist attorneys would join a party and many would run for and win a seat in Parliament. The mothers and some student leaders not professionally trained to challenge the regime in court, turned to public protests.

Motivational Issues

The interviews carried out for this study shed light on tactics used and provide the activists' own explanation concerning motives. The archival record of activism is a way of corroborating the claims by the activists as to what they actually did. To some extent, tracking the behavior of early activists in later years offers some insights on whether they stayed true to stated motives. But one's actions – and motives – may change over time with changes in circumstances. Some simply burned out and took jobs that offered better pay. A few joined the ruling party after fighting it for years. But later actions do not negate earlier resistance.

There were divisions among activists as to the best tactical approach, especially during the organizational activism phase discussed in chapter 5. The divisions and personal ambition for power, especially among opposition presidential candidates led to some bitter personal antagonism and disappointments within the activist community, leaving some resentment that carried through to the end of the study period (2002). These introductory remarks before examining the question of motivation more closely are given to underscore the fact that there are few saints in the world of political activism. Ambition for political power, money, and status all play a part in any political struggle.

The constraint/opportunity nexus for the individual and organizational phases of activism are distinct enough to provide a basic observation. It was risky being an organizational activist; it was much more risky being an individual activist before there were many domestic organizations to offer a measure of protection and support and before the regime had moved away from its use of torture and threatened executions of those it considered to be enemies of the state.

"Most of them [the activists] were very genuine human rights defenders, placing themselves at risk. [As for] anything else they were getting out of it in the early

---

23 As we shall see in chapter 4, the main form of resistance during the organizational phase of activism was systemic. Although activists would continue to seek the release from prison of fellow activists, most of the resistance, with long lulls of activism between election years, focused on winning passage of constitutional amendments or passage of an entirely new constitution.

stages – there weren't rewards; there were only risks, really," according to Martin Hill, a former researcher on Kenya for Amnesty International.[24]

The Importance of Models for Activists

It is an argument of this study that examples of resistance encourage others to join that resistance. Individual activists don't topple pillars of an authoritarian regime, but they can help erode them and encourage others to resist. Their record may not be flawless, nor is it likely to be without danger. Rumba Kinuthia, detained and tortured, was an activist attorney who represented accused dissidents.

> We had seen examples of people, of lawyers, being victimized because of representing clients who were unpopular with the government of the day, and some of them being detained like Dr. John Khaminwa, Dr. Kuria…People were quite scared of defending these people who were perceived to be anti-government, because it was at the height of the one-party dictatorship."[25]

Kinuthia took some controversial human rights cases in the 1980s, including some 25 detainees accused of membership in the Mwakenya underground. When Kinuthia was himself detained in 1990, Khaminwa was his lead defense attorney. "Khaminwa was acting as an individual, motivated by his notions of what justice is…" said Willy Mutunga, one of Kenya's most consistent leaders in the human rights field, starting from the 1980s.[26]

What the few early resisters had done in Kenya in the early 1980s was built on a long, historical tradition of resistance in Kenya (as described in chapter 2) and set an example of personal courage and principle. Their work did not go unnoticed. Many of the activists of the late 1980s and early 1990s spoke of Khaminwa, for example, as one who had been ready to defend human rights when most others were not. There is no quantifiable measure of the impact of such an example. But the fact that other attorneys and student leaders who became activists still mentioned their admiration of him in 2002 is an indication of the importance of models in establishing a culture of resistance.

Wafula Buke, for example, was a student leader at the University of Nairobi when he was arrested in 1987, charged with spying for Libya, and tortured. A year earlier he had organized a campus protest over the U.S. bombing of Libya. In an interview he referred to Khaminwa as one of the few lawyers willing to defend human rights in the 1980s. He called him "a great man."[27]

A Model Individual Activist. Khaminwa was wearing a blue and green pullover sweater one evening in August 2002 at his law office in downtown Nairobi. He had

---

24 Martin Hill, in an interview with the author in London, July 2002, speaking for himself, not Amnesty International.

25 Rumba Kinuthia, in an interview with the author in Nairobi, Kenya, August 2002.

26 Willy Mutunga in an interview with the author in Nairobi, Kenya, September 2002.

27 Wafula Buke, in an interview with the author in Nairobi, Kenya, October 2002.

just finished another full day of legal work, still challenging President Moi's powers in various cases. Khaminwa was detained for a few weeks in 1990 for helping plan the attempted political rally in July of that year to promote multiparty government despite a constitutional ban on opposition parties.

He said he had always been "committed to certain values" and had strongly opposed detentions.[28] But there was a price to pay for such activism. His son, Arthur, was at Leeds University, in his third year when the government began pressuring his father's law practice. With security agents discouraging potential clients, Khaminwa senior's income dropped. As a result, his son was unable to finish his studies. "People come to you if the government is on your side" because the judges are appointed by the President and lacked security of tenure, said Khaminwa. But loyal clients still kept coming to him.

Activist attorney Gibson Kamau Kuria said "[h]uman rights work entails sacrifice.... The clients don't have money to pay." He added that there is also "the risk, to your profession, your life…"[29] Another prominent activist in this period, Paul Muite, was also the victim of state harassment aimed at slowing down his work. The state tried to "tire you financially . . . in terms of time . . . exhausting you deliberately . . . to destroy you or co-opt you."[30]

Khaminwa was not the only model who inspired other Kenyan activists. Kinuthia said he had looked up to a group of lecturers at the University of Nairobi for inspiration. Among them was the novelist Ngugi wa Thiong'o, whom he admired for his "sincerity and his devotion…to the cause of the betterment of the people of Kenya, and his singular opposition to the mercenary attitude of the rulers."

Martha Karua named fellow-attorney Pheroze Nowrojee, an activist in the 1980s and 1990s as a mentor and model for her own activism. For example, in the midst of handling a difficult human rights case as a new lawyer, she said "I remember Pheroze Nowrojee finding us outside the court and coming in to help us and to lead us. He really rescued us. He came into give us guidance. He led us in a very gallant manner."[31]

Nowrojee said that he never lacked human rights cases to defend under the Moi regime. There were cases defending "the right of assembly…charges [of] sedition; there were charges against unlawful assembly, illegal meetings. There was press censorship. Each and every one of these represented a violation of a specific right within the Bill of Rights [of the Kenyan Constitution]."[32]

---

28 John Khaminwa, in one of two interviews with the author in Nairobi, Kenya, August 2002.

29 Gibson Kamau Kuria, in an interview with the author in Nairobi, Kenya, July 2002.

30 Paul Muite, in an interview with the author in Nairobi, Kenya, July 2002.

31 Martha Karua, in an interview with the author in Nairobi, Kenya, August 2002.

32 Pheroze Nowrojee, in an interview with the author in Nairobi, Kenya, August 2002.

Alternative Motivational Explanations

Max Weber confronted the materialistic and deterministic explanation of societal change by Karl Marx. Commenting on his own famous essay *The Protestant Ethic and the Spirit of Capitalism,* Weber said it was "a factual refutation of the materialist conception of history."[33] Weber wrote in his essay that it might "in a modest way form a contribution to the understanding of the manner in which ideas become effective forces in history." He adds, "[c]ountless historical circumstances, which cannot be reduced to any economic law, and are not susceptible of economic explanation of any sort, especially purely political processes, had to concur in order that the newly created Churches should survive at all."[34]

In Kenya it was the idea of human rights and greater democracy that motivated and invigorated many of the individual activists and gave them a focus in their resistance to state repression. The economy during the study period was practically a constant, bad, for most people. It limited the resources activists could bring to bear in their resistance, but it did not dissolve their determination and effort. Financial sacrifice was often a feature of individual activism.

Weber argued that ideas are the engines that drive social change, that "... ideas in their presence or through their absence are the main determinants of the social." For Weber, "... the economy itself is a limiting, though not determining influence on society. Marx's simple economic materialism, Weber believed, dissolves under such considerations."[35]

Weber's emphasis on ideas did not mean that he ignored rationality; rationality formed a major part of his analysis, not only of social change but also of bureaucratic behavior. To Weber an act is rational "when it can be described as being in accord with the canons of logic, the procedures of science or of successful economic behavior..." But he went beyond instrumental rationality to include value-based rationality based on "religious, moral, or aesthetic" values. People are moved not just by the hopes of material gain but "by affections and passions ... this is when ends and means are both derived from emotions." This calculation represented an "opposite pole in Weber's system from the calculating, rational deed."[36]

Rational choice. Most considerations of a rational choice explanation for individual action eventually go back at least to Mancur Olson.[37] But in a passage seldom cited in such explanations, Olson states that the rational argument does not always work.

---

33 Macrae, Donald G. 1974. *Max Weber.* New York: Viking Press, 62.

34 Weber, Max. [1930] 1992. *The Protestant Ethic and the Spirit of Capitalism.* London: Routledge, 90–91.

35 Macrae, 64.

36 Macrae, 74–75.

37 Olson, Mancur. [1965] 1998. *The Logic of Collective Action: Public Goods and the Theory of Groups.* Cambridge, MA.: Harvard University Press.

"The theory developed here is also not very useful for the analysis of groups that are characterized by a low degree of rationality, in the sense in which that word is used here. Take for example, the occasional band of committed people who continue to work through their organizations for admittedly "lost causes." Olson would surely have written off as a lost cause the attempt by some Kenyan activists, especially those acting primarily as individuals, to challenge an authoritarian government that tortured dissidents. Political scientists often tend to skip over Olson's caveats about applying economic-based rationality to noneconomic groups and what he terms "non-rational" endeavors such as struggling for "lost causes." Olson also goes on to suggest that in general rational choice theory is not the best way of analyzing such phenomena as mass movements.[38]

There is another problem with applying rational choice theory to try to explain the motivations of human rights and pro-democracy activists in the early phases of resistance when costs far outweigh likely benefits. Early activists risked possible detention and torture; their gains might be additional legal clients, or brief notoriety. It is an argument of this study that the normal rational choice explanations fail to reveal why most individual activism took place in Kenya.

Community model. Amitai Etzioni offers another model, a different way of looking at choices, of pursuing goals one acquires from our communities. He looks at "inner moral and emotive developments...."[39] In Etzioni's model, man is seen as moral and not just economic. Man considers his community as well as himself in making decisions. Etzioni credits Martin Buber for this "I & We" view of life. One makes decisions not just to further one's self interest but also to advance the interests of the community. The communitarian model of Etzioni challenges Hobbes' view of man[40] as so self-centered that he must surrender power to a Leviathan to keep order among people.[41] Anderson takes a middle position that sometimes peasants act out of self interest and sometimes for community interests, though some community-oriented actions carry with them the hope of long-term personal benefits in terms of community help for themselves in times of future need.[42]

This study agrees with the conclusion of Mansbridge regarding motivation in political life: that sometimes it is out of self-interest and sometimes out of "concern for the common good." Mansbridge points to numerous conceptual advances in political analysis through application of a rational choice model. "But the claim that self-interest alone motivates political behaviour must be either vacuous, if self-interest can encompass any motive, or false, if self-interest means behavior that

38 Olson, 161–162.

39 Etzioni, Amitai. 1988. *The Moral Dimension: Toward A New Economics*. New York. Free Press/Macmillan, 14.

40 Hobbes, Thomas. [1651] 1997. *Leviathan*. New York: Norton.

41 Etzioni, 8.

42 Anderson, Leslie E. 1994. *The Political Ecology of the Modern Peasant: Calculation and Community*. Baltimore: Johns Hopkins University Press.

consciously intends only self as the beneficiary." She argues that "both self-interest and concern for the common good [have] a significant role in political action."[43]

One could reasonably argue that as the resistance expanded in Kenya to include political parties and nongovernmental organizations, at least some Kenyans joined such groups for reasons of self-interest and not strictly community interests. Former Amnesty researcher on Kenya, Martin Hill, notes that once the aura of invincibility of the Moi regime was broken, "some [activists] went into politics; some were forming NGOs themselves and getting a living from it whereas before, they suffered. And this is very, very, very proper. That's the way it should be. You need professional human rights workers. They...usually do better than the part-time volunteers who are voluntary people who don't have the time or the resources and are at great risk. And their families, too."

Principled Ideas

"I believe in democracy and human rights," was Kuria's concise explanation of his work when asked about his motivation. As a youth during the Mau Mau conflict some freedom fighters had come to his family's house looking for food. One day he saw bodies of Kikuyus left near the market of his hometown, killed by the British. He could see that the colonial system was "very unjust and [Kenyan freedom fighters] had really made a sacrifice."

In secondary school, he was impressed by the play A Man for All Seasons about Sir Thomas Moore, who stood firmly for the law against the Crown and was executed. He saw a link between Moore and the Mau Mau fighters: "both were fighting for justice," he explained in one of several interviews for this study. At Oxford University he was influenced by British law professor Ian Brownley who combined theory and practice, and by an American professor, Ronald Dorkin. Kuria decided he wanted to become a scholar, a teacher, and a practicing attorney, which he did. He didn't set out to challenge an authoritarian state, but that's where his principles led him.

In 1988 Kuria was honoured by the Robert F. Kennedy Memorial Center for Human Rights for his dedication to the principles of human rights in the face of danger. He showed consistency in his commitment to human rights. In 2003, Kuria, like Khaminwa, was helping the new government investigate corruption of the past regime, a task considered dangerous enough for the government to assign him a bodyguard.

Kinuthia, who was inspired in his own human rights legal work by Kuria and a few others, said "they made me feel I'd be ready to sacrifice for the betterment of the common man's lot." Kinuthia's defence of Mwakenya detainees landed him in detention from 1990 to 1993, during which time he was tortured "very badly," he

---

43 Mansbridge, Jane J., ed. 1990. "Self Interest in the Explanation of Political Life". In *Beyond Self-Interest*, ed. Jane Mansbridge. Chicago: University of Chicago Press, 20–22.

said. He had been helping plan one of the most important political opposition rallies in the pre-multiparty period of the early 1990s, in July 1990.

A nonactivist Kenyan who has been a close observer of what took place during the establishment of a culture of resistance is historian Macharia Munene, author of a book on political transition in Kenya. He notes that much of the individual activism was by "people who are very principled...who in their mind...are very clear that when something is wrong, it is wrong; and whether you suffer or not is not the issue."[44]

Tactics of Individual Activists

Informal Networks

Most studies of resistance begin with organizations, which are easier to locate and map. The informal networks of activists, often outwardly invisible that may precede the formation of organizations are critical, however, in the establishment of a culture of resistance. This was the case in Kenya where the regime attempted to strengthen its hegemony by gaining control of as many formal bases of power in civil society as it could, including co-opting the unions and a national womens' organization, as well as keeping tight control over university student activism through the use of informants and quick police response to disturbances. In such a police state, as former Amnesty researcher Hill notes, there was a need for secrecy and informal networks in the resistance to avoid government spies:[45]

Quite often these individuals were connected, but not openly and not organizationally. Behind the scenes they knew each other and they were all working to similar objectives... They wouldn't dare to form organizations. And they were fearful of being seen together... there were secret contacts among some of them.

One way or another most activists get in touch with each other in an authoritative regime. Lacking the formal protection of organizations, individual activists in Kenya also tried to watch out for each other. Activism was risky.

"War room." One example of this informal networking among individual activists in the late 1980s in Kenya involved a "war room," as Martha Karua (Martha Njoka at the time) and others called it. The "war room" was a downtown office of Kenyan attorney Japheth Shamalla, a former Permanent Secretary for Foreign Affairs who had become a human rights and multiparty democracy advocate. It became the informal headquarters for a group of young attorneys who were challenging Moi to support greater human rights, using the courts to air political criticism of the

---

44 Munene, Macharia. 2001. *The Politics of Transition in Kenya: 1995–1998.* Nairobi, Kenya: Quest & Insight Publishers.

45 Martin Hill in an interview with the author in London, July 2002.

regime. They would plan legal strategies there. Karua, one of the activist attorneys, explained how it worked: [46]

> We used his office daily, even when the multipartyism came [in 1992]. It was his telephone that everybody used; it was his fax that we were faxing [to international human rights groups]...It was really a war room. And whenever one [of the activists] failed to come in the evening, frantic calls [were made] to find out [about them] because they could have been picked up [by police].

One day at the "war room" word was received that police had surrounded the downtown office of one of the main human rights activists, Imanyara. His controversial law magazine, launched in 1987, had been publishing scholarly articles by lawyers and others pointing out how the Administration was abusing the law and the rights of Kenyans.[47] Imanyara stands out in the resistance in Kenya to repression in the late 1980s and early 1990s. Among Kenyan activists and others interviewed for this study, attorney/journalist Imanyara was named more times by Kenyan activists and others than anyone else other than attorney Muite.[48] Although Imanyara was the editor of *Nairobi Law Monthly*, his activism was largely as an individual. He financed the magazine, prepared in his small, fourth-floor law office in downtown Nairobi with the help of only a few loyal and courageous staff members. It became, along with Pius and Lloyce Nyamora's family-run *Society* magazine and, for a while, *Finance* magazine, one of the few sources of news and opinion contradicting the official statements of the Moi regime on human rights and the rule of law.[49] He quickly became a target of the State.

"Gitobu, for me, was very, very, very courageous," said Kenya Human Rights Commission's Executive Director Mutunga. "And he suffered a lot for it...He was a glaring example of somebody who was acting as an individual." Nowrojee considers Imanyara a "sustained voice speaking through a lot of hardship and suffering."[50]

---

46 Martha Karua in an interview with the author in Nairobi, Kenya, August 2002.

47 While some might consider Imanyara an organizational activist because he headed his own small publishing firm, this study considers him an individual activist in a weak organization. His firm was family-run, had only a small staff and it offered him little or no protection. Imanyara was detained several times, beaten up by thugs under suspicious circumstances once, and his magazine was shut down numerous times by the government.

48 Others among the top ten individual or organizational activists, in order of the frequency of their ranking by Kenyan activists and other Kenyans were: attorneys James Orengo and Gibson Kamau Kuria; former academic and human rights advocate Willy Mutunga; Dr. and Rev. Timothy Njoya; attorneys Kiraitu Murungi and Mirugi Kariuki; environmentalist Dr Wangari Maathai; attorney Pheroze Nowrojee. See Appendix for a listing of the top 30 activists.

49 Imanyara's political machinations in the late 1990s left him isolated and with little public support, but in the late 1980s and early 1990s, he was seen by many Kenyans unhappy with the Moi regime as a hero.

50 Willy Mutunga, in an interview with the author in Nairobi, Kenya, September 2002.

In March 1990 police banned Imanyara's magazine and arrested him, charging him with sedition. He was released in July and immediately rearrested for publishing an article related to the multiparty debate. He was released in a few months, after 20 lawyers offered to defend him and after attracting considerable negative, international publicity from human rights organizations. He quickly filed a law suit seeking to overturn the 1982 constitutional amendment making Kenya a one party state, claiming it bars freedom of expression. This marked the first time the multiparty debate moved into the courts.

In March 1991 Imanyara was arrested again at the same time police confiscated the latest issues of *Nairobi Law Monthly*, *Society* and *Finance*. Moi personally attacked the editorials of Imanyara's magazine. At one point Imanyara, ill, was sent to a hospital where he was handcuffed to the bed to keep him in custody. After another round of international publicity on his behalf, he was freed in May 1991 and the ban on his magazine lifted in July. On the occasion that word reached the "war room" that Imanyara was being arrested, Karua responded in a way that highlights the informal networks activists nurtured.

> We rushed to his office. The police, when they learned we had arrived, took him out through the back door.... I gave chase...they would jump traffic lights; I would jump them, too. They realized they were not going to lose me and I was right on their tail. So they eventually ended up at [a city] Police Station...with me hot on their heels.

She got out of her car to try to talk to Imanyara, when suddenly the police took off again with Imanyara. As she tried to reenter her car, a senior police officer grabbed her arm and took the keys forcefully, tearing the button of her jacket off in the process. Karua told him she would sue the man; he gave her back the keys. She guessed that the arresting officers might have taken Imanyara to his home to search it, and she was right. When the police saw her approaching, they fled with Imanyara, blocking her attempted pursuit with other police cars. The whole incident she explained was "not something I had planned. We had some very interesting times. If one were to think about it you'd actually laugh."

Karua did sue the police Superintendent who grabbed her keys and damaged her designer suit. She was awarded damages of 83,000 Kenyan Shillings in 1993. When the government refused to pay the damages, she sued the Superintendent personally for the amount, putting a claim on his property. That forced the officer to go to the President's office where he finally was issued a check to pay her. In 1994 when police threatened to break up a political opposition meeting in Karua's Parliamentary constituency, she dared the police to touch her, citing the case in which she successfully sued the Superintendent in Nairobi. The effect on the police is an example of how news of resistance, which passed quickly through the general public by word of mouth, newspaper and magazine accounts, also made an impression on state personnel, as Karua recalled.

> When I quoted to them the case...there was nobody to touch me and put me in the police vehicle. Which leads me to the belief that if we stood up for our rights by suing... many

times...the overload of cases would force the government to sit down and change their policy of deliberately abusing the law.

The reason for presenting these details is not to show how brave the activists were, but to show the kind of unplanned, spontaneous actions many of them took that helped put pressure on the regime. Given the authoritarian nature of the state at this time, such actions were seen by both the regime and the general public as brazen defiance of the claimed legitimacy of the state. What the activists were doing is showing that (1) the state could be challenged; (2) there were people willing to challenge it – though not many at first.

Such acts of defiance were helping establish a culture, a pattern of resistance that would grow stronger, not simply because of the state's reluctance to stamp it out entirely, which was a factor, but the accumulation of acts of resistance was revealing a hidden vulnerability of the state. This was not pact-making with an out-going regime; this was a battle of tactics, a struggle for legitimacy on both sides: the state seeking to maintain control and hold on to some public support; activists seeking to keep the momentum of resistance building while trying to keep themselves free from harm.

Karua's informal network with a number of other activists was not the only one operating in the late 1980s and early 1990s. Those pushing for multiparty elections were talking to each other secretly, too. Out of this came the first opposition parties in the new multiparty era after 1992. In addition, former detainees who still had the courage to resist were contacting each other. There were "individual groupings" of activists, according to Edward Oyugi, a psychologist who had been imprisoned for his earlier activism.[51]

Institutional Learning: A Chess Game of Tactics

Isaiah Berlin cautioned against a belief in "one great universal pattern, and one unique method of apprehending it...."[52] There is sometimes in political science a tendency to come up with a theory or a methodology that would fit many cases, an explanation that attempts to satisfy. Yet before long, the explanation of today usually is overtaken by another challenger. Berlin's approach to finding answers was different. The Latvian-born historian of ideas probed deeply but always with modesty, a willingness to concede that he was unlikely to ever find a universal answer or pattern.

Institutional learning is a process by which an institution adapts to the behavior of others and changing conditions in society. In the case of Kenya, the state adapted its tactics to counter those of activists; and vice versa. As used in this study, the

---

51 Dr. Edward Oyugi, in an interview with the author, in Nairobi, Kenya, October 2002.
52 Berlin, Isaiah. 1991. *The Crooked Timber of Humanity: Chapters in the History of Ideas*, ed., Henry Hardy. New York: Knopf, 201.

concept of institutional learning applies to both the state and activists, each learning from each other's moves, as in a game of chess.[53]

Learning is a basic concept, yet it is often not part of the explanations we offer for political change. This study argues that there are certain general patterns that may be detected as a culture of resistance is established through individual and organizational activism of opponents to an authoritarian regime. But within this general pattern are many varieties of activism that can not be described by any formal, predictive laws. This variation is seen in the kinds of tactics activists used and how they change in response to state behavior; it is seen in the unpredictable role minor characters play in chains of events that lead to an act of resistance. It is also seen in the way the state, though with less flexibility and subtlety than activists, adapts to the tactics of its adversaries.

The focus in this study is on process, a process that involves learning. In the individual activism phase, especially, the actors were constantly learning from their successes and failures. When the State blocked one avenue of resistance, they tried another.

The State was learning, too. The State shifted its tactics to try to block moves by activists. Thus the dangerous chess game progressed, though at times one saw evidence that both sides failed to improve their moves and sometimes reverted to old habits. Several examples will help illustrate this chess game/learning process.

Throughout the controversy of the torture and detentions of Kikuyus and others in the late 1980s President Moi maintained a verbal adherence to the rule of law, a stance he continued through the 1990s. In comparison to some of the neighboring countries such as Somalia, Sudan, and Ethiopia, there was a greater professed respect for the law in Kenya. But it was the State's own insistence that law was to be respected that gave activist attorneys, especially in the early 1990s, the room they needed to carry out an elaborate battle of tactics. The scene of most of these battles was the courtroom. Attorney Nowrojee explained that one tactic human rights attorneys turned to in order to get their message of reform out was to use the courtroom as a political platform.

> In these political cases, you seek to win, but by definition, winning is not allowed. Therefore the trial has to be used to make the maximum gains. You show the contradiction between the claim that we are a legitimate government and the illegitimate steps that it keeps taking. You make it [the courtroom] a platform for the accused, for the opposing view.[54]

Activists kept learning new tactics from the changing political response by the state to their initiatives, as human rights attorney Muite, explained. He is recognized by other Kenyans as the most prominent and consistent human rights and democracy activist during the establishment of a culture of resistance. He was elected to

---

53 Dr. Lawrence C. Dodd of the University of Florida introduced the author to the concept of institutional learning.

54 Nowrojee interview.

Parliament several times, including in the opposition sweep of Parliament and the Presidency in 2002. Activist attorneys, he recalled, realized that although the mainstream newspapers often were avoiding serious critical statements about the government, they would report court proceedings.

> And the government would be mad, but since it [was] in court, you know, they couldn't hammer the papers because the papers were merely covering it…That was a strategy that Gibson Kamu Kuria and I promoted. We still use it, even today [2002]. It doesn't matter that the case is going to be decided against you. The objectives [of exposure of state repression] can not be stopped.[55]

Though most of the activism at this time was a matter of day-to-day tactics rather than strategic planning, exposing abuses through the media would help get a sense of momentum going that could help sway the uncommitted to support the resistance. The State tried to stop the exposures with a countermove: using what Muite called "shameless judges." Judges' tenure in office had been removed a few years earlier by the Parliament at the President's wish. Thus the courtroom chess game became a tactical match with activist attorneys proceeding on their own initiative, facing off against judges dependent on an entrenched President determined to stay in power. The lawyers were insisting on the rule of law to enable them to expose, case by case, abuses of law by the regime and by using a state institution to do so – the courts.

Once the Attorney General's office realized that activist attorneys were using the courts to get publicity about the regime's abuses of human rights into the newspapers, the State tried a countermove: silence the attorneys in the courtroom. One judge sought to avoid giving reporters a chance to hear arguments in court by ordering Muite to submit his arguments in writing. Muite argued that the constitution called for cases to be "heard," which means statements had to be spoken aloud. The State made another countermove, threatening him with contempt of court. Muite moved again; he said his client did not want the statements to be submitted in writing. And with that, he walked out of court.

As Njeru Kathangu, an activist who was tortured and charged with sedition, explained, lawyer walk-outs became part of the game. "Whatever motion was in court and [our attorneys] wanted to speak and the magistrate would refuse us, then we would temporarily dismiss our lawyers so that we had to speak for ourselves."[56]

As another countermove to the State's attempt to minimize publicity surrounding a case, defense attorneys made use of a loophole in the law. In filing the initial court papers in a case, the rules require merely a synopsis. But activist attorneys knew reporters had access to such initial filings. So they began submitting detailed arguments, laying out all the abuses of human rights in detail; and the papers published them.

Another tactical move was to drag the trials out as long as possible to allow for maximum negative publicity against the state and time to attract international attention and support. "For more than one year our case was headline news" said

---

55 Muite interview.
56 Njeru Kathangu, in an interview with the author in Nairobi, Kenya, July 2002.

Kathangu of his own trial. Martha Koome, a new attorney at the time and involved in some of these trials, explained that slowing a trial down was not "a strategy" but a day to day tactic. [57] Such shaming tactics would have had no effect if the regime had not pretended to subscribe to the rule of law.

Implications of Individual Resistance

This chapter has shown that in the late 1980s and early 1990s, the phenomenon of individual activism emerged as a challenge to the authoritarian regime of President Moi. Building on a long and historic tradition of resistance in Kenya, it was a phase of activism distinct from the later phase of organizational activism.

Why did individual activism emerge? There were no sudden changes in the economy, which remained poor throughout the period. Donors were not putting pressure on the regime, except in the later months of this five-year period; in fact foreign aid was increasing. Class structure experienced no major changes, and civil society was still relatively weak and unorganized. Levels of state repression were high, posing a major constraint. For the most part the public was cowed into silent discontent or deference, nothing like the public defiance that would emerge during the period of organizational activism.

Repression triggered response by activists willing to take a risk. A rational choice explanation fails to explain why individual activists would risk detention and torture to satisfy the needs of a few clients who were victims of repression and willing to challenge the regime's human rights abuses. Later, when more freedom had been won from the regime, there would be more opportunities to get jobs and political position via activism, but not in the initial phase. Alternative explanations include a sense of community and principle as motivational factors.

This chapter shows that the typical individual activist was a well-educated professional with a family and living in the capitol. Many were lawyers with contacts abroad that at times helped provide publicity from human rights groups when they got into trouble. Patterns of activism varied according to timing, professional background, and the goals (institutional or individual). Both the activists and the state adapted to each others' tactics in an ongoing chess game of learning.

---

57 Martha Koome, in an interview with the author in Nairobi, Kenya, October 2002. She later became chair of the Kenya Chapter of the International Federation of Women Lawyers (FIDA). In 2002, in the new government, she was appointed a High Court judge.

Peaceful Resistance

Table 3.2   Individual activists in Kenya 1987–1991

Name	m/f	Profession	Degree	Ethnicity	Religion
Muite	m	attorney	law	Kikuyu	Christian
Kuria	m	attorney	law	Kikuyu	Christian
Orengo	m	attorney	law	Luo	Christian
Murungi, K	m	attorney	law	Meru	Catholic
Kariuki, M	m	attorney	law	Kikuyu	Anglican
Maathai	f	academic	science	Kikuyu	none
Nowrojee	m	attorney	law	Indian	Parsi
Khaminwa	m	attorney	law	Luhya	n.a.
Odinga, R	m	activist	n.a.	Luo	n.a.
Wamwere	m	activist	none	Kikuyu	Catholic
Karua	f	attorney	law	Kikuyu	Anglican
Odinga, O	m	politician	n.a.	Luo	n.a.
Kababere	f	insurance	business	Kikuyu	Christian
Matiba	m	business	n.a.	Kikuyu	Christian
Rubia	m	business	secondary	Kikuyu	Anglican

Individual activists in weak or opposing organizations

Name	m/f	Profession	Degree	Ethnicity	Religion
Imanyara	m	attorney	law	Meru	Methodist
Njoya	m	clergy	political science	Kikuyu	Presbyterian
Nyong'o	m	academic	political science	Luo	Anglican
Kibwana	m	academic	law	Kamba	Catholic
Buke	m	student	none	Luhya	none

Source. Interviews; archival records. Individual activists are considered those whose activism was recognized as significant by fellow Kenyans, including other activists, corroborated by archival records. They are listed in each section in order of the ranking by fellow Kenyans. See Appendix for a full explanation of selection criteria and a listing of the top 30 activists with first and last names. Note. n.a. = information not available

Finally, this chapter shows that an authoritarian regime that pretends to uphold the rule of law, that prides itself on how it is seen at home and abroad, can be shown vulnerable and respondent to domestic pressure for change. As seen here, at first the pressure may come not from organizations but from a small group of individual activists willing to try to force the regime to live up to its own supposed standards. Such individual activism in Kenya challenged the legitimacy of the regime, and with international support helped win a return to multiparty elections that set the stage for the next phase, organized activism aimed at changing the distribution of political power – and at defeating the incumbent rulers.

Chapter 4

Opening the Door:
Organizational Activism

Paramilitary troops set up roadblocks, and riot police with their usual batons, shields and teargas, spread out around that morning to try to block an illegal political rally in a poor neighborhood near downtown Nairobi. But crowds arrived at the site on foot in defiance of warnings from the government. It was November 16, 1991, a turning point in the growing resistance to authoritarian rule in Kenya.

Political opposition leaders had chosen for the rally a site known as Kamakunji, where many historic political meetings had been held. President Daniel arap Moi was determined to prevent the gathering because it challenged the basis of his authoritarian power: continuation of a one-party system in which he was the only candidate for re-election as head of state.

For several days the police had been looking for the organizers of the rally to detain them, but they had gone into hiding. Now, the morning of the intended rally, a car with tinted windows slowed then stopped in front of the U.S. Embassy. Normally the street was jammed with traffic; but this morning it was practically empty. A rear window of the car was lowered. Some international journalists, including the author who was a correspondent at the time for *The Christian Science Monitor*, had been tipped off by the Embassy. Martin Shikuku, one of the rally organizers, was sitting in the back seat. He and several other organizers of the rally had eluded the police dragnet so far and now were planning to try to reach the protest site and address the crowds in open defiance of the President.

Just as Shikuku began speaking to the journalists, a police car approached. Shikuku's driver sped off with the opposition leaders, slipping through a roadblock being set up and managing to reach the rally site where he made a few quick remarks from the roof of a van he had switched to. Then he was driven away to elude approaching police. What followed was one of the symbolically defiant moments in the resistance to President Moi's hold on power.

Riding atop the van, he and several other opposition organizers waved to the crowds that lined the streets near the rally site. With police in hot pursuit behind them, Shikuku drapped his legs over the luggage rack and raised his arms over his head, giving a V sign with each hand, a sign that had come to symbolize support for multi-party elections. National and international newspapers caught the image of Shikuku atop the van. Police soon caught and arrested him and the other rally organizers, though they were soon released.

At the rally site itself, police were now doing what they did well, clubbing people with their long wooden batons as everyone attempted to scatter to safety. At a corner near the rally site, I spoke with some of those who had run away. Though shaken, they were also angry and determined not to flee the area; some of them headed back toward the rally site. But now it was our turn to flee as a truckload of police disembarked and began running toward us. Another reporter and I reached my car and took off down the median strip (both lanes had been blocked) just as the first police reached within a few feet of the back bumper.

Organizational Activism Builds on Individual Activism

In the approximately four years leading up to this November 1991 illegal political rally, President Moi had been drawn into a game of tactics by individual human rights activists starting in 1987. They had banged on the door of power and won a few concessions, including a reduction of torture by the state.

In 1991, organizational activism started to emerge with a much broader goal: opening the door to power and ushering in a democracy that would lead to the ousting of the incumbent President through an election in which more than one party could present candidates. The President and his ruling party had banned opposition political parties. But now opposition leaders were calling for an end to the one-party system. They had organized into something they called the Forum for the Restoration of Democracy, or FORD, an informal organization that differed from the early phase of individual activism. Though small, it was backed by an array of opposition politicians and was soon to emerge as the first opposition party of the 1990s. It was FORD that organized the November 16 rally in support of multi-party elections. The illegal rally highlighted a new wave of resistance – this time an organizational one that would soon replace individual activism.

This chapter examines the period 1991–1996, a period marked by the institutionalization of a culture of resistance through the efforts of organizational activism. It begins with a look at why organizational activism arose and how it differs from individual activism; who the main activists were, and what they did. The chapter then examines the role of donors and their inconsistency in using aid as leverage for reform. It was domestic activism, not donors that were of primary importance in establishing a culture of resistance in Kenya.

In this institutional/organizational phase of activism in Kenya, the major catalyzing events were the political protest rally in November 1991, the decision by the Moi government to allow multiparty elections; creation of political opposition parties; and the emergence of a demand for wider constitutional reform. In this period, President Moi made some concessions but did not concede any of his vast constitutional powers that kept his regime authoritarian. Organizational activism emerged against major obstacles, building on the gains of individual activism and with some international support.

Structural and Institutional Factors

The class structure had not changed in Kenya between the period of mostly individual activism and organizational activism; and the economy continued to be poor. What did change was the international dynamics after the end of the Cold War and the domestic dynamics of civil society after the regime was forced to drop its constitutional ban on opposition parties. Along with this step toward democratization (an insincere step on the part of the regime, as it turned out) came the legal registration of many nongovernmental organizations whose efforts helped augment the resistance against the regime.

The symbolic end of the Cold War in 1989 was followed by abrupt change of regimes in a number of former Communist countries. One change that surely caught the attention of President Moi and other authoritarian leaders holding on to power in the early 1990s was the overthrow and murder of President Nicolae Ceauşescu of Romania. Western donors including the United States began showing more interest in human rights and democracy now that Kenya was no longer a proxy in the global struggle for influence against the Soviet Union. But on the whole, donors proved to be inconsistent in their funding, sometimes praising the regime, sometimes cutting off funds, in a usually uncoordinated fashion (see below).

Modern civil society[1] at the beginning of the 1990s was still fairly weak in Kenya due to regime control and co-option tactics. But it flourished after 1992 as the government allowed pluralism and more nongovernmental organizations (NGOs) to form and as donors stepped forward to help fund them.

Regime Behavior. In the late 1980s, in the face of domestic resistance and some international publicity, the regime had reduced its use of torture of detainees and the practice of detention itself. But political activists such as Kenneth Matiba and Charles Rubia were detained in 1990 for their role in organizing an unlicensed political protest rally. The number of political prisoners remained high; many of them having been tortured into confessions in the crackdown on suspected Mwakenya members. And critical publications were periodically shut down with force. Regime

---

1   In his study of the impact of foreign aid on democratization, Thomas Carothers argues that Western democracy advocates often overlook the subtle mix of civil society that does not fit the usual Western, institutional definitions (Carothers 1999, 248–249).

"The romanticization of civil society has roots in Americans' rather mythicized Tocquevillean conception of their own society, but it entails a gross oversimplification of the makeup and roles of civil society in other countries around the world. American democracy promoters have made few efforts to understand civil society on its own terms in complex traditional societies in Africa, Asia, and the Middle East. They basically ignore the many layers of clans, tribes, castes, village associations, and the like as essentially unfathomable complexities that do not directly bear on democratic advocacy work. Democracy promoters pass through these countries on hurried civil society assessment missions and declare that "very little civil society exists" because they have found only a handful of Westernized NGOs devoted to nonpartisan public-interest advocacy work on the national scale."

behavior remained erratic and arbitrary and always defensive regarding challenges to the authoritarian power of the President.

Through this period, the regime and activists had matched wits as they had during the earlier phase of activism. Each time the other side tried to advance, in terms of more repression or more activism, the other side would respond. The learning process described in chapter 3 continued, but this time the activists had at least some semblance of organizational backing. And the game had more players, including opposition parties and newly-emerging NGOs.

At the same time, donors and the regime were playing their own game. The donors as a whole failed to use their aid leverage for reforms collectively except for a dramatic moment in November 1991. Otherwise they sent conflicting signals to the regime that in turn attempted to play the game well enough with concessions aimed at staving off real threats to its power and at keeping aid money flowing.

Agency Factors

In the earlier individual activism phase, participants had learned that the regime was vulnerable to pressures and willing to make some concessions. Through a process of accumulated learning, activists had managed to publicize abuses of power through various tactics and gained some improvements in human rights (e.g., less torture; fewer detentions). But it had become evident that the President would not willingly concede or share power, nor would he support constitutional changes that would reduce his power. In other words, individual activism had come to a kind of fortress wall the regime had constructed against incursions to prevent regime change or reduced presidential power.

Short of staging a coup, which activists seemed neither willing nor able to do, they saw no other way to proceed other than to organize for more effective pressure against the regime. "You [had] an imperial presidency with undemocratic institutions," said activist attorney and politician James Orengo.[2]

Comparing Individual and Organizational Activism

There were key differences between individual and organizational activism, in addition to the central fact that the later had some important support from an organization. Table 4.1 shows these differences.

---

2   James Orengo, in an interview with the author in Nairobi, Kenya, July 2002.

Goals. In the organizational phase of activism in Kenya, the main goal became pluralism; specifically elimination of the constitutional provision making Kenya a one party state. Improving human rights, the main goal of individual activism, was still a goal in the organizational activism phase, especially for a number of the new NGOs but in the later phase the main goal of the activists was pluralism. Human rights could no longer "take a front line any more because there [had] been a reduction of violations of human rights," noted a leading Kenyan activist.[3] Instead the focus shifted to democratization.

Activists. The main actors in the individual phase – attorneys, journalists, and some clergy members – continued their activism but were joined, significantly, by some former members of the ruling party, the Kenya African National Union (KANU) who had gone into opposition politics. It was the politicians who took the lead in organizing the illegal protests in 1990 and 1991 that helped transform the resistance from a scattered effort to a national issue, from a small band of courageous activists to a political movement drawing in political opponents to the regime and discontented members of the pubic.

Target of activism. While getting dissidents out of detention and winning improved treatment of detainees was a target of this new activism, most of it now focused on systemic changes such as pluralism and a new constitution. It took a while for the focus to shift toward a new constitution, but when it did, that helped sustain and energize the sometimes flagging resistance movement whose political leaders and followers were dispirited after losing the controversial election in 1992 which Moi won through manipulation, including rigging, and the lack of a united front among his opponents.[4] KANU won 53 percent of the seats in Parliament in 1992, aided by disproportionate districts that favored the ruling party. It was enough to form a government but not enough to amend the Constitution, which required a two-thirds majority.

---

3   Activist attorney and politician Paul Muite in an interview with the author in Nairobi, Kenya, July 2002.

4   Throup, David, and Charles Hornsby. 1998. *Multiparty Politics in Kenya: The Kenyatta and Moi States & the Triumph of the System in the 1992 Election*. Oxford: James Currey, chapter 11. President Moi won with 1, 962,866 votes, or 37 percent of the total against four major and three minor rivals, none of whom was able to expand his base of support much beyond his own ethnic region. Matiba finished second, with 1,404,266 votes. Under the constitutional election rules the regime had fashioned to its benefit, a presidential candidate had to win at least 25 percent of the popular vote in at least five of the eight provinces. No other candidate but Moi got more than 25 percent of the vote in more than three provinces (Throup, Hornsby, 1998, chapter 11).

Table 4.1   Individual vs. organizational activism 1987–2002

	Phase I: Individual Activism 1987–1991	Phase II: Organizational Activism 1991–2002
Goals	human rights	pluralism; new constitution
Activists	attorneys, journalists clergy	politicians, attorneys, NGOs churches
Target	individuals	political system
Tactics	use courtroom as political platform; exposure by alternative media; public protest	political opposition rallies citizens' constitutional convention human rights reports by NGOs
Actions	often illegal	mostly legal
Global	Cold War on or just ended; little Western interest in human rights, democracy	Post-Cold War Western interest in human rights, democracy
Donors	Little use of funding leverage Little funding for reform efforts	Greater use of funding leverage More funding for reform efforts
Domestic	Modern civil society weak; opposition parties illegal	Modern civil society robust; opposition parties legal

Tactics. In the individual phase of activism, one of the main strategies was use of the courtroom as a political platform. In the organizational phase, the main forum was the political rally. Before multipartyism was restored at the end of 1991, such rallies were illegal. After that, opposition party leaders held many rallies across the country, though the police often tried to interfere with them.

In the buildup to the change to multiparty politics, activists organized two major public protests, in 1990 and 1991 that drew large numbers of people and had a ripple effect in other parts of the country. Both of the public demonstrations were dramatic and violently repressed by state security personnel. They marked important milestones in the establishment of a culture of resistance in Kenya for two reasons: (1) they challenged the regime's legitimacy[5]; (2) they provided the first major public forums for expression of opposition to the regime despite the fact that they were broken up by police.

What the organizational activists with the second rally in 1991 did that individual activists had not been able to do was to bring together a political coalition that crossed ethnic lines and would soon emerge as the main opposition party. After opposition parties were legalized again in December 1991, the first legal public rally of the Forum for the Restoration of Democracy (FORD), in January 1992, drew at least 100,000 according to the British Broadcasting Corporation (BBC).[6]

Primarily in the run up to the elections in 1992, 1997, and 2002, opposition parties held many rallies for their candidates. Here the focus was neither human rights nor democratization – the focus was on winning the elections. Presidential candidates anxious to assume power seldom spoke out for a new constitution that would bring presidential powers more in line with the other branches of government.

In the 1990s human rights and other pro-rights and pro-democracy NGOs began investigating abuses, reporting them, and educating the public about their civil rights, often attracting international funding. This had a double ripple effect: (1) it kept human rights abuses before the Kenyan domestic public and international donors; (2) it helped rouse the dormant understanding of the Kenyan public about what rights they had, especially after the legalization of opposition parties. A national network of human rights activists was nurtured by Nairobi-based organizations that helped establish grass roots support for reform.[7]

Domestic strength. Regime repression blocked formation of most advocacy groups before 1992. But after the switch to multiparty elections in 1992 there was a proliferation of NGOs, including many advocacy groups. Despite continuing selected repression of individual activists and key advocacy groups, organizational activists operated in a climate of expanding freedom of speech and assembly, with some opposition activists in Parliament, and with the drawing power of opposition political rallies, despite regime attempts to block many of them.

---

5   In the absence of regular opinion polls on support for the President during the late 1980s and early 1990s, a measure of the legitimacy of the regime in the view of the public can be seen in the growing public resistance to it, which is highlighted in this book. Once multi-party elections began, the lack of support for the President became clearer; though he won re-election in 1992 and 1997 it was with a low plurality each time.

6   *Weekly Review January* 24, 1992, p. 9. An opposition newspaper said the crowd was much larger.

7   Mutuma Ruteere of the Kenya Human Rights Commission, in an interview with the author in Nairobi, Kenya, September 2002.

Motivational Issues

After the regime dropped the constitutional ban on opposition parties (December 1991) and allowed more NGOs to register with the government, organizational activists had more options than the earlier individual activists. This gave them a choice of ways to pursue their goals. In interviews, all activists said they had wanted a regime change, but they chose different ways to express their resistance.

The main organizational options open to activists at the time were (1) joining a political opposition party, running for Parliament, or working in the party; (2) working for an activist NGO advocating human rights and/or democratization.[8] There are two broad categories of motivations that one could surmise from statements and actions of activists from this period.[9]

First, there were the more idealistic motivations. Some activists were ideologically motivated and wanted "an ideological change of the system," according to Edward Oyugi an activist and psychologist who chose the NGO route.[10] Some of these ideologues, including Marxist-Leninists or socialists, ran for political office while others joined NGOs and pushed for human rights and democracy.[11] Other activists saw a need for a government more ethical, more broadly based in terms of ethnicity, more democratic and more respectful of human rights. Some of these joined an opposition party or one of the NGOs.

Still others focused on a more open civil society capable of protecting human rights and advancing democracy. Mirugi Kariuki was one such activist. Suspected of involvement in the underground movement Mwakenya for his defense and association of some accused of membership, he had been arrested in 1988 and tortured. But even after his release he continued his human rights legal work into the 1990s. He was also active in the International Commission of Jurists, both at the national and international levels. Principle "is *important* (his emphasis)", he said. Without it, why would you live? . . . I get more satisfaction out of matters of principle than just going with the wind."[12]

Second, there were more practical motivations. Some of the politically-motivated activists, especially former members of the ruling party who had been eased out, "simply want[ed] to take over the system" and assume power, Oyugi explained. They were not inclined to seek constitutional changes that would reduce the power of the President; they preferred to inherit such powers. This helps explain why the main opposition presidential candidates showed little interest in a new constitution.

---

8   A few activists from the individual phase never aligned themselves with an activist organization but carried on some resistance in their own professional roles.

9   One could argue that the two categories are not mutually exclusive: an activist may be idealistic but still need a job, for example.

10 Edward Oyugi in an interview with the author in Nairobi, Kenya, October, 2002.

11 Ideologues working for an NGO should leave their "ideological baggage" behind, says Oyugi.

12 Mirugi Kariuki in an interview with the author in Nairobi, Kenya, August 2002.

Another group of activists used the NGOs as an entry point into politics. "Civil society was a halfway house to political society," or an active role in opposition politics, notes law Professor Kivutha Kibwana, an intellectual architect of some of the resistance efforts by elites in Kenya.[13] Human rights thus became a means to an end for some activists. Still others simply sought employment through an NGO. They could carry on their activism, but they could also pay their bills.

Identifying Organizational Activists

Analysis of the top 30 Kenyans identified by other Kenyans as the most active in pushing for human rights and democratization in the study period shows several patterns.

First, of the top 20 Kenyans identified as individual activists (chapter 3) in the first period (1987–1991), all but one of them were active in the second period starting in 1991, this time with an organizational base. They carried on the resistance they had started in the earlier period, though most shifted their focus from human rights to democratization. This time they had some kind of organizational backing. Some went into the opposition political parties, some into NGO work, and some carried on their legal work but with the active support of the Law Society of Kenya (LSK) with regards to human rights and democratization cases. Other organizational activists joined them.

Second, a number of key activists were elected to Parliament in the new multiparty elections of December 1992. They simply moved their activism from the streets to their seats in Parliament. Now they had a base in an important state institution from which to continue their activism.

Third, opposition politicians and their parties replaced lawyers and independent journalists as the main actors in the push for multiparty politics.

As organizational activism grew, individual activism faded, no longer needed in a vanguard role of knocking at the door of authoritarianism. Some of the non-lawyer activists, politicians including Matiba and Rubia, took their activism into the new political parties. Through the parties they were able to mobilize large numbers of supporters at campaign rallies, despite the regime's continuing efforts to block some of those events. Oginga Odinga and his son Raila Odinga both pursued activism through the political party route. Those who helped lead the various opposition parties often were in close contact with the public and in a position to try to keep public excitement for political change building. Opposition parties tended to do very little between elections, rallying voters only in time of pending votes. This had the effect of numbing the reform movement during long lull periods between elections.

Fourth, other activists went into NGOs, where they began earning a more steady income. These groups, such as the Kenya Human Rights Commission (KHRC) kept the spotlight on human rights but for the most part were not activist organizations in terms of holding mass public protests. They and some other NGOs did carry

---

13 In 2002, Kibwana ran successfully for Parliament on the opposition ticket of the National Alliance Rainbow Coalition (NARC).

out an important sensitizing campaign helping citizens become more aware of their rights, sometimes through small, local protests. This was a less obvious part of the establishment of a culture of resistance. It provided people legal and other information to help them register, vote and realize that human rights were not just a privilege but also something they could expect. This process helped people in many parts of the country come to see basic democratic and human rights not as a privilege to be handed out by an authoritarian/patrimonial regime, but as a normal part of a democratic society.[14]

Biographical Characteristics of Organizational Activists

The typical profile of the organizational activist in Kenya closely resembled the characteristics of the individual activists since almost all individual activists became organizational activists. Table 4.2 profiles the characteristics of the top thirty individual and organizational activists combined, based on interviews for this study.

Table 4.2 indicates some interesting biographical characteristics of the Kenyan activists. If one were to describe a typical organizational activist, he would be an attorney with a graduate law degree, a Kikuyu and Christian. For the most part, these organizations were led by urban, middle class elites, mostly professionals. More than half were attorneys; others included several members of the clergy, a few key academicians, and several who can best be described as political activists.

Table 4.2   Top 30-ranked Kenyan activists 1987–2002: biographical characteristics

Profession		Sex		Degree		Ethnicity		Religion	
Attorney	13	male	27	graduate	14	Kikuyu	15	Anglican	7
Clergy	4	Female	3	bachelor	6	Luo	4	Catholic	5
business	3			secondary	3	Meru	3	Methodist	1
activist	3			unknown	7	Kamba	3	Presbyterian	1
academic	2					Luhya	2	Christian$_b$	6
Other$_a$	5					Indian	2	Other$_c$	10
						Kalenjin	1		

Notes: [a] other includes a biological scientist/environmentalist, a journalist, a politician, an architect, and an engineer; [b] did not specify a denomination; [c] other includes a Parsi, a Muslim, a Sikh, three with no religion, and four whose religion was undetermined.

---

14 One sign of the growing commitment on the part of the public to greater democracy was the increase in the number of Kenyans who monitored elections. For the 1992 election there were some 5,000; for 1997, there were nearly 28,000. The re-election process "reinvigorated civil society and the press – two fundamental components of any democratic system (Barkan, Gordon 1998).

Nearly half of the activists were Kikuyus. As part of its drive to consolidate power, the Moi regime had "sought to fragment and capture all independent bases of authority to reduce his dependence on institutions controlled by ethnoregional interests that were never part of his political coalition. The Moi regime undermined through corruption and maladministration the coffee and tea sectors – the mainstay of the Central Kenya (Kikuyu, Embu, Meru) economy.[15]

Most of the activists in both periods lived in Nairobi most of the time. Resistance in Kenya was not only a middle class elite-driven effort, but also most of the key acts of resistance happened in the capitol. In the later half of the 1990s, resistance would spread to smaller cities and towns and some rural areas, as NGOs spread out encouraging more active participation in local reform efforts as well as in voter preparation. But the main theater for resistance was Nairobi, the capital, where most of the activists lived.

The capital had the advantage of being close to the home of the key news media, including a growing independent press. The press offered some degree of notoriety and thus a degree of protection in that the activists' international contacts were likely to lodge complaints against the regime if the activist were arrested, as happened with activist attorney/journalist Gitobu Imanyara on several occasions. But prominence also increased the risk of arrest.

Lesser-known activists might attract little attention in the capital but were more likely to stand out in rural areas. Under the constitution, independent Kenya gave colonial-like powers to its President, including a top-to-bottom political spy system based on presidential appointment of provincial, regional, and district officers as well as local chiefs.

> [T]here is much more exposure and spotlight [on abuses] in urban areas than in the rural areas. In the urban areas police are bound to be much more careful in dealing with suspects than in the rural areas…in the rural areas the officers know they can do [harm] and get away with it.[16]

Most of the organizational activists were quick to join opposition political parties once they were legalized in 1992. As more parties came into being and the original FORD quickly split into two factions (and more later), the activists spread out and into a variety of parties. Some became officers in those parties. A number were elected to Parliament. Their human rights and democracy advocacy helped bring them publicity and electoral credentials, though no guarantee of election or reelection.[17]

---

15 Barkan, Joel D. 1993. "Kenya: Lessons from a Flawed Election." *Journal of Democracy* 4(3):85–99, July, 188.

16 Mutuma Ruteere interview.

17 Imanyara later joined KANU only to be dumped by the President in 2002, a move that left him in a political wilderness. He had burned his bridges with the opposition; suddenly he was left without a party, his political career apparently over despite his years of risky activism in the late 1980s and early 1990s.

Institutionalization of Resistance

Institutionalization of resistance in Kenya came mostly through four prominent groups: (1) churches; (2) professionals, especially attorneys; (3) nongovernmental organizations (NGOs); and (4) opposition politicians. In the case of churches, institutionalization of resistance began in the previous period of activism. It is an argument of this study that activists were able to increase the pressure on the authoritarian regime to make concessions on human rights and democracy despite the relative weakness of their organizations. Often the organizations were poorly staffed, poorly financed, and poorly equipped. More important was the accumulating effects of their resistance on both the public and the regime.

The accumulating acts of resistance, first by individuals then those working within organizations, had two effects: (1) it encouraged public support for reforms as seen in the public's participation in mass demonstrations and other expressions of dissent, including riots; and attendance (often massive) at opposition party rallies; (2) it served as evidence to the regime that demands for reform had transformed from individual acts of resistance to an informal resistance movement that had wide appeal.

Activist organizations that had the widest appeal were the new political opposition parties. Political coalitions that brought together key ethnic groups signaled widespread opposition and worried the regime. Later as such coalitions emerged into political parties and fractured they presented less of a threat, but the large crowds turning out for their rallies still indicated the scope of the opposition. Coalitions that brought together a variety of civil society organizations such as those that later focused on a new constitution were another sign of the strength and breadth of the resistance.

Institutionalization Slows Resistance

While institutionalization strengthened the establishment of a culture of resistance in Kenya by giving it organizational support and some continuity, in some ways it also slowed it. The 1992 elections saw a number of individual-turned organizational activists elected to Parliament, including Muite, Martha Njoke, Peter Anyang' Nyong'o, and Kiraitu Mirungi. These and others had provided the intellectual planning for much of the resistance and the institutionalization of the resistance in the form of political parties.

As one account noted, "[i]n terms of brainpower alone, the opposition would appear to be miles ahead of KANU and probably has the capacity to go on the assault on a number of issues that would have the government on the defensive."[18] Now the activists had two fronts: one inside government, and the various groupings outside, including the churches, NGOs, and professional organizations.

---

18 *Weekly Review*, January 1, 1993, p. 44.

Instead of performing solo acts of defiance, which usually brought publicity, activists elected to Parliament spent more time preparing budgets, visiting donors, holding staff meetings, than on the streets or in the courtroom challenging the President. What might have been seen as a new opportunity for activism on the outside supported by members of Parliament on the inside proved to be just the opposite: street activism diminished. As activist political scientist Anyang' Nyong'o, first elected to Parliament in 1992 noted:[19]

> Once you elect those people to an institution called Parliament, that institution does not necessarily lend itself to further political mobilization because they are now functioning under certain rules of the game which you may not necessarily have understood when you were mobilizing for them to go and represent you there. Those rules essentially mean that you slow down the mobilization. The dynamics of that institution leads to political decay – a loss of mobilization.

Anyang' Nyong'o noted that after the opposition had won nearly half the seats in Parliament, there was less energy and direction going into efforts to rouse public awareness and provide public opportunities for expression of discontent. Mobilization declined after 1992. The lull lasted until the next election year in 1997.

Institutional Resistance by Churches

Churches were one of the few organizations the regime was reluctant to try to shut down. A handful of activist clergy who were outspoken during the period of individual activism continued to speak forcefully in the name of human rights and democracy during the organizational phase. They had the benefit of a loyal audience (their congregations), employment as members of the clergy, and the prestige of the churches themselves. Their remarks critical of the political leadership of Kenya brought them notoriety and popularity among many Kenyans dissatisfied with the regime.

Activist clerical 'quartet'. The Catholic Church as an institution became more vocal in its defense of human rights. Four esteemed members of the Kenyan clergy were the most outspoken church leaders in favor of greater human rights and democratization. Resistance by such esteemed activists helped build public resistance to the regime. This clerical quartet was composed of Bishops Henry Okullu, David Gitari, and Alexander Muge of the Anglican Church of the Province of Kenya; and Rev. Dr. Timothy Njoya of the Presbyterian Church in Kenya.

Catholic Bishop Ndingi Mwana 'a Nzeki joined their outspoken resistance when state-manipulated ethnic clashes broke out in the region of Nakuru in 1990 where he was serving. The Catholic Church Bishops also united from time to time in issuing public pastoral letters critical of the regime's abuses of human rights and

---

19 Peter Anyang' Nyong'o, in an interview with the author in Nairobi, Kenya, August 2002.

democratic principles, more so in the 1990s. And the National Council of Churches of Kenya (NCCK) also spoke out as an institution. Peter Njenga, Provost in the early 1990s at the Anglican All Saints Cathedral in downtown Nairobi, was also a strong government critic on issues of human rights and democracy.

This study does not focus on the inner workings of activist NGOs, including churches. But it is worth noting an observation by one Kenyan activist whose professional focus has been NGOs and who is well aware of the role the clerical quartet played in establishing a culture of resistance in Kenya. Oduor Ong'wen, chairperson of the National Council of NGOs in Kenya at the time he was interviewed for this study, suggested that the clerical activists were speaking more as individuals than as institutional representatives. All four were highly-respected in Kenya and in their congregations, but "you can't say the entire church was very happy with what Muge, Okullu, Gitari and the rest were doing."[20] The Rev. Dr. Njoya was openly opposed in his church by several senior members of the church hierarchy who were supporters of President Moi and KANU.

President Moi was in a difficult position when it came to trying to silence the criticism from the clergy. He had a fairly tight control over NGOs and would-be political opposition parties as the 1990s began. He simply did not register those he didn't like; without being registered, they could not operate legally. No rival political party was registered before the President finally agreed in December 1991 to allow more than one party.

But the churches were long-established institutions. The President himself attended church. In the face of very strong criticism from the clergy, Moi would, nevertheless, verbally and publicly chastise outspoken members of the clergy. And since only a few spoke up consistently, his targets were few. But the more he condemned the clergy, the more attention he drew to their charges. The outspoken clergy took steps to make their sermons available to the media so the public would hear their condemnations of rights abuses, for they intended for their message to reach far beyond their own congregations.

There was an intriguing linkage between the outspoken clergy members and some of the intellectual activists such as Anyang' Nyong'o, who would provide information that wound up in the sermons of the late Bishop Okullu,[21] according to Gitari, who had just retired as Archbishop of the Anglican Church in Kenya when interviewed for this study:[22]

---

20 Oduor Ong'wen in an interview with the author in Nairobi, Kenya, October 2002. In a separate interview in Nairobi, November 2002, Archbishop (Retired) Gitari said there were "some Bishops who did not support me," but that the Archbishop never tried to stop him from making political sermons. He did note that he was strongly criticized from time to time by President Moi for his critical statements.

21 In the acknowledgements of his autobiography (1997), Bishop Okullu thanks Professor Anyang' Nyong'o for giving him "a lot of encouragement" to write his book. "We worked together very closely," said Anyang' Nyong'o in an interview with the author in Nairobi, Kenya, August 2002.

22 David Gitari, in an interview with the author in Nairobi, Kenya, November 2002.

We [the four clerics] became the spokesmen of the people because it was so dangerous [in the 1980s] for an individual to attack the government because they could easily be detained without trial…So people [were] scared. But they would find it very difficult to arrest Bishop [Henry] Okullu or Bishop [Alexander] Muge or myself. If they arrested me, within a very short time, the whole world would be protesting.

Gitari, according to activist attorney G. B. M. Kariuki, was "very courageous, and he spoke with a lot of courage and pointed out incidents where government was failing in its duty, ranging from the ethnic cleansing that was ongoing in the Rift Valley and other places, to political violence, to subversion by government of the…economy…"[23]

Sometimes Bishop Gitari's critical sermons were on local issues but had national implications.[24] A sermon in May 1991 was preached at the base of Kamuruana hill in Kirinyaga to condemn allocation of a large part of the environmentally sensitive hill by the Kirinyaga County Council to two local politicians.[25] Land grabbing by regime allies was a major problem during the Moi years, as Kloop has documented.[26] "As a result, that hill not taken. Because the sermon was heard all over the nation, it became the key passage in the struggle against land grabbers in Kenya," said Bishop Gitari.

Bishop Gitari believed that "all good preaching must be relevant to us today." When in 1988 the government imposed a system of voting called queuing (lining up in public behind the name of a candidate), candidates favored by the government were still rigged into office. When some of the newly elected officials came to his church, he wound up his sermon by announcing that the majority of the newly elected officials, including members of Parliament have been elected in a "rigged election."[27]

A week after police broke up Matiba and Rubia's intended pro-democracy rally of July 7, 1990, which was followed by riots in several cities, Bishop Okullu gave one of his most forceful sermons against the KANU/Moi regime:

> I stand before you as an old man in body but a young man at heart….I remember so clearly the ideals our people stood for in our nationalist struggle…democracy, social justice, truth, peace, personal integrity, human dignity, equality before the law, the rule of law, and above all, the just government of men . . . Kenyans are rightfully frustrated with this

---

23 G. B. M. Kariuki, in an interview with the author in Nairobi, Kenya, October 2002.

24 Some of his sermons are collected in a book edited by the Rev. Joyce Kirigia and published in 2002 by the Anglican Church in Nairobi, Kenya: *Eight Great Years: October 1994 to September 2002, To God be the glory great things He has done; Achievements of the ministry of the retiring Archbishop The Most Rev. Dr. David Mukuba Gitari as the 3rd Archbishop of the Anglican Church of Kenya.* Some of his sermons were also published in a book by Gitari (1996).

25 Gitari, Bishop David. 1996. In *Season and Out of Season: Sermons to a Nation.* Carlisle, U.K.: Regnum, 102–110.

26 Kloop, Jacqueline Maria. 2001. "Electoral Despotism in Kenya: Land, Patronage and Resistance." PhD dissertation. McGill University (Canada).

27 Gitari, 70.

government, and there is no other way of putting it than that we want to elect a new and proper government.[28]

The clerical quartet was never far from condemnation or threats from the regime or its supporters. Rev. Njoya was exiled by senior members of the Presbyterian Church to a rural area in an attempt to silence his criticism of the regime. And Bishop Gitari was attacked by a mob for his outspokenness. "I have suffered more in the process of fighting for human rights than I have gained," said Gitari. "When I preached so much against rigging of elections, my house was raided by a big number of thugs on 21st April, 1989."

Bishop Muge was killed in early 1990 in a mysterious road accident that many Kenyans suspect was intentionally set up by the regime. Muge, a Kalenjin, the same cluster of ethnic groups as the President, had long been a critic of regime excesses. Not long before his death he had spoken out against corruption, "suggesting that a prominent local politician...," a close ally of President Moi, was involved.[29] Just before his death, local Member of Parliament and Minister of Labour Peter Okondo had threatened that Muge would be killed if he set foot in a particular district (West Pokot) where he went despite the threat.

President Moi had managed to muzzle most of the academic activists in the 1980s through repression. Some had fled into exile; others had been arrested, some tortured. He had neutralized the trade unions, the women's organization, and refused to register rival parties or most NGOs which threatened to challenge him. But he had not been able to silence the churches. The words from the clerical activists stirred the public, encouraging the push for multiparty democracy.

Institutionalization of Resistance by Professionals

The institutionalization of activism by attorneys occurred rather suddenly in 1991, a year that proved critical in Kenya's transition toward democracy. Activist lawyers and sympathetic members helped politicize their Law Society of Kenya, ending a long-standing internal debate over whether the LSK should play an obvious political advocacy role. The conservative, neutral position was soundly defeated with the election of activist Paul Muite as LSK chair.[30]

From that point on, activist attorneys on their own or in the name of the LSK had the LSK support, not so much in the traditional organizational way (financial, clerical, etc) but by having the endorsement of the group. A pattern of open solidarity among activist attorneys that had begun to emerge in the late 1980s, was now formalized in the name of the LSK. Once politicized, the LSK lent its full prestige to the resistance

---

28 Okullu, Bishop Henry. 1997. *Quest for Justice: An Autobiography of Bishop John Henry Okullu.* Kisumu, Kenya: Shalom Publishers and Computer Training Centre, 151–155.

29 Throup and Hornsby, 200.

30 Muite was ranked as the number one activist for the study period by fellow Kenyan activists and others interviewed.

efforts. Often a number of its members would sign on as defending attorneys in cases in which another activist had been charged with some offense. And the organization itself generated a number of key law suits challenging the government on a variety of democratization issues.

Lee Muthoga and others had helped keep the LSK on the sidelines in terms of advocacy for political reform in the 1980s. In 1990, Fred Ojiambo was elected chair by a vote that many in the Society felt was improper, and outraged them. At the end of the controversial proceedings, "Ojiambo walked away with the Chairmanship but [candidate Paul] Muite left with the LSK."[31] Members angry with Ojiambo were now ready next time to elect Muite, who wanted to pull the LSK directly into the middle of the mounting resistance against the Moi regime.

Muite was elected chair in March 1991 along with an activist Council that included former detainee and human rights advocate Willy Mutunga as Vice Chairman; another former detainee G. B. M. Kariuki, as well as activists Njoke and Japheth Shamalla, were also elected. In his opening speech as the new Chair, Muite said, "[u]nder my chairmanship, your Society will endeavour to work with the government and judiciary but not, and I repeat not, at the expense of compromising on issues of principle. The rule of law must reign supreme."[32]

Muite called for the registration of Oginga Odinga's National Democratic Party (NDP) that Moi was blocking because of the constitutional ban on more than one party. He also called for the release of detainees Raila Odinga, Kenneth Matiba and Charles Rubia. Thus the stage was set for a major confrontation between the regime and the organization which included the same individual activist attorneys who had been forced to proceed earlier on their own, without the LSK backing, but who now had a chair fully behind their efforts to challenge the government on human rights and democratization.

A tactical battle began. Four pro-government attorney members of the Society quickly filed a suit aimed at preventing Muite from acting as chair. A Moi-appointed judge issued an injunction that prevented Muite from assuming the chairmanship. In defiance, Muite chaired a Council meeting, claiming that they were only discussing nonpolitical matters. The pro-government attorneys filed suit to obtain a contempt of court order; proceedings on that issue lasted some five months.

By now the regime was losing ground. Muite was becoming a political hero in the eyes of many Kenyans. "Kenyans saw him as the bastion of resistance to tyranny. Hundreds of people appeared outside the court to listen to the submissions and they would carry Muite shoulder-high as he left the courts." International human rights organizations began sending representatives to the proceedings.[33]

When the decision was finally made in October 23, 1991, the court apparently did not want more international publicity by sending more attorneys to jail. Instead

---

31 Mwangi, Paul. 2001. *The Black Bar: Corruption and Political Intrigue within Kenya's Legal Fraternity*. Nairobi, Kenya: Oakland Media Services, 163.

32 Mwangi, 171.

33 Mwangi 176.

the defendants were found guilty of contempt and fined. In his closing remarks before the court ruling was announced, Muite said:

> The LSK Council is before your Lordship today and on the doorsteps of prison because those in power are determined to remain in power courtesy of the security forces and the judiciary but without the consent of the people of Kenya...Our faith while in prison will be the knowledge that the present leadership will not and cannot stop the tide – the LSK and its Council will have played its part and paid its share of the sacrifice.[34]

The politicized LSK under Muite's chairmanship is an example of institutional learning, or a tactical chess game between an organization of resistance and an authoritarian regime. A similar game had played out during the phase of individual activism. But now that the LSK had a political activist for chairman, the game took on an organizational aspect. Now instead of meeting in a secret downtown "war room" to clandestinely plan their moves, activist attorneys met in the LSK office and planned bold moves to challenge the regime.

There was another change, as Muite explained. His goal was always pluralism, not human rights per se, though human rights are included in his definition of pluralism. But human rights were no longer a big enough goal to insure both rights and democratization. Pluralism, multiparty democracy had been his real goal from the start, he said. In the 1990s, his tactical games with the administration were centered on challenges to the one-party system and the legal underpinning the regime attempted to use to justify it, he said. It took a convergence of domestic and international forces to bring concessions, he and most others interviewed argued.

Resistance by Nongovernmental Organizations

The institutionalization of resistance by NGOs came as an adjunct to the creation of political opposition parties in 1992. The institutionalization was not so much achieved as granted by a regime forced into accepting pluralism. But the concession was a very limited one: civil society organizations had to struggle to gain the political space for effective resistance.

Once launched, the NGOs began looking for and often found funding abroad, money not forthcoming from domestic sources. There was a gradual widening of the scope of NGO activities and many direct challenges to which the regime responded with an occasional de-registration. While usually small in staff, many of the NGOs hired full-time staff that at least could provide some clerical, publicity and other office support for advocacy of human rights and democratization. But few organizations engaged in direct confrontational politics such as organizing mass rallies, with the major exception of 1997, when many joined the coalition effort seeking a new constitution.

---

34 Mwangi, 179.

In President Moi's bid to expand his power, especially after the aborted coup of 1982, he had not only sought to weaken Kikuyu and other ethnoregional bases of political and economic power, he had tried to get control of NGOs through a system of government registration. He was suspicious of their often outside funding and sponsorship. Civil society activists resisted the original registration Act and fought hard (successfully) to get it amended. NGO activists continued to face threats of arrest; and their families, an often-overlooked element in Kenya's resistance, suffered anxiety over the fate of their loved ones.[35]

Institutionalization of Opposition Politics

The process of institutionalization of resistance by the political opposition began with the regime's bowing to pressures for pluralism. The creation of opposition parties put another major set of actors in motion on behalf of democratization. The legalization of an opposition acted as magnets for a wide variety of activists, including many former ruling party politicians seeking a way to get back into elected office.

But the contribution to the institutionalization of resistance had little to do with the formal structures of the parties. For the most part, they were seldom well-financed, and divided by rivalries that led to the splitting and further splitting of the original party, FORD. Most parties operated out of small, poorly-staffed offices with little in the way of modern equipment or the usual trappings of modern political parties in Europe or the U.S. Kenyans had gone more than two decades without an opposition party. The number of politicians and party professionals still available from the previous era of multiparty politics was limited.

The institutional strength of the parties came not from the usual organizational capacities. It came more from their presence as beacons of hope for political change, helping galvanize a previously dormant public into shifting from deference to defiance of the regime.

From Networks to Parties

Two of the most important mileposts in the establishment of a culture of resistance were the aborted, public, pro-multiparty rallies on Saba Saba (July 7, 1990), and the Kamakunji[36] rally (November 16, 1991). They galvanized the public, even though both rallies were banned by the regime. They also highlighted abuses by the regime by triggering police brutality that brought increased public support for change as well as negative international publicity. Together, the two cases illustrate the transformation from individual to organization activism.

---

35 Davinder Lamba, activist NGO leader, in an interview with the author in Nairobi, Kenya, September 2002.

36 Kamakunji is the name of the open grounds in a poor neighborhood near downtown Nairobi used for the rally, an historic site for political speeches in Kenya.

Both cases also illustrate another characteristic of the resistance in Kenya, that it often involves informal networks that become more formal as protest is institutionalized. The most dramatic transformation from informal networks to formal organizations in the resistance movement in Kenya in the early 1990s was in the growth of the political opposition from a loosely-connected group of politicians before opposition parties were legal to the formal establishment of such parties after they became legal in 1992.

In their aborted attempt to organize a mass political rally in 1990, individual activists Matiba and Rubia accomplished what earlier, individual activists had been unable to accomplish. "Over a few weeks, Matiba and Rubia effectively transformed the long-repressed underground movement for multiparty democracy into a mass movement which for the first time threatened the government's control."[37]

Behind the scenes there was an informal network of activity aimed at ensuring a good turnout for what would be the first public opportunity for Kenyans to express their discontent with the regime at an open rally. Had few turned up it might have dampened the move toward greater opposition to the regime, slowing the establishment of a culture of resistance.

"In those days there were no proper structures for organizing protests," said Raila Odinga, an activist detained on several occasions during the 1980s and 1990s. So the organizers of the rally turned to their own, informal constituencies to insure a crowd would turn up, as Odinga explained. "Mr. Matiba had contact with matatu [minibus taxi] operators which he said he would mobilize. And I had the football... fans, which I could use. We agreed that he would mobilize the matatu touts [fare collectors] and drivers, and I would organize the fans... I have been involved in football administration for a long time."[38] Odinga had been a member of a football club, a secretary of their organization, a coach and trainer. Matiba's links to Matatu drivers is less clear except that when he was a Cabinet Minister, he said, he approved the first commercial matatu drivers.[39]

The 1990 press conferences by Matiba and Rubia calling for multiparty democracy and the attempted Saba Saba rally was a form of resistance that straddled

---

37 Throup and Hornsby, 61–62.

38 Raila Odinga, in an interview with the author in Nairobi, Kenya, October 2002. Odinga was encouraged by Moi to cooperate with the regime by offers of a substantial post in a new government to be elected in 2002, including either as a presidential candidate or a Prime Minister, in an attempt to rebuild a Kikuyu-Luo alliance that had been created during the initial years of the Kenyatta presidency.

39 Matiba's personal charisma and his stature as an elder in society were still evident in 2002, despite his defeat in two presidential races. I was in his chauffeured car with him entering Nairobi after an interview in his country home when he spotted a matatu driver who had stopped illegally in the middle of our lane to let off a passenger. Angered, Matiba ordered his driver to stop. He got out of the car and walked hurriedly over to the vehicle. The offending driver's expression changed from cocky confidence to humbleness and he asked for forgiveness as soon as he realized it was Matiba. He repeatedly apologized for what was normal behavior among many such drivers.

individual and organizational activism, with two prominent individuals out front but a loosely-organized set of activists in the background. There was little in the way of organizational follow-up, however. It was not an example of the institutionalization of resistance in Kenya. They were detained, and the democracy project seemed to end there. But it did not.

Emerging Party. In 1991, a more serious challenge than the Matiba-Rubia pronouncements emerged. This time instead of two Kikuyu politicians, the challengers represented a number of key ethnic groups, including Kikuyu and Luo, the political combination the regime most feared.

There had been many behind-the-scenes discussions preceding the two Matiba-Rubia press conferences in 1990, but no lasting organization emerged as a result. This time an organization, FORD, emerged from many conversations and plans behind the press conference in July 1991 that announced the start of a forum to unite various opposition factions.[40] It was clear from the start that this was the nucleus of a political opposition party. But by limiting the number of identified founders, they escaped the law then in effect which required government registration.

The creation of FORD marked a turning point in the resistance movement in Kenya. "The strategy here was to widen the allies, to increase the momentum, to up the stakes, to get more people involved in the drive for pluralism,"according to Muite, a key architect of the plan and part of a group of activists known as the Young Turks. Muite said they recruited members of an older and respected generation of politicians to step forward as its original members, which they did at a press conference July 4, 1991 announcing its formation.[41]

Major Rally. FORD's leaders quickly called for a national rally November 16, 1991 at the same location as the aborted multiparty rally of 1990, in Nairobi at Kamakunji, an historic site for political speeches located in a low-income area just off the city center. They challenged the legitimacy of the regime by declaring the peoples' right to assemble and support an end to one-party rule, ignoring threats by the regime to

---

40 In separate interviews for this study, several organizational political activists claimed credit for launching FORD, including James Orengo, Raila Odinga and Martin Shikuku. Orengo said it was his idea to form a civic group not to exceed nine members so that the group would not have to seek formal registration as a society under restrictive laws at the time and in view of the failure of Oginga Odinga to register an opposition party. Shikuku said he was the one who helped bring people into the group that became FORD; but Raila Odinga said he was the one who invited Shikuku to join the organization in the first place.

Odinga's version of events is cited by Throup and Hornsby (1998, 78) who attribute it to a *Weekly Review* article of April 3, 1992.). Shikuku said he contacted others to join the group and he ended up attracting international attention when he was chased by police in a vehicle after the rally was violently aborted by security personnel.

41 Paul Muite, in an interview with the author in Nairobi, Kenya, July 2002. The original members of FORD included: Oginga Odinga (Raila's father), Martin Shikuku, Masinde Muliro, Philip Gachoka, George Nthenge, and Ahmed Salim Bamahriz.

forcefully prevent the event. Although the Moi regime quickly declared the new FORD organization illegal and warned against participation in its planned rally, the momentum for change was increasing. Some details of this event are important as illustrations of the public mood and the tactics of the still-illegal political opposition, soon to be free to institutionalize their dissent through formation of legal parties.

The morning of the intended rally, large crowds began heading toward the site. Police and paramilitary forces were on the streets leading to the rally and at the site itself. Starting the night of Nov. 14, the government began a sweep to arrest the organizers of the rally, snagging Oginga Odinga and Imanyara, among others. Muite, Masinde Muliro and Shikuku went into hiding; Shikuku took refuge at the home of Fred LaSor, public affairs counselor at the United States Embassy.[42]

Diplomatic Pressure. To emphasize their united stand in favor of free speech and democratization, German Ambassador Bernd Mutzelberg and U.S. Ambassador Smith Hempstone jointly met with Bethuel Kiplagat, Permanent Secretary in the Ministry of Foreign Affairs, to protest the arrests. Both of the Ambassadors had infuriated President Moi by their repeated, blunt criticism of the regime and their endorsement of democratic reforms. Ambassador Hempstone, admired by most activists as an outspoken and sincere ally in their quest for pluralism, offered to try to broker a compromise between Moi and the FORD team, seeking to get the President's agreement for a rally at a specific date and site to be agreed upon by the two sides. But the negotiations fell apart when the government was unwilling to make any compromise.[43] Germany recalled its Ambassador temporarily in protest over the arrests.

Regime's Violent Response. Crowds arriving at the rally site were met by riot police who attacked. Having escaped a police dragnet just before the rally, FORD founders Shikuku, Orengo, Muliro and Philip Gachoka, made a brief appearance at the rally site before being driven off through the streets of a working class neighborhood nearby. That is when Shikuku climbed atop raising his hands in the two-finger salute that signaled support for opposition parties.

There couldn't have been a clearer symbol of defiance at the moment, a symbol witnessed by crowds along the way. It was also a dangerous gesture: he was exposing himself to any gunfire by pursuing police or other supporters of the regime along the way. Shikuku and Orengo, in separate interviews, later stated that shots had been fired at them. Shikuku explained their defiance:

---

42 Hempstone, Smith.1997. *Rogue Ambassador: An African Memoir.* Sewanee, TN.: University of the South Press, 251. Hempstone was Ambassador to Kenya from 1989 to 1993.

43 Hempstone, 250.

We were determined; we were ready to die. Who would see us inside the pick up? And of course the masses were there and they wanted to see their leaders coming. We didn't want to have that repeat of the Saba Saba where...Mr. Matiba and Rubia got cold feet [and called off the multiparty rally in July 1990].[44]

Photos of the dramatic police chase, with Shikuku riding atop the vehicle flashing the multiparty sign were splashed all over the domestic media and made its way into the international press. One of Kenya's individual activists, Rev. Njoya described the events shortly after they happened as a "milestone. It brought together a lot of people – thousands from all directions of the city. It shows also the confidence people have with the alternative to what we are having now – autocratic and dictatorial leadership."[45]

Major Concession. A few days later, donors meeting in Paris imposed a freeze on new funding to Kenya pending reforms. A few days after the Paris meeting, on December 2, 1991, President Moi addressed a national conference of KANU. After a number of delegates, including several top party officials among the approximately 3,600 attending had soundly denounced the idea of abandoning a one-party system, the President rose to speak. Toward the end of his remarks, he stunned delegates by announcing that the provision of the constitution making Kenya a one-party state would have to be dropped.

As presented in chapter 1, this study argues that concessions are most likely to come when there is a convergence of forces including domestic and international, with domestic activism acting as the catalyst to international pressure. Both elements came together in November 1991 at the major, illegal rally in Nairobi to which large crowds of Kenyans responded but which was violently suppressed by security forces. As argued later in this chapter, domestic unrest and growing public opposition to Moi, not the freeze on new aid funds, provided the major threat to the regime, possible instability, that led a few days after the suppressed rally and Paris donors' meeting to the President's concession of allowing competitive, multi-party elections starting in 1992.

Accumulating Resistance

Organizational activists continued playing a game of tactics with the regime from 1991–1996. Each side was trying to counter the moves of the other, each side learning from the other. Strategies shifted among activists and the regime, but the goals of each side did not: activists wanted power; the regime wanted to keep it. Ideologies

---

44 Martin Shikuku in an interview with the author in Nairobi, Kenya, July 2002. Matiba and Rubia did call off the rally. Rubia explained in an interview with the author (in Nairobi, Kenya in October 2002) that this was done because the government had not issued a permit for the rally. A few hours after their decision to call it off, they were detained by police.

45 Press, Robert M. 1999. *The New Africa: Dispatches from a Changing Continent.* Gainesville, FL.: University Press of Florida, 115.

would play only a minor role in the game; the main struggle now was over who would win control of the country.

The 17 months between the aborted Saba Saba pro-democracy rally of July 1990 and the decision by the President to adopt multiparty politics in December 1991 was a period of transition between individual activism and organizational activism and involved elements of both. There was evidence of a growing public anger at the way the Moi regime was running the country. Both sides, the regime and the activists, began to look for ways to harness this public anger, to channel it, to institutionalize it to their benefit.

The evidence of public anger was clear. After the aborted rally of 1990, where crowds defied the Presidents warning not to show up and had been driven away by baton-swinging police, there were riots across parts of Kenya. When popular and outspoken Bishop Alexander Muge was killed in August 1990 in a vehicle crash the next month, there was more public anger. In September that year, the regime came under heavy criticism in the press when it refused to release a report by Scotland Yard that its author later testified pointed to two top aides of President Moi as suspects in the 1990 murder of popular Minister of Foreign Affairs Robert Ouko.[46]

The regime would be hard-pressed, its institutional capacity strained, were it to try to quell such a popular sentiment. Instead it chose to try to appease it through a series of national hearings chaired by the Vice President on the conduct of the ruling party. The hearings surfaced further public discontent, however, and signaled that it was not just the sentiment of a few individual activists. On the resistance side, several activist clergy members sought a way to institutionalize the anti-regime sentiment surrounding the aborted Saba Saba 1990 rally. They wanted to try to shift the resistance from rather chaotic mass protests in the streets to a longer-lasting and more broadly representative forum; they called for a national convention to remap Kenya's political system.

As 1991 began, activist Imanyara sought an even broader way to formalize the resistance: he sued in Kenyan court to allow multiparty elections, claiming that a single party limitation violated free speech rights protected by the constitution. This was the first time the growing demands for competitive politics had reached a court. The Moi regime responded to this fundamental attack on its power by reverting to its former pattern of detaining perceived troublemakers. But Imanyara's detention prompted further outcries from domestic activists and brought down international criticism on the regime as well.

---

46 *Weekly Review*, November 29, 1991. At the commission set up by President Moi to investigate the murder, Scotland Yard Detective John Troon, who headed the Scotland Yard team the President earlier had asked to come investigate said: "...I cannot rule out either of these two gentlemen – [Nicholas] Biwott and [Hezikiah] Oyugi – or eliminate them from the death of Dr. Ouko. Those are my principal suspects. There may well be others involved on the periphery but certainly those two gentlemen are my principal suspects."
Immediately before the Paris Club meeting of donors in November 1991, President Moi arrested these two senior Kenyan aides to the President, releasing them shortly after the meeting.

Moi faced further legal challenges on human rights and democratization issues when Muite, as chair of LSK, called for repeal of detention laws. The Catholic Church made a similar demand. By mid-1991, the regime was facing a convergence of domestic forces from organized civil society including the professional middle class (mostly lawyers), churches, former politicians now in the opposition, some business leaders, and from an angry, unorganized public. Donors were also beginning to show more interest in demanding reforms.

In both 1991 and 1997, when donors united to freeze new funds, their actions followed rising domestic resistance. If the cutoff of funds was the key pressure on the regime, then one has to ask why it was not quicker for the regime to work out a favorable position with donors to end the freeze. At later stages of resistance, domestic pressure in an authoritarian regime may reach a level at which it can largely replace the role of international pressure for reform. The accumulating domestic activist pressures, the public turnout at the attempted pro-pluralism rally at Kamakunji by FORD in November 1991, and the subsequent freezing of funds by donors had been followed quickly by the regime's first major concession to the growing activism, a decision to allow multiparty politics.

Resistance: Peaks and Valleys

Resistance peaked in election years and declined in between. The opposition parties began 1992, an election year, with several massively-attended public rallies organized by FORD in January and the Democratic Party of Mwai Kibaki in February. This first year of renewed multiparty politics brought a shift in the pattern of activism by the political opposition. Having succeeded in their call for pluralism after a period of transition from individual to organizational activism, they began the year focused on coalition building within the various parties, shifting their attention from the regime. Ethnic clashes and the protest by mothers of political prisoners, meanwhile, would further stir resentment against the state.

Criticism Over Ethnic Clashes. Ethnic clashes had begun in November 1991, just as domestic pressures for pluralism were reaching a new high; the clashes reached an intense level by May 1992. During this period, clergy in several Kenyan churches, the National Christian Council of Kenya (NCCK), and the often-reticent Catholic Church increasingly spoke out. The churches were strident in criticism of the clashes and the presumed role of the government. The clergy spoke clearly as representatives of their churches.

The NCCK became more outspoken during the clashes, calling for a halt to the violence. The clashes served to chase potential nongovernment supporters out of an area in central Kenya that the government hoped to win in the upcoming multiparty election. But the clashes also galvanized opposition to the regime and further challenged the legitimacy of the government, and by association, the President, even prompting some calls for massive civil disobedience to a government that could no longer protect its citizens and which seemed to condone violence against its political enemies. In a meeting with the President, church leaders gave him a blunt assessment: "People have lost confidence in you."[47]

As the clashes continued, the opposition parties sought a strategy to counter the clashes, which they considered domestic terrorism. At an all-parties meeting in May, the so-called Young Turks within FORD attempted to turn the gathering into a national convention with sovereign powers, the way opponents of the regime had done in the tiny West African nation of Benin (resulting in a regime change) and Togo (resulting in a regime clampdown). But party leaders refused, despite the fact that this was probably the widest gathering of opposition groups to date, including professional associations, the parties, and the main religious groups.

Mothers' Strike. In March 1992, when the mothers of political prisoners staged their sit-down protest in a downtown park in Nairobi, its violent ending after several days by police using batons and tear gas revealed the limits of protest activists. The regime would strike back whenever there was any direct challenge to its power, especially one that seemed based on a convergence of domestic forces. The strike had brought together mothers, a potent and esteemed group; then members of the general public, opposition politicians, and activist members of the clergy joined them.

Anxious to test its political power beyond its capability of drawing a mass crowd, FORD threatened a strike March 2 if all political prisoners were not released. The regime began a pattern that would mark this period, making small concessions in the face of larger demands. Moi released four detainees, including George Anyona, who had been jailed on trumped up charges.

Fragmented Opposition Loses Election. Institutionalization of the political opposition did not mean unification. It was becoming clear that the parties were not going to unite behind a single presidential candidate. Instead the opposition split, fracturing the vote, and leaving political opponents attacking each other instead of the President. Disproportionate districts favoring the ruling party, maladministration and outright rigging further helped insure the President's election in December 1992.

In 1993 and into 1994, halting the clashes provided a goal behind which the opposition could unite, both inside Parliament and outside. Several reports had blamed the government for either a passive or active role in promoting them. Thousands were displaced and several hundred killed in the clashes. Several activists were arrested

---

47 *Weekly Review*, May 8, 1992 pp 20–21. The article also noted that the next day the President must have noted the solemnity of the crowds who "simply stared sullenly without acknowledging the President's salute" as his motorcade drove to Uhuru Park, site of the previous Mother's protest to visit the headquarters of the Central Organization of Trade Unions.

for entering clash areas the government had sealed off.[48] Several journalists were arrested for reporting on victims of the clashes.[49]

New Regime Strategy. In 1995, Moi seemed bent on slowing the further institutionalization of activism. Having lost many seats in Parliament, been attacked for the clashes, and challenged at opposition rallies, the Moi regime sought to regain the momentum by claiming a new opposition group based in Uganda was seeking to overthrow his regime. Opposition leaders cried foul, charging that the President was simply returning to his mid-1980s repression in which many suspected dissidents had been arrested and tortured into confession. This time, however, Moi avoided the negative domestic and international publicity and sought to garner public support through staging a series of pro-government rallies.

Also in 1995, the regime tried to slow the institutionalization of resistance in a more targeted way. This time the target was the rapidly growing and active network of NGOs advocating democratization and greater human rights. The churches had grown quieter, but NGOs had begun "digging deeper into some of the underlying corruption of the Kenyan society."[50]

The regime's new strategy in the chess game began with a move to deregister the first of many organizations registered under the 1991 NGO Co-ordination Act.[51] That Act had left in the hands of the government the power to register all NGOs.

The second apparent part of the regime's new strategy was violence: the Legal Advice Center, an advocacy group, was attacked several times, including with a petrol bomb. In one attack, hooded gunmen burst into the group's office demanding to know the whereabouts of activist Willy Mutunga, its director, who was not found. He later went on to head the Kenya Human Rights Commission. Another petrol attack was made on the offices of FORD Asili Member of Parliament Njehu Gatabaki, editor of the then-defunct *Finance* magazine that had been exposing alleged government corruption. But the attacks may have been a ruse to draw attention away from the recently-emerged constitutional reform movement.[52]

Activism Declines. As the activism of rallies, and protest demonstrations tapered off after the 1992 elections, another attempt at institutionalization of resistance began with a citizen's campaign to form a representative constitutional convention to adopt a model constitution that would include further advances in democracy and human rights. An organization was formed known as the Citizens Coalition for Constitutional Change (4 Cs). It had roots dating back to 1992. It began building

---

48 Among the arrested activists were The Rev. Dr. Timothy Njoya, Bedan Mbugua, Mirugi Kariuki and Koigi Wamwere.

49 *Weekly Review*, April 22, 1994, pp. 18–19.

50 *Weekly Review*, Mach 24, 1995, pp 24–15.

51 The organization was Clarion that had been critical of the government on corruption, constitutional reform and land reform issues (*Weekly Review* February 24, 1995, p. 18.)

52 *Weekly Review*, March 31, 1995, p. 4; 11–12.

support among various elements of civil society. Except for the occasional political rally, it became the driving engine of resistance, a nonviolent resistance aimed at persuading enough elements of society to join in calling for a new constitution that it would make its adoption by Parliament inevitable. Their climactic efforts would come in the election year of 1997.

Donors' Mixed Signals on Human Rights and Democracy

Can donors help institutionalize resistance to a regime abusing human rights and dragging its feet on democratization? The record in Kenya is mixed.

For the most part, the Cold War kept the focus of Western donors on supporting allies and undermining leftist regimes in Africa. Kenya was seen as a stable country in a turbulent region where Uganda and Sudan had experienced civil wars, and Somalia and Ethiopia (at different times) had received military aid from the Soviet Union. Kenya was a pro-market capitalist state. Any international concerns about human rights abuses and lack of democracy in Kenya until after the fall of the Berlin Wall in late 1989 were given low priority.

Despite mounting abuse of human rights by the regime in the months leading up to the freeze in late 1991 on new funds, donors were often inconsistent, sometimes increasing funding, sometimes slowing it down; some donors praising the regime, others condemning it. It was only after dramatic mass public protests that they finally united, temporarily, to cut off funds, which was followed by a tactical concession by the regime on pluralism – a concession never fully implemented.

There is evidence of informal, diplomatic encouragement from the United States and the United Kingdom of institutionalization of domestic resistance. Through much of 1990 and 1991, the United States, particularly Ambassador Hempstone, complained, sometimes publicly, about human rights abuses. A political officer at the U.S. embassy suggested to one Kenyan activist that formation of a unified opposition group would be a good idea.[53] The British were quieter about any disagreements with the Moi regime, however, although two activists met with a British politician who encouraged them to organize a civic forum of the kind formed in Czechoslovakia and East Germany prior to 1989.[54]

Hempstone warned the Moi regime in May 1990, that future aid money would likely be concentrated on nations supporting human rights and democratization.[55] And the

---

53 Raila Odinga, in an interview with the author in Nairobi, Kenya, October 2002. Odinga said he met with the American diplomat in June 1991.

54 Throup and Hornsby, 76.

55 Ambassador Hempstone's remarks came at the end of a speech to the Rotary club in Nairobi. He said that "a strong political tide is flowing in our Congress, which controls the purse strings, to concentrate our economic assistance on those of the world's nations that nourish democratic institutions, defend human rights, and practice multiparty politics" (Hempstone 1997, 91). His remarks provoked a barrage of criticism from officials in the ruling party (KANU).

United States was beginning to back up his words, holding up funding: first $5 million in August 1990, then $25 million in November, specifically pending human rights reforms. But signals from the donor community were mixed, as Table 4.3 shows.

Table 4.3   Development aid to Kenya 1987–2002

Year	Dollars (millions)	Donor Actions	Regime Concessions and Abuses
1987	753	87–90: aid increased	torture; detention
1988	954		torture reduced
1989	1,092		detentions reduced
1990	1,615		protests suppressed
1991	1,102	donors freeze funds	protests suppressed; multiparty accepted
1992	987		multiparty election
1993	870	Inconsistent aid	
1994	731	flows send ambiguous	
1995	1,021	signals to regime	rights abuses continue
1996	743		
1997	448	IMF freezes funds	protests suppressed; constitutional reforms
1998	415		
1999	310		
2000	512	donors freeze funds	Corruption
2001	452		Corruption unaddressed
2002	n.a.		Rallies suppressed; Moi allows election on time

Source: World Bank study for 1987–1996; Organization for Economic Co-operation (OECD) for 1997–2001; Human Rights Watch World Reports 2002 and 2003.
Note: n.a. = not available

By coincidence the same day as Hempstone's speech , two former KANU members who had served in President Moi's cabinet but had resigned and been expelled from the party, Kenneth Matiba and Charles Rubia, held a press conference calling for Kenya to move to a multiparty system. They were later detained.

Inconsistency in the use of donor aid as a leverage for reform not only slows the institutionalization of resistance, it can send signals to the abusive regime that it need not make major reforms in order to keep money flowing. Geopolitical needs of donors are also likely to trump any intended penalties for abuses by allies whose help might be needed in regional conflicts.

The U.S. freeze of $25 million was followed a week later by a promise from donors in the so-called Paris Club of $1 billion in new aid, with no mention of human rights abuses. Then in January 1991, the U.S. switched its own signals. With the start of the Gulf War, the U.S. was now looking for ways to help the Kenyan government, with an eye to possible use of its ports in the conflict. The U.S. moved to cut some of the debt owed to it from Kenya; the Danish promised new aid.

Next month donors were complaining about the arrest of activist Gitobu Imanyara, who by now had developed numerous contacts with journalist and human rights organizations in Europe and the United States. By August, however, the donors were once again giving the regime mixed signals; some were linking aid to reforms, while the British went out of their way to praise President Moi.

Overall, donor assistance to Kenya had been increasing from 1987 to 1991. But in late November 1991, shortly after the disrupted, pro-multiparty rally Shikuku and others helped lead, bilateral donors meeting in Paris decided as a group to freeze some $350 million in new aid pending reforms.[56] This was one of only two major freezes in donor funding during the study period (1987–2002).[57] A World Bank official at the 1991 donors' meeting recalls that the main concern at the meeting was Kenya's poor economic performance but that donors also wanted Kenya to adopt a multiparty system.[58]

---

56 One year earlier Western donors had considered reducing their aid to Kenya, "which financed nearly 30 percent of government expenditure" (Throup and Hornsby 1998, 74).

57 The first freeze lasted from November 1991 to mid-1993, though some donors, including France, increased funding before that. The second major halt in funding in mid-1997 by the International Monetary Fund (IMF) came amidst mounting public demonstrations put down with police violence in which a number of protestors were killed. It lasted for three years without an agreement with the Moi regime. (O'Brien, F.S. and Terry, C.I., Ryan, 2001). *Kenya: In Aid and Reform in Africa*. Washington: World Bank, 477; 515.

58 Stephen O'Brien, in e-mail communication with the author, June 2002. The freeze of funds resulted "from concern primarily over poor economic management and corruption and from the desire to force Kenya to adopt a multiparty political system," according to O'Brien.

Another official at the meeting, a governance official who has worked for the World Bank, says he can not recall anyone at the meeting mentioning "human rights," though there was talk of the need for better "governance," which was understood to include "basic human rights such as freedom to associate, freedom to assemble, and freedom of access to information" (e-mail communication with the author from a governance official who worked with the World Bank and requested anonymity, January 2003).

According to the World Bank press release at the time, donors conditioned a resumption of aid to the "early implementation of political reform," which included "greater pluralism, the importance of the rule of law and respect for human rights, notably basic freedoms of expression and assembly, and... firm action to deal with issues of corruption" (Brown 2000).

Domestic Protests Key

Domestic resistance was more critical a factor than the aid freeze in wresting a reluctant decision from President Moi to accept multiparty elections. The 1991 freeze followed the brutal suppression of the rally for multi-party elections. In 1997 when a funding freeze by the International Monetary Fund (IMF) followed a series of domestic protests, brutally put down by police with numerous deaths of civilians, the regime agreed to partial constitutional reforms.

The timing of the aid freeze and Moi's adoption of multiparty politics, one of only four major concessions during the study period,[59] is so close that there was at least correlation. However, had the freeze come with no domestic resistance, the President might well have decided to forgo the aid temporarily, especially given the on-and-off pattern of donors. Since Moi was not being asked to adopt multiparty elections – a point the U.S. went out of its way to emphasize – he might have appeased donors with a set of economic reforms. But that would not have appeased the increasingly active Kenyan opposition.[60]

It is an argument of this study that the decision by the President to adopt a multiparty system was done primarily as a result of accumulating and converging domestic forces calling for multiparty. A study of donors came to a similar conclusion: "In the case of Kenya, the reform movement was mainly domestically driven, with donors lending their support after a critical mass had already been achieved and actually discouraging more fundamental political reform.[61]"

By 1995 aid levels were back to approximately the same levels as just before the freeze and yet many of the democratization reforms that one would expect to have accompanied a change from a one-party system to a multiparty system, such as freedom of speech and assembly, were still significantly limited by the regime.

Donor Leverage Impact Limited. Overall, conditionality of donor aid did not have a major effect on reform adoption in Kenya, according to a study by the former head of the World Bank team in Kenya at this time and co-authored by a former

---

Although donors did not require multiparty democracy, the repeal of the constitutional ban against more than one party was necessary, according to one scholar who focuses on Kenya (Barkan 1993: 91).

59 The other three were (1) the decision in 1987 to sharply reduce the use of torture and detention of prominent accused dissidents; (2) agreeing in 1997 to constitutional amendments passed in Parliament to drop most restrictions on freedom of speech and assembly; (3) allowing an orderly election to take place on schedule in 2002, despite built-in electoral advantages to the ruling party.

60 A former senior aide to the President who spoke with him on the morning he made his surprise announcement at the Party conference that he had decided to allow multiparty elections, said that the President still had not revealed to aides that morning what he was going to do. (As noted, some donors favored multi-party elections).

61 Brown, Stephen. 2000. "Donors' Dilemmas in Democratization: Foreign Aid and Political Reform in Africa." PhD dissertation. New York University.

senior financial and economic official in the Kenyan government. The study found that "donor aid can have an influence on the form of agreement reached and on the agreed timetable for implementation, but whether implementation is carried out depends in the end much more on domestic political and economic factors than on donor money." [62]

The role of donors in Kenya pushing for reforms was not only inconsistent, it may have slowed Kenya's transition toward democracy. Brown argues that the funding freezes of 1991 and 1997 did help push the Moi regime to make concessions. But he adds, "[d]onors twice knowingly endorsed unfair elections [which Moi won in 1992 and 1997] (including suppressing evidence of their illegitimacy) and repeatedly undermined domestic efforts to secure far-reaching political reforms, which were a prerequisite for an opposition victory and a full transition to democracy."[63]

Activists' Coordination Limited. Donor aid also had mixed results when it came to promotion of human rights in Kenya. Kenyan human rights activists have been helped and protected by international networks but those same networks may also have had negative, long-term consequences. The networks operated on a vertical basis and did not develop broader horizontal support. This actually left the human rights movement in Kenya weaker than it might otherwise have been.[64]

---

62 O'Brien, F. S., and Terry C. I. Ryan. 2001. "Kenya." In *Aid and Reform in Africa.* Washington: World Bank. The study was by Stephen O'Brien, a former head of the World Bank delegation in Kenya, and Terry C. I. Ryan, of the University of Nairobi and former senior Kenya Treasury official. It focused on aid to Kenya between 1980 and 1998. The report noted: "Certainly Kenya has received massive amounts of aid over a sustained period of time more than US $15 billion between 1970 and 1996. This substantial flow of financial and technical assistance has given donors leverage, but much less than the aggregate numbers might suggest," the authors note. Several World Bank staffers calculated the grant-only portion of aid to Kenya and found that it was some $4 billion or 25% less than the $15 billion that counted loans and grants. That means the government "sees" less tangible benefit from the aid since loan repayments pose a financial burden, the report notes. The study stated: "On balance, we conclude that government ownership and political will have more to do with the timing, extent, and sustainability of the reform program than does the volume of donor aid."

63 Brown, Stephen. 2001. "Authoritarian Leaders and Multiparty Elections in Africa: How Foreign Donors Help to Keep Kenya's Daniel arap Moi in Power." *Third World Quarterly* 22 (5):725–739. Brown notes that the internal version of the final report of the Election Observation Centre (Kenya General Elections 1997: Final Report for Donors' Democratic Development Group, Nairobi, January 1998, p i) includes the following sentence: "...the irregularities in the poll and count were so great as to invalidate the elections in these particular constituencies [eight] and consequently, the legitimacy of the overall KANU majority in the National Assembly." But at "the behest of Canada, France, the USA and especially the UK," the sentence was deleted in the public version of the report. "In other words, *donors deliberately suppressed evidence that KANU had not legitimately won a majority in parliament*" (emphasis in original).

64 Schmitz, Hans Peter. 2001. "When Networks Blind: Human Rights and Politics in Kenya." In *Intervention and Transnationalism in Africa: Global-Local Networks of Power,*

While some human rights activists in Kenya stated that there was horizontal cooperation among organizations, that cooperation may have been more superficial than substantial. Activist journalist David Makali, who headed the Media Institute in 2002, a private watchdog NGO, noted that human rights advocates in Kenya did get together for meetings. "We got together, planned and [made] proposals and [for example] said we are going to look for funding, all of us, and...publish a journal... [but] nothing happened," Makali emphasized loudly. " Nobody follows through."

Makali attributed this lack of coordination not to donors but to what he calls "destructive individualism. And it permeates in the opposition, politics, and everything, in the political parties...It is human nature, I think. Human nature doesn't allow sacrifice; the egos ...have been standing in the way. It will be a long time before we overcome that individualism that blocks all our initiatives."[65]

One study of the effectiveness of foreign donors on the democratization process of developing countries concluded that the impact was minimal and often makes false claims related to causation. "In any society, the political environment is a swirl of events, institutions, personalities, processes, attitudes, and trends. It is rarely possible to know with any precision how external influences affect internal factors to produce political outcomes."[66]

Implications of Organizational Activism

From 1991 to 1996, organizational activism transformed the resistance movement in Kenya from one of individuals acting bravely against a mostly-intransigent regime to an institutionalized effort that had shown itself capable of achieving a major concession.

This institutionalization of a culture of resistance arose out of a shift of tactics by activists when it became clear that the (1) the regime was vulnerable to domestic and international pressures and willing to make some concessions; (2) the regime would only make major reforms under greater pressure than individual efforts could generate.

Activists sought to channel and organize a widespread public discontent in Kenya against the regime. A number of different forums, including a nascent political party, were planned and attempted in an effort to marshal a convergence of domestic opposition forces. Before 1992, such efforts were met with force; after 1992, with the legalization of opposition parties, the regime still used force from time to time, especially when it felt some combination of resistance threatened its power.

By the end of this period, a culture of resistance had been more firmly established in Kenya. There were several indicators of this. Building on the earlier activism of

---

eds. Thomas Callaghy, Ronald Kassimir, and Robert Latham. Cambridge: Cambridge University Press.

65 David Makali, in an interview with the author in Nairobi, Kenya, September 2002.

66 Carothers, Thomas. 1999. *Aiding Democracy Abroad: The Learning Curve.* Washington: Carnegie Endowment for International Peace, 283.

individuals, organizational activists, with some help from donors, had won the right to establish opposition parties. Though the opposition lost the presidential election in 1992, they won many seats in Parliament, turning it into a public venue for resistance as numerous activists were elected. Along with the new pluralism came a wave of NGOs with a goal of pressing for more human rights and/or democratization. These organizations offered not only employment but a formal channel for activism. The new organizations provided the general pubic with a variety of ways to express their own resistance, including rallies, strikes, and the start of a constitutional reform drive.

Both the illegal, pre-1992, and legal rallies signaled to the regime and the general public that many Kenyans were tired of silent deference to a regime abusing human rights and democratic principles. In a country whose farthest reaches are linked by the media and a constant flow of travelers, word of each rally spread rapidly across the country. The regime's repressive efforts to curb such events seemed only to add to the determination to hold more.

Dankwart Rustow wrote that "[t]he forces of conservatism may yield from fear that continued resistance may lose them even more ground in the end."[67] This was the case in Kenya. The regime was not sincere in its concessions, blocked their full implementation, and never made any effort to reduce the disproportionate powers given the President in a constitution with authoritarian aspects carried over from the British colonial rule.

One very thorough account of the 1992 election and its buildup concluded that the advent of multiparty politics "did not really change anything because Kenya remains an authoritarian state[68]" If the sole criterion of change is whether or not the regime remained authoritarian, then the authors are correct. But several major changes had taken place.

In the face of domestic and international challenges, the fairly frequent use of torture in the mid to late 1980s had subsided. Detention of political opponents had dropped dramatically. In the new multiparty era people were suddenly fairly free to voice criticism of the regime. The press became bolder, though still subject to occasional repression from the state. Individuals and organizations spoke out against the regime and called for further democratization.

The 1992 election provided another significant change: instead of a chorus of sycophancy regarding the President, the new Parliament became a beehive of heated debates. The opposition had few successes in scuttling authoritarian laws or restrictions in the constitution, but the open dissent in this new Parliament signaled to the public that their days of silent fear were largely over.

A culture of resistance had taken root in Kenya. Activism in Kenya was shown to be an independent variable. There would have been no concessions without it. Donors were too inconsistent to have provided sufficient pressure alone, and in any

---

67 Rustow, Dankwart. 1970. "Transitions to Democracy: Toward a Dynamic Model." *Comparative Politics* 2(3):337–363.

68 Throup and Hornsby, 602.

case they did not act until public support for the resistance was evident and had been met with police brutality. Regime concessions, few and incomplete and never fully-implemented, came not in the face of strong organizations, however, but in the face of growing domestic resistance expressed through many channels and evidencing a growing culture of resistance.

The institutionalization of the resistance by the clergy, professionals, nongovernment organizations and politicians provided a way to harness the underlying discontent among Kenyans and to keep pressure on the regime. Resistance was not constantly increasing. There were ebbs and flows. As 1997, an election year approached, however, the level of resistance began to grow once again.

Chapter 5

Entering the Bastille (Peacefully): From Resistance to Elected Power

From 1997 to 2002, both election years, the culture of resistance in Kenya came of age.

This study has argued that a culture of resistance involves a process of public challenges to an abusive regime, starting with individual activists and expanding to include organizations and a visible segment of the general public. There was strong evidence to support this argument in this period. Activists tried new combinations of actors, used new tactics, and recruited new activists. Resistance, which had started with a few lonely and courageous voices around 1987, was becoming the norm for many Kenyans.

This study also has argued that contrary to the structural bias in one of the most dominant social movement theories, political process, activists created most of their own opportunities to challenge the authoritarian regime rather than waiting for a change in structural conditions to provide such openings. Several other theoretical perspectives presented in Chapter 1 were also in evidence during this period. In the model of resistance, the dynamics start with activists responding to regime repression, which was the case in this period. Repression had only partially abated since the first multiparty presidential election in 1992.

By 1997, it was quite apparent to most Kenyans that the regime had no plans to allow the kind of freedom of speech and assembly and other rights normally associated with a democratic government, despite the fact that the first multiparty presidential elections had been held in 1992. The regime continued to harass opposition politicians, breaking up rallies and even arresting some outspoken members; critical nongovernment organizations (NGOs) were under verbal and sometimes physical attack; torture continued to be used on common criminals; and the President was dragging his feet on constitutional changes that could reduce his powers.

There was also evidence of political learning, a theoretical concept introduced in the first chapter. Both sides continued to engage in a chess game of politics, each seeking to outmaneuver the other. There was further evidence that a convergence of forces – domestic and international – were at play when concessions were won during this period, though this study argues that the role of donors in winning reforms was less important than domestic resistance and that domestic resistance was even more critical in 2002, another general election year.

Finally, the period provides clear evidence of a revised version of cycles of contentious politics, this study presents, building on Tarrow's work.[1] The ebb and flow of activism continued, peaking in election years, which provided activists with a useful focal and rallying point. Except for a slow build up of a constitutional reform effort, between the 1992 and 1997 elections, there had been relatively little in the way of political advances; one analyst writes that there were "no true domestic political advances" in this period.[2]

Between 1997 and the election in 2002, which saw the defeat of the ruling party, there was again a slow buildup of constitutional reform efforts. Major activism tapered off, however, until the election year itself drew massive crowds to rallies of opposition political candidates. There was also some expansion of smaller-scale demonstrations and activism around the country, not just in the urban areas.[3]

Questions. Several questions arise at this point in the examination of the establishment of a culture of resistance. For example: what evidence is there that such a culture has been established?

Resistance came in many forms: lawsuits, speeches, articles, rallies, marches, etc. The resistance may be very small, as it was at first when only a few individual activists were taking public stands against the regime. Later many more Kenyans were involved, including in the period covered by this chapter. Establishing a culture of resistance does not mean, however, that there is one culture that suddenly, or even gradually, encompasses a particular number of people. Any regime has its supporters; many others are reluctant to demonstrate their opposition for one reason or another.

How does one determine if such a culture has grown or expanded? One way to do this would be to count the instances of public challenges. But it is not the number of events that counts; what counts is their importance in terms of citizen and regime reaction to the challenges. As we have seen, the regime responded to the challenges with concessions, not many, but enough to change the political character of Kenya.

Instead of a quantitative analysis of the number of challenges to authority, this study takes a different course in tracking the resistance: examining the political process involved, a process which involved expansion of resistance from a small group of individual activists to include various organizations and in the process

---

1   Tarrow, Sidney. 1998. *Power in Movement: Social Movements and Contentious Politics.* 2nd ed. Cambridge, U. K.: Cambridge University.

2   Brown, Stephen. 2000. *Donors' Dilemmas in Democratization: Foreign Aid and Political Reform in Africa.* PhD dissertation. New York University. Professor Kivutha Kibwana, an activist elected to Parliament in 2002, sees the election periods of 1991–1992, 1996–1997, and 2000–2002 as high points in the ebb and flow of activism in Kenya.

3   The evidence for this is still sparse and comes mostly from accounts in a few interviews. Future research on the extent of activism in this period, especially in rural areas, would be revealing but would also require considerable time since it is not likely that much of the activity would be recorded in the handful of national newspapers and magazines or in reports of human rights or other NGOs except for activities connected directly to those organizations.

pulling in a segment of the general public in support of protests. (Public support, a key element in the establishment of a culture of resistance, will be analyzed in Chapter 6.)

With a focus on the theoretical perspectives of this study, this chapter first examines the virtually unchanged structural constraints against resistance in 1997. Next, the chapter looks at how activists took the initiative in spite of such constraints to challenge the regime in new ways in 1997 with a goal of adoption of a more democratic constitution.

After that the chapter examines the period leading up to the 2002 general election with examples of a broadening out of resistance and more frequent public challenges to the regime as the culture of resistance became a more normal part of the society. The purpose here is not to document the final negotiations among the opposition and among the parties over constitutional issues, for example. By the late 1990s and early in the new century, the culture of resistance had been well established. The focus is on the broadening of a culture of resistance. (It is worth noting once more here that this study does not claim an automatic link between activism and democratic elections of the kind that occurred in Kenya.) The chapter closes with some implications of the evidence presented.

Overcoming Barriers

By 1997, the main, elite-organized resistance movement in Kenya, except for plans for a national constitutional convention organized by various elements of civil society, had slowed significantly after the loss by opposition candidates in the 1992 presidential election. Opposition parties were having difficulty holding rallies because the police would frequently and violently break them up, claiming that they had not been permitted.[4] Permits were a political tool of the regime and seldom given. Although Kenya was now a multiparty system, it was still a de facto one-party system with an authoritarian President.

If political process theorists were correct about their structural bias regarding opportunities for action, there would have been little activism in the period of 1997–2002. Not only were key structural constraints showing no signs of change or weakening, but the resistance movement itself was showing some signs of institutional weakness. Yet in this period, especially in the two election years of 1997 and 2002, resistance peaked again.

A weak economy actually worsened during this period, with gross domestic product (GDP) declining from 2.3 percent in 1997 to 1.5 percent in 1999. But this was not a dramatic enough shift to suddenly stir an outpouring of resistance. Regime strength had not weakened. Activists in 1997 were clubbed and several dozen were killed demonstrating for a new constitution.

---

4   *Human Rights Watch World Report* 2001; and 2002: Kenya.

After the September 11, 2001 terrorist attacks on the United States, the U.S. shifted its attention even further from human rights and democracy in Kenya to counter-terrorism activities in Kenya. The shift in international focus regarding Kenya could be seen in meetings between top United States officials and President Moi. In June 2001, President Bush and Vice President Dick Cheney met with Moi in Washington and encouraged him to make more progress on democratization and economic reform. But when President Bush met with Moi not long after the terrorist attacks the talks focused on anti-terrorism efforts and peace initiatives for Sudan and Somalia.[5]

Opposition parties were weak. By not allowing the normal kind of opposition party campaigning, the ruling party looked set to continue its hold on Kenya indefinitely, especially given the rivalries and ethnic voting patterns that kept the opposition leaders competing with each other. The President's party, the Kenya African National Union (KANU) in the 1990s was "the only national political force," while "[t]he centrifugal impact of ethnicity on Kenya's opposition parties …produced a series of factional breakaways and realignments, which…over time seriously undermined the opposition's legitimacy…" Civil society was still narrowly based and not very strong. After the multiparty election in 1992 there had been an explosion of new NGOs including some dedicated to expanding democratic practices and human rights in Kenya. Many of the influential human rights and democracy advocacy groups and "think tanks" were "Kikuyu dominated" and had a "narrow constituency of middle-class intellectuals, largely based in Nairobi, and [had] little impact on the wider community.[6]" The government retained the power to register such organizations and the threat of de-registration was always a factor for organization leaders to consider.[7]

Under such circumstances, the opportunities or openings for activism seemed bleak. Yet during this period, activism not only revived but spread beyond urban centers, despite continuing risks of repression from the regime.[8] The explanation this study offers for such an expansion of activism is that structural conditions were not the determining factors in the level of activism. As mentioned in earlier chapters, this

---

5   *Human Rights Watch World Report* 2002: Kenya.

6   Throup, David W. 2001. "Kenya: Revolution, Relapse, or Reform?" *Africa Notes.* Washington: Center for Strategic and International Studies.

7   When the human rights organization, the Centre for Law and Research International (CLARION) was de-registered in early 1995, two days after holding a seminar describing widespread government corruption, the organization won an appeal to the government that reinstated their status. But the message was clear: criticize the regime and risk de-registration.

8   For the purposes of this study, activist organizations are considered ones that openly advocate for improvements in human rights and/or democratization in Kenya. Many other NGOs in Kenya are educational or offer training in economic or social issues. The growth of human rights groups was not dramatic, but it was significant because their presence marks such a contrast with the late 1980s and early 1990s when there were few such open challenges to the status quo.

study treats activism as an independent variable, not beyond the influence of such factors as regime repression, economic hardships and international issues, but not controlled by them either. Regime repression continued to be a catalyst for activism. Each stage of activism helped open wider the door of opportunity for additional resistance to the regime.

According to Mutuma Ruteere, a researcher for Kenya Human Rights Commission (KHRC), the main human rights NGO in Kenya, there were approximately 15 small human rights groups in rural parts of Kenya by 2002. Their work was dangerous in some cases. For example, two such human rights activists, Nicodemus Mutuku and Alois Mwaiwa Muia, were charged in 2002 with murder in Machakos, a provincial town. They claimed it was an attempt by the government to silence their protests over the illegal grabbing of public land by powerful politicians.[9]

A group of youth activists joined veterans in helping plan and carry out a key series of protests marches that led to important reforms. And in the period leading up to the presidential election in 2002, civil society and political society, energized by the prospect of a regime change, combined forces temporarily to counteract the regime's delaying tactics on a new constitution.

It had become obvious to Kenyans and international observers alike that the regime was not going to give more ground unless forced to do so. An independent legal team from the United Kingdom concluded that the legal system of Kenya was deeply flawed and that Kenya "lacked many aspects of an established pluralist democracy, such as a free and organized opposition and a network of appropriate NGOs." Attorneys belonging to the Law Society of Kenya, whose members individually and later as an organization were in the vanguard for reform, faced "harassment" for taking politically sensitive cases.[10] The Kenya Human Rights Commission published a series of reports on abuses.

The regime stretched the law to curb dissent. Having publicly subscribed to the concept of the rule of law, the regime claimed it was only using its constitutional powers to avoid chaos and a threat to stability when it clamped down on activists. "They [the government] always wanted to point out some kind of legal basis for the things they have been doing," noted one activist attorney, Kathurima M'Inoti.[11]

Synergy in the Resistance Movement

In the ongoing chess game of politics in Kenya between the resistance movement and the regime, the regime had lost a move: Kenya was now a multiparty state. But repression and curbs on freedom of speech and assembly continued. Activists

---

9   Human Rights Watch, New York. News release, Dec. 27, 2002.

10   International Human Rights Working Party of the International Committee of the Law Society of England and Wales: Report on a Visit to Kenya 27 –31 January 1997, by Gerald Shamsh, Andy Unger, and Katherine Henderson, p 26–27.

11   Kathurima M'Inoti, in an interview with the author, July 2002, in Nairobi, Kenya.

needed a way of merging the various strands of resistance forces closer to produce a synergetic effect. No one part of the movement alone could accomplish a great deal at this stage in pushing the country toward greater democratization. The regime had grown adept at resisting resistance, granting partial reforms to stave off more complete ones, and keeping control of the electoral process with its built-in advantages for the ruling party. Activists began to focus on the goal of a new constitution as a way to reduce Presidential powers and pave the way for a fair election they hoped would result in a regime change.

There was very little coordination among elements of the resistance movement in Kenya, despite dialogue and meetings of human rights organizational representatives. And opposition political parties were rivals and seldom worked with NGOs on common goals. From 1992 to 1997, many NGOs actively opposed the regime's restrictions on basic freedoms, including the government's attempt to control all NGOs. Some groups focused on the continuing instances of torture; others aimed at slowing land-grabbing by members of the ruling party; still others worked to educate voters about elections and their civic responsibilities. It was an active period. But for the most part, political opposition leaders and the rest of civil society were not working together on most issues.[12]

"We [NGOs] didn't link up with groups – trade or ethnic groups," said Kivutha Kibwana, an Associate Professor of Law and former Dean of the Law School at the University of Nairobi, a leader in the civil society drive for constitutional reform. "We didn't make good links [or have] cross fertilization."[13] But by 1997, civil society and opposition political parties had agreed to work together in a "confluence" of pressure that led to a national meeting of reformists calling for a new constitution.

Though the initial planning for a new constitution began several years earlier, it was not until 1997 that the various pieces in the planned pressure for its adoption came together. By timing their protests to coincide with an election year, civil society activists behind the initiative were able to capture wider public support and participation in their efforts. "Elections will not be peaceful, free nor fair if certain minimal constitutional and legal reforms do not take place," said one statement from a coordinating group in the drive for a new constitution, the Citizens Coalition for Constitutional Change, better known as the 4Cs.[14]

Rallying Slogan. The rallying cry became "no reforms, no elections," which was aimed at putting pressure on the President to make concessions in order to keep

---

12 A number of Kenyan activists, however, including Kivutha Kibwana and Willy Mutunga, distinguish between civil society and political parties, calling political leaders part of "political society" or a "political class." Mutunga uses the later term in his work on the citizens' constitutional reform effort in Kenya (Mutunga 1999) but said in an interview in 2002 that the term was too loose and not clear enough to merit continued use.

13 Kivutha Kibwana, in an interview with the author in July 2002, in Nairobi, Kenya.

14 Mutunga, Willy. 1999. *Constitution-Making from the Middle: Civil Society and Transition Politics in Kenya, 1992–1997.* Nairobi, Kenya: SARET, 111.

the election on its constitutionally-mandated schedule of every five years. Snow's theory of framing a message to win the broadest appeal was evident.[15]

A National Convention Planning Committee was organized to plan during 1996 for a National Convention Assembly (NCA) in April 1997 in Limuru, outside of Nairobi. It was led by various segments of civil society, including business, religious, youth, women, and other groups. When the Convention was held, the NCA in turn elected a National Convention Executive Committee (NCEC). The planning was carried out mostly by urban, middle-class elites, though efforts were later made to form local assemblies around the country with a wide representation of Kenyans.[16]

The NCA marked the most expansive grouping to date in Kenya of those seeking major political reforms. The goal was a new constitution, one that reduced the powers of the President, among other things. President Moi had several times expressed a willingness to have a new constitution but repeatedly delayed efforts to arrive at one. The Constitutional Convention was an attempt to move beyond this impasse and win enough public support for one that the ruling party-dominated Parliament somehow would be obliged to adopt.

At the constitutional Convention, youth delegates lobbied hard for mass action while, they claim, older activists, especially political opposition leaders, were more inclined to settle for other forms of resistance such as petitions to the government. "The older people and the politicians…were saying 'Let's draft petitions and take them to the Office of the President.' And we were saying that [petitions] can only be part of the larger strategy which is protest, which is resistance – public demonstrations, what we call mass action…the language of this protest and resistance," said Cyprien Nyamwamu, a youth activist who attended the NCA in 1997.[17]

Ultimately the constitutional convention endorsed a series of mass actions including rallies, demonstrations, processions, strikes, sit-ins, vigils, and prayers and even "parading coffins of the dead at police stations before burials. All these activities were in defiance of the law."[18] They were aimed at challenging the legitimacy of the regime. The mass actions began May 3, 1997 and ended October 20. The actions that drew the most concerted violence from the regime to stop them were the public demonstrations, usually involving a short public walk as part of the protest in favor of a new constitution.

---

15 Snow, David, E., Burke Rochford, Steven Worden, and Robert Benford. 1986. "Frame Alignment Processes, Micromobilization, and Movement Participation." *American Sociological Review* 51(4):464 –81; Snow, David E., and Robert Benford. 1992. "Master Frames and Cycles of Protest." In *Frontiers in Social Movement Theory*, eds. Aldon Morris and Carol McClurg Mueller. New Haven, CN: Yale University Press.

16 Defenders of the resulting assemblies around the country claim they involved many Kenyans in a participatory process; others contend that most of the assemblies have a leadership appointed by elites and have not accomplished much.

17 Youth activists who were at the convention took an active part in the negotiations. At one point, according to Mutunga, they also heckled a speaker whom the youth considered insincere in his stated dedication to a new constitution.

18 Mutunga, 156.

Mutunga credits youth with a key role in organizing non-violent demonstrations, including such undramatic but essential tasks as distributing handbills announcing their start and leading the first one May 3. "The leaders of the mass action at Kamakunji ...were the youth."[19] It was extremely dangerous work. At least 14 people were killed during the July 7, 1997 protests in a public contest in which the government was "losing the remains of its moral authority."[20]

Cycles of Resistance, Repression, and Reform

Activists had devised a new mobilization technique by combining strands of the resistance movement. In 1992 and 1997, this posed a greater threat to the regime than when the strands were operating separately. Now key elements of civil society such as churches, along with opposition politicians were brought together to demand a new constitution. It would strip the presidency of its disproportionate powers that allowed the regime room to operate in an authoritarian way despite having become, at least officially, a multiparty state.

There were no formal negotiations between the regime and activists; pact-making was not part of the scenario as it often had been in Latin American democratization. But the new resistance, which was met with a new round of repression, amounted to an indirect cycle of negotiations. Tilly describes such a phenomenon as "mobilization-repression-bargaining cycles."[21]

Regime Learning

What happened next symbolizes the kind of political learning mentioned in Chapter 1 and the earlier empirical chapters as both sides sought to apply lessons they had learned in previous confrontations to win the current one. Activists had learned that the separate elements of resistance were not as effective as a potential merger of forces. They had watched the resistance movement dissolve into a competition among political opposition parties at the polls in 1992, based not on platforms of human rights or even democratization but on a desire to push the incumbent President out of power and seize the office and its over-sized powers. The regime, on the

---

19 Mutunga, 173.

20 Peters, Ralph-Michael. 2001. "Civil Society and the Election Year 1997 in Kenya." In *Out for the Count: the 1997 General Elections and Prospects for Democracy in Kenya.* Kampala, Uganda: Fountain Publishers, 42.

21 Tilly, Charles. 2000. "Processes and Mechanisms of Democratization." Sociological Theory 18(1):1 –16. In Goodwin, Jeff, and James M. Jasper, eds. 2004. *Rethinking Social Movements: Structure, Meaning, and Emotion.* Oxford, U. K.: Rowman & Littlefield. These are cycles "during which currently excluded actors act collectively in ways that threaten survival of the government and/or its ruling classes, governmental repression fails, struggle ensues, and settlements concede political standing and/or rights to mobilized actors." That is approximately what happened in Kenya at this time.

other hand, had learned that it could make some piecemeal concessions and not be pushed into more drastic reforms, though the 1992 election had posed uncertainty for the regime. It had learned to manipulate part of the vote through intimidation (the ethnic clashes) and through disproportionate districts that favored the incumbent party. Once the regime learned how to win a contested election at the polls and hold its Parliamentary majority, the focus became how to block further reforms, not agree to more. It had also learned how to play on the egos of the resisters, as would soon become more evident in dealings with the clergy and opposition members of Parliament to block a new constitution.

Activists might have ended up with nothing more than a popular constitutional convention had it not been for the series of public marches in support of a new constitution. After repeated attacks by police, in which some marchers were killed, and after domestic and international publicity on the violence, the President made what most Kenyan activists concede were several politically shrewd moves in the series of tactics that marked the resistance-repression cycles in Kenya. First, he invited the clergy to leave the coalition of reformists and assume a neutral, mediating role between them and the government. But as soon as they had pulled out of the reform movement, they were ignored by the President.

New Reforms

Having neutralized the clergy, the President then lured opposition members of Parliament away from the citizens' reform movement by offering to strike a deal in Parliament on key constitutional amendments. Most of the politicians jumped at the chance to achieve some changes they could campaign on for re-election. President Moi backed the establishment of an Inter-Party Parliamentary Group (IPPG), which brought KANU and opposition parties into dialogue that resulted in the rapid dropping of key constitutional limits on freedom of speech and assembly that, in theory, would make election campaigning easier since police routinely blocked many opposition rallies and speeches. The concession also brought the drive for a new constitution to a dead stop as most eyes turned toward the upcoming election.

Donors who had been helping fund the citizens' constitutional reform initiative pulled back when the conference split up; instead, they expressed their support for a compromise in Parliament. Many non-Parliamentary activists considered the agreement by opposition politicians to participate in the deal a sell-out for the reform effort. It was a "betrayal" and the reforms adopted by Parliament were a ruse, a "safety valve which defused the steam pressure that had built up" for a new constitution that would have reduced the President's powers.[22] International support for reforms had weakened since 1992; donors supported only "minimal reforms"[23] and were more focused on corruption than human rights or democracy. It was only

---

22 Activist attorney Pheroze Nowrojee, in an interview with the author in August 2002, in Nairobi, Kenya.

23 Brown, 275.

after the street protests were renewed in 1997 and ran into brutal regime repression that the International Monetary Fund (IMF) announced a temporary suspension of new funds. But the reforms they sought focused on personnel and other bureaucratic issues.[24]

By one interpretation, the aid freeze "prompted KANU to seek an accommodation with the opposition parties."[25] This study has argued, however, that it was the domestic resistance and not the international funding cut-offs that was the main pressure moving the regime to make concessions in 1991 and in late 1997 shortly before the election. Each time the funding freezes followed domestic resistance that drew a repressive response from the regime.[26] In 1997 as in 1991, the regime appeared to be in no hurry to get the funding restored.[27] And as in 1991, the concessions on the part of the President followed evidence from a series of massive street protests in the face of police threats that the public was restless and tired of an abusive regime.

Further Growth of a Culture of Resistance

After the 1997 election, which Moi won again with a plurality and his powers practically intact, there was another lull in activism. With an eye to the 2002 election, civil society groups seeking to restoke the fires of reform, looked once more toward mounting pressure for a new constitution. But once again opposition party leaders failed to make constitutional reform their rallying cry. Another rallying cry, however, united many Kenyans unhappy with the 1997 election results: "Moi must go."

Activists had not managed to achieve a regime transition in 1997, but they had helped further establish a "culture of resistance," according to Maina Kiai, who

---

24 *Weekly Review*, August 8, 1997. The writer complained that while Rome was burning, the IMF was merely examining the strings on the fiddle.

25 Brown, 285.

26 One gets a glimpse of the official view of the effect of IMF and World Bank imperatives from the biography of Moi, a flattering one, which states: "While wider democratization and economic liberalization have dramatically changed the social landscape of Kenya, the pace of this change has been dictated as much by the World Bank, the IMF and the international donor community as by the country's sovereign government" (Morton 1998, 183).

The President and his biographer avoided accrediting activists with prompting any reforms, which was consistent with the President's frequent and strong denunciations of reform efforts and activists.

27 Later, in January 2000 the IMF and World Bank set anti-corruption conditions that the Kenyan government had to meet and withheld new funds from January 2001 until it did. But two years later Kenya had still not met the conditions and was instead accusing lenders of "shifting goalposts" when they added other conditions. In March, 2001, nineteen diplomatic missions urged Kenya to respect the constitutional review process, which further angered President Moi.

had started the Kenya Human Rights Commission.[28] "In 1997 I was so depressed," he recalls. "I thought victory meant massive change." But then he realized that the early protests and expanding activism was permeating through society and people were more informed about their democratic rights and demanding them. It was that "culture of activism…that culture of demanding that forced politicians to come together [in late 2002]," he said.

The activism that took place in the period leading up to the 2002 election was a far cry from the first bold ventures of individual activists in the late 1980s. No longer was there simply an occasional, dramatic lawsuit challenging the President's powers on human rights issues, with small and mostly spontaneous demonstrations of public support for activists. Now such lawsuits were common. Newspapers were full of photos of Kenyan attorneys striding toward yet another courtroom battle.

The once-a-year, illegal political rallies of 1990 and 1991, smashed by police, had long since been replaced by frequent ones drawing large crowds across the country, including a series organized by veteran activist James Orengo from 1997 onward as he sought to lay the base for his own political party. Police still broke up some rallies, but this had little effect in slowing them down or keeping people from attending.

Small demonstrations of various kinds had become frequent across the country, some of them focusing on economic issues. In other instances, political protestors took bodies of alleged victims of police killings to the local police station to demand justice. Teachers were no longer afraid to go on strike and did so. Bookstores carried personal accounts of earlier activists who had been tortured by the regime. Once-banned accounts of corruption in Kenya's government were also on sale.

Goal of Regime Change. An unfocused culture of resistance may make open criticism the norm, but it is a norm an authoritarian regime may learn to live with and remain in power. Unfocused resistance is not effective in accomplishing major political goals. Activists had two goals in the run up to the 2002 election, however: regime change and a new constitution. For many Kenyans the two became intermingled.

One measure of the effectiveness of activism in a culture of resistance can be seen in the political jousting and pressure politics that took place between 2000 and the election itself in December 2002. In December 1999, Parliament formalized President Moi's decision to appoint activist Raila Odinga, the National Democratic Party (NDP) leader and new de facto coalition partner of KANU, to initiate a constitutional reform process. Odinga named 15 individuals to a constitutional commission, subject to approval by the ruling party-dominated Parliament and appointment by the President.

---

28 Maina Kiai in a telephone interview with the author, September 2003. Kiai was preparing to return to Kenya to accept a government post as head of the state's human rights commission. Under President Moi the organization had accomplished little. Under the new regime, Kiai hoped to make it an active watchdog for human rights.

Odinga, a former leader of the opposition, had stunned many of his political colleagues by joining the President's party. He said later he had joined KANU "to democratize it or destroy it," though he made little attempt to hide his hopes of winning the party's presidential nomination for 2002."[29] He later challenged the presidential nomination procedures of KANU, openly confronting President Moi, sometimes face to face in Party meetings. Kenyans had never seen this type of open challenge to the head of State. It "excited the masses," which veteran activist Paul Muite said was always the goal of resistance tactics in order to win greater public support.[30]

Two Centers of Resistance. Two centers of resistance quickly took shape in the face of the President's apparent plan to control the constitutional drafting process with Odinga's help. The first was within Parliament itself. When the vote came up on the Constitutional Review Act, not only opposition members of Parliament walked out, but also some members of KANU. Odinga's merger of the NDP had further changed the makeup of KANU. These new members had no history of subservient agreement to the President as old-time KANU members had.

The resistance to a one-party regime had had its effect on KANU itself in the two previous elections. In order to win support in the first multiparty presidential election in Kenya's history, in 1992, the party had opened its nomination process to "democratic participation by ordinary voters," as it did again in 1997. Voters jumped at the opening, turning out many veteran KANU politicians. Sixty-six of the 107 KANU MPs elected in 1997 were new, including some "20 to 40 Young Turks" who were outspoken against the regime on certain issues. "Indeed in many respects, the biggest impact of the advent of multiparty politics has been within KANU."[31] Voters for the opposition showed a similar independent streak when it came to incumbent reformists in 1997. Approximately sixty percent of the opposition members elected that year were new to Parliament.

The second center of resistance to the regime's plan to steamroller its own version of a new constitution through Parliament was civil society. Afraid of losing their role in shaping a new constitution, church leaders and NGO representatives

---

29   Raila Odinga in an interview with the author in Nairobi, Kenya, October 2002. At the time of the interview he had bolted from the party and was supporting opposition candidate Mwai Kibaki. He claimed his bold confrontations with President Moi, sometimes face to face in party meetings, had given courage to other KANU members, some of whom also bolted the party before the election. Though he had failed to further democratize the presidential selection process, he said he felt he had achieved his alternative goal to "destroy" Kanu, which lost the 2002 election.

30   Paul Muite, in an interview with the author in July 2002, in Nairobi, Kenya. During my field research at that time, almost every Kenyan I met was talking about Odinga's challenge to President Moi.

31   Throup, 2001.

quickly launched another initiative to come up with a draft constitution.[32] This led to a public debate over the makeup of the constitutional commission and two rival bids to shape a draft constitution.

Faced with this twin resistance, the President gave some ground. After some "hectic shuttle diplomacy" by Professor Yash Pal Ghai, an eminent Hong Kong-based Kenyan legal scholar and appointed Chair of the constitutional review commission, the two initiatives were merged. President Moi made the concession of appointing 12 civil society nominees to the commission.[33] By early 2001 the Constitution of Kenya Review Commission was finally formed and began a series of national public hearings to get citizens' views on what kind of constitution people wanted. But the Commission Chair, Professor Ghai, faced opposition within the Commission itself from some Moi supporters.

Nevertheless, the Commission "held a remarkable number of public meetings of all kinds: from public hearings, consultations and 'meet-the-people' tours; to conferences and seminars with various local and international experts and specific interest groups; to smaller caucuses and focus group discussions."[34]

Resistance Becomes Normal

For a culture of resistance to take root, resistance has to become the norm for a visible segment of society.[35] To have much impact, there must be outward participation in various forms of resistance by more than just a few individuals or groups. By 2002, resistance to the still-authoritarian regime had grown to take various forms and was happening so often among so many that it had become a norm for many Kenyans.

By late September 2002 when the draft constitution was published, in defiance of a court order not to, election fever had engulfed Kenyans. The President had chosen as the KANU candidate Uhuru Kenyatta, son of the late Jomo Kenyatta, a Kikuyu and Kenya's first President. Opposition within KANU erupted over the choice; Odinga quit the party shortly before the official party vote on Kenyatta's nomination. He had been attracting massive crowds while still in KANU battling for the nomination himself; now out of the ruling party, he continued to draw huge crowds at his public rallies.

The opposition had not united, though Mwai Kibaki looked like the strongest candidate. Peter Anyang' Nyong'o, a long-time academic activist and Member of

---

32 The civil society initiative was known as the Ufungamano initiative after the meeting site where they held their planning sessions in Nairobi.

33 Human Rights Watch World Report 2002, covering 2001.

34 International Commission of Jurists (Kenya Section). 2001. *State of the Rule of Law in Kenya 2000*. Nairobi: International Commission of Jurists (Kenya Section).

35 Norm, which comes from the Latin *norma*, meaning a carpenter's square or rule, is generally defined as a "standard of conduct that should or must be followed" (Webster's 1988). Normative theory "seeks to understand not simply the way things *are* but also the way things *ought* to be [emphasis in original]" (Thiele 1997, 20).

Parliament, was working behind the scenes to try to bring the opposition candidates together to avoid a third election loss.

The regime had lost legitimacy in the eyes of many Kenyans. Not only were presidential warnings against participation in protests not heeded, but also the President had become a target of public heckling and his handpicked intended successor an object of ridicule in the independent press. The declining legitimacy of the President appeared to encourage more resistance in various forms. The focal point of the confrontations with the regime in late 2002 was the proposed constitution that a state-approved commission had drafted but which it now appeared the regime wanted to block. A sampling of news accounts in late 2002 shows the level of defiance that had been reached by some of those leading the resistance at this point:[36]

Sept. 27 (2002):

"The High Court yesterday confronted a tidal wave of protest by issuing an order stopping public debate on the judicial reforms proposed in the Constitutional review report." Law Society of Kenya chair Raychelle Omamo vows LSK opposition to the order.

Sept 28:

The 280-page draft constitution is released by Professor Ghai who, along with opposition members of Parliament, claims the right to publish it under Parliamentary orders that supersede court orders not to. The Federation of Kenya Women Lawyers Chair Martha Koome threatens demonstrations if the judiciary persists in efforts to block the review process. The Commission notes it has found "overwhelming evidence" that judges had been appointed for political reasons under Moi and had demonstrated neither competence nor integrity.

Sept. 29:

President Moi claims the constitutional review commission did not consider his views because he did not appear (he was invited) and claims that most Kenyans did not have a chance to air their suggestions, claims strongly denied by Professor Ghai.

LSK announces plans to support the review process: with press statements and disobedience of court orders against discussing the judiciary section of the draft constitution; filing a motion of censure against the two advocates who filed the suit to block the review; staging a yellow ribbon campaign in support of the review; boycotting of the courts; lobbying MPs to censure the judiciary; organizing mass action marches led by NGOs, with the LSK providing legal support; networking with regional African court and legislative bodies such as the East African Community, East African Legislative Assembly, East African Court of Justice, and the African Union.

---

36 Taken from *The Nation*, the main daily newspaper in Kenya, strongly critical of many government positions.

Oct. 3:
> Members of Parliament attack efforts by Moi's courts to silence debate over the draft constitution. More than 1,000 lawyers sign a protest note to Chief Justice Bernard Chunga over the courts' attempted interference in the review process.

Oct. 4:
> President Moi is jeered and heckled at a political rally in his own territory, Eldoret. Moi threatens those calling for mass action in favor of adoption of the draft constitution before elections. Crowds along the road wave the two-finger opposition salute and chant "Rainbow…" the name of the KANU faction opposed to Moi's selection of Uhuru Kenyatta as the party's presidential candidate. Kenyatta's convoy is stoned near Eldoret.

Oct. 10:
> "Most of Kenya's 3,000 lawyers held prayers, demonstrated in the streets (Oct. 9) and shunned the courts for one day to protest attempts by the Judiciary to block the work of the Constitution review team."

Oct. 29:
> Police block the entrance to the National Constitutional Conference on its opening day in Nairobi, one day after Moi announced the Ghai commission was disbanded.

Oct. 30:
> Moi's Attorney-general Amos Wako contradicts the President, stating publicly that the Constitutional Review Commission can not be disbanded by the President but only when a new Constitution is enacted or unless Parliament repeals or amends the Review Act.

Ultimately the constitutional debate and review was not completed before the election in late December 2002. After Odinga left KANU, realizing he would not win the party's endorsement as its presidential candidate, he joined the other key opposition presidential contenders in uniting behind Mwai Kibaki, who was elected President. It marked the first defeat of the ruling party since Independence.

Implications of a Culture of Resistance

Resistance moved beyond the role of icebreaker and became more and more institutionalized, more routine in this period, more a norm for many Kenyans. From the late 1980s, activists had wrested a series of concessions from the President; not many, and never fully implemented, but enough to encourage continued resistance. By the mid 1990s, however, many of those who stayed in human rights work were victims of fatigue and disappointment over the prolonged transition. Some went into other work abroad. The approaching general election in 1997 energized activists anew (as it did again in 2002).

The period of 1997 through 2002 illustrated a deepening of the culture of resistance in Kenya along the lines of the concepts and model introduced in Chapter 1. Activists renewed their pressure in another cycle of resistance despite persistent structural constraints, creating their own political opportunities instead of waiting for societal conditions to provide an opening. They tried new tactics and recruited new activists, including youth street-level organizers. In various parts of the country small civic organizations were educating people about their rights and in some cases organizing protests to protect those rights.

The resistance of previous years had served as a foundation for the expanded efforts in this period, providing further evidence that activism was an independent variable. As acts of resistance accumulated in this period they emboldened and encouraged further resistance, though there were clear peaks and valleys in the efforts.

By 1997, the culture of resistance had taken on a new form – an attempt to merge the various strands of the resistance movement that previously had not been coordinated. Each side – resistance activists and the regime – sought to apply lessons learned in previous confrontations. When the regime unleashed a new wave of repression, that and the domestic and international publicity further de-legitimized the regime. A convergence of mostly domestic forces and some donor pressure convinced the President to allow more human rights but not a new constitution that would have weakened his powers.

The last concession the President made was to allow a reasonably free and fair election without postponements, without the kind of state-sponsored violence that preceded the elections in 1992 and 1997, and without apparent massive attempts at rigging. Any of those deviations would certainly have cost him an outcry of foul play from his critics at home and abroad. The election went ahead on schedule, peacefully. When Mwai Kibaki won, President Moi quickly handed over power to him.

Intellectuals such as Kivutha Kibwana, who played a key role in the push for a new constitution in Kenya, hoped that two things would happen in the establishment of a culture of resistance to help insure continuing protection for human rights: (1) new activists would emerge from the movement to create civic awareness of rights; (2) civil society and what he terms "political society," or political parties, would work together to protect rights and in the process, human rights would become a regular part of the "legislative agenda." He hoped human rights would become a regular feature of society and not just a wedge used by one group of politicians to replace another.

One of the main elements in the establishment of a culture of resistance had been the public support given to activists and their events. They were the audience that resistance actors need under any regime to help legitimize demands for reform and are the focus of Chapter 6.

Chapter 6

Mass Public Support:
A Key Element in a Culture of Resistance

In 1997, another election year, just when it looked like police would no longer attack crowds at political opposition rallies, they did so with a vengeance.

On May 31, police and demonstrators clashed as police tear-gassed the crowd. But on the Kenyan scale of violence, it was nothing like what happened in Nairobi at the next rally, July 7, a traditional day for protest. At the July protest, hundreds of police and paramilitary personnel were dispatched throughout the downtown business district and at the intended rally sites, including Uhuru Park, and at the Kamakunji grounds, site of the first rally in 1990.

Some opposition leaders, including ones who had been individual activists earlier then became organizational activists later, including James Orengo, Martin Shikuku, and Paul Muite, managed to reach one of the rally sites and briefly addressed the defiant crowds. But police broke into the area "in a mad frenzy," charging the crowds and beating everyone they came across in "unprecedented" violence. As people fled, the police chased them, even into the All Saints Cathedral, where in 1992 mothers protesting for release of political prisoners found sanctuary after being chased from Uhuru Park. This time there was no sanctuary. The Presidential guard stormed onto the church grounds and into the Cathedral itself. The Rev. Timothy Njoya, a leading activist for human rights was attacked and beaten, surviving with the help of local journalists who used their own bodies to deflect blows aimed at Njoya.[1]

More than a dozen people were shot dead by police that day. Smaller clashes with police took place in some other towns in Kenya.

Despite all this state violence, the public protests continued later in the year. Release Political Prisoners, a private organization, held another peaceful demonstration the very next day, July 8. On July 13, a crowd gathered at All Saints Cathedral; and on July 17, memorial prayers for those killed in the demonstrations were offered at Uhuru Park. Additional public demonstrations were held in other parts of Kenya in July and August. "The defiance reflected by the mass action had confirmed the growing culture of resistance in the country…"[2]

Crowds play an important role in the establishment of a culture of resistance. If few people show up at public rallies organized by a political opposition, an authoritarian

---

1   *Weekly Review*, July 11, 1997, p. 5.
2   Mutunga 1999, p. 189.

leader like President Daniel arap Moi of Kenya can argue that the opposition's demands for more human rights and democratic reforms have little public support.

Starting in the early 1990s, activists organized public protests only to have riot police repeatedly break them up, forcing people to flee. Even after the regime reluctantly agreed to allow more than one political party, many opposition party rallies were attacked. People kept showing up only to be chased away. But the fact that they tried to show their support for change signaled to the regime that public unrest was growing.

After a divided opposition lost the first new multi-party election in 1992, civil society leaders took the lead in the reform drive. They tried to unite people behind a demand for Parliament to adopt a new constitution that would trim the powers of the President. In comparison to 1987, when most Kenyans dared not criticize the regime in public for fear of arrest, by 1997 and even more so as the next election in 2002 approached, massive crowds attended rallies for the opposition. People everywhere were talking openly about their frustrations with the regime. The independent press had shed most of its self-censorship and was strident in its criticism of the President. A local cartoonist who boldly had started drawing only the mace and hand of the President now showed his whole body in true cartoon style. A popular national television show even mimicked the President himself in front of a live audience. The cameras often showed the audience erupting with laughter.[3] The wall of silence around much of the general public had cracked. Many Kenyans had shifted from public deference to the regime to open defiance of it. For them resistance had become the norm.

This chapter focuses on the role mass public support plays in establishing a culture of resistance, including these points:

1. By their own activism, activists provided an opportunity for the general public to express their preexisting dissatisfaction and anger with the regime over various economic, social and political issues.
2. People were drawn to protests by the accumulating examples of activists challenging the regime and making some headway, which encouraged the idea that change was possible.
3. The public never lost their fear of possible reprisals for their participation in public protests due to continuing attacks by police; but people demonstrated openly anyway because of their hope for change that would improve their lives.
4. Public participation in protests played an important role in the establishment of a culture of resistance: without visible public support, activists would have had a difficult time arguing that many people wanted change. The presence of crowds at protests sends a signal to the public that a resistance movement is underway; it also signals the regime that pressure for change is coming from more than just a small band of activists.

---

3   In 1999, the author saw a performance by street children in a downtown park in which one youth did a credible job imitating the President, something that caused convulsions of laughter among the audience.

The chapter begins by examining the conditions under which public support for resistance is likely to occur and how this applied to the case of Kenya. Constraints are weighed against opportunities. Next the chapter examines different categories of mass public participation and their different forms, risks, and the strategies behind them. The chapter concludes with implications of the public protests and the role they played in establishing a culture of resistance.

As one social movement scholar puts it, "people construct their own history – not under circumstances chosen by themselves, certainly, but under circumstances they have the power to change. Opportunity ultimately is what people make of it."[4]

The focus in this chapter on pubic support for activism builds on the literature that notes, as one Africa-wide study does, that political protests are the "core" aspect of "how transitions start."[5] It also builds on the literature that recognizes the important role civil society has played in bringing about political transitions in Eastern Europe, Asia, Latin America and Africa.[6] But in contrast to many studies, the Kenya study recognizes more clearly the power of people to change things.

Civil society and political society (parties) in Kenya were never that strong during the study period. Despite their role in helping organize protests, it was not their militancy, force, or organizational strengths and skills that attracted crowds. Rather it was the power of an idea – the hope that change could come. Similarly it was the hope of change that impelled hundreds of thousands of protestors to go to the streets in Eastern Europe, helping bring an end to the Communist era, as previously noted. "Communism was not defeated by military force, but by life, by the human spirit, by conscience..." according to Vaclav Havel,[7] one of the architects of that change.

The Kenya case, however, differs from explanations of the massive protests in Eastern Europe which argue that participation by groups was the key to the protests.[8] In Kenya the crowds were smaller, less organized and more a collection of individuals. Contrary to the Karklins and Petersen study which explains how protestors overcame their fear as the crowds grew in size, most Kenyans who turned out for protests never lost their fear of reprisals because the regime kept attacking

---

4 Kurzman, Charles. 2004. "The Poststructuralist Consensus in Social Movement Theory." In *Rethinking Social Movements: Structure, Meaning, and Emotion*, eds. Jeff Goodwin and James M. Jasper. Oxford, U. K.: Rowman & Littlefield, 117.

5 Bratton, Michael, and Nicolas van de Walle. 1997. *Democratic Experiments in Africa: Regime Transitions in Comparative Perspective*. Cambridge: Cambridge University Press, 128.

6 Examples of this literature include: Tarrow, Sidney. 1998. *Power in Movement: Social Movements and Contentious Politics*. 2nd ed. Cambridge, U. K.: Cambridge University; Diamond, Larry. 1999. *Developing Democracy: Toward Consolidation*. Baltimore. Johns Hopkins University Press, chapter 6; Giugni, Marco, Doug McAdam, and Charles Tilly, eds. 1999. *How Social Movements Matter*. Minneapolis: University of Minnesota Press.

7 Havel, Vaclav. "The End of the Modern Era," *New York Times*, 1 March 1992.

8 Karklins, Rasma, and Roger Petersen. 1993. "Decision Calculus of Protesters and Regimes: Eastern Europe 1989. *The Journal of Politics*, 55(3):588–614.

demonstrators. The crowds in Kenya never grew to the massive size seen in the Philippines, the Ukraine, or some Latin American countries in recent years.

The Kenya study also contrasts with a path-dependency explanation of protests that links them with characteristics of previous regimes.[9] Instead it focuses on the contemporary dynamics of activism and offers a closer look at resistance dynamics than one can expect from such an archival study.[10] In Kenya, the power of personal example of activists did much to create the conditions for public participation in protests. When, for example, two former politicians-turned activists boldly called in 1990 for change from a one-party to a multiparty system and for a rally to support the idea, despite regime threats to crush such an initiative, many Kenyans began to "gather courage…because there was an example set," notes a Kenyan historian who has studied the process.[11]

Constraints that did not Constrain

We have seen in the previous chapters that activism does not take place in a vacuum; neither does public support for that activism. Constraints may include the strength of a state's security apparatus (police, military, paramilitary forces, intelligence system); the willingness of a regime to use force to overcome opposition; geopolitical realities

---

9   Bratton, Michael, and Nicolas van de Walle. 1997. *Democratic Experiments in Africa: Regime Transitions in Comparative Perspective.* Cambridge: Cambridge University Press, makes such a link.

10 In their archival study, Bratton and van de Walle use correlation data that found that political protests occurred most often in sub-Saharan Africa between 1985 and 1994 in countries that (1) had the most trade unions under the previous regime; (2) had the most elections under all previous postcolonial regimes. "Simply put, our model suggests that protest was more likely to break out where there was some semblance of institutional tradition of competition and participation" (150).

While the correlations may be exact, their meaning is subject to varying interpretations. For example, how long does a past set of circumstances affect the present? Would the presence of trade unions in a previous regime have an effect on the minds of those joining a public protest years later? Further, the correlation on trade unions leaves open the question of just how free they were. Simply counting a list of unions in past issues of Africa South of the Sahara, which is what Bratton and Van de Walle did, tells us little about the degree of "competition," their category, in those unions. Under Moi, for example, the regime was able to minimize the independence of the trade movement.

Another variable, elections, poses other problems. Counting the number of elections tells us little about the quality or nature of them. Was there an open choice of candidates? Was there rigging? "Political participation," their category for elections indicates only that people could vote. But did their vote have any meaning? Kenya was long a one-party state with much participation but not much competition. Nevertheless, their study provided a probing, continent-wide analysis of the dynamics of democratization in Africa.

11 Macharia Munene, in an interview with the author in Nairobi, Kenya, September 2002.

(e.g., Cold War-era tolerance by the West of authoritarian regimes because they were not Communist); politically-manipulated ethnic rivalries that tend to divide people and thus weaken reform efforts; poor economies that might render some too busy making a living to join protests; and a tenuous middle class that is too vulnerable to losing material possessions to take risks.

Structural Constraints

The socioeconomic status of Kenyans worsened during the late 1980s and 1990s. A 1992 report by the United States Embassy summarized the situation this way: "Kenya has fallen on hard times, largely of its own making... [except for exports] all major economic indicators are in decline...much of it is the result of simple, if all pervasive government mismanagement."[12] Aside from some improvements in literacy and infant mortality rates, and life expectancy, the average annual percentage of growth in the economy from 1985–1992 was only 0.9 percent;[13] in a longer period of 1987 to 1997 it was 0.0, no growth at all. Average annual population growth in Kenya began declining in the 1980s, but was still one of the highest in sub-Saharan Africa by 1989 at 3.3 percent.[14]

By 1991, as demands for multiparty politics were reaching a climax in Kenya, at least 10 percent of the urban population was living below "absolute poverty" as was 43 percent of the rural population.[15] Such estimates hide the real extent of poverty since they blend in the rich and the poor to arrive at an average. By 1997, Kenya was often portrayed as the "world's fourth most unequal society with the top 10 percent controlling 48 percent of national income." Things kept getting worse through the 1990s: from 1997 to 1999, the gross domestic product declined from 2.3 percent to 1.5.[16]

What happened in Kenya does not fit the model Samuel Huntington offered that linked demands for democratization to a growing economy with an expanding middle class which put pressure on the government for greater participation.[17] He argued that a growing economy, improving levels of education, and a growing

---

12 *Kenya: Economic Trends Report*, October 1992, prepared by the American Embassy in Nairobi.

13 World Bank. 1995. *African Development Indicators* 1994–1995. Washington: World Bank, 6.

14 World Bank. 1999. *African Development Indicators* 1998–1999. Washington: World Bank, 6–7.

15 Absolute poverty was defined as a level of income "below which adequate standards of nutrition, shelter, and personal amenities cannot be assured" (World Bank 1995, 363). The actual poverty rates were probably much higher than this, especially in urban slums. In 1994, for example, the per capita gross national product was only $260, compared to a sub-Saharan average of $550 and a world average of $4,740.

16 Throup, 2001.

17 Huntington, Samuel P. 1991. *The Third Wave: Democratization in the Late Twentieth Century*. Norman, OK.: University of Oklahoma, 65–69.

middle class combine to produce support for democratization. In Kenya, however, the economy was heading downhill, the middle class was shrinking, and yet demands for democratization were increasing. But while the economy worsened, there was no precipitous drop of the kind noted in some social movement literature as a trigger giving a social movement an opening or opportunity to take off.

There is wide disagreement among scholars over the linkages between economy and democratization.[18] It seems that for every argument in one direction about the economy-democratization question, there is an argument in the other direction. Bratton and van de Walle note that ". . . every plausible scenario mapping out the exact link between economic crisis and regime transition can be counterbalanced by a logical argument, buttressed by empirical evidence, against such a link." Economic approaches are "compelling only if and when they are embedded within a political approach," they argued.[19] Some scholars emphasize the actions of people (agency) over the structural or background constraints such as the economy as a key variable in democratization.[20]

The discouraging economic picture in Kenya, one might argue, inspired people to join protests. But a counter-argument might be that the very poor were too busy making a living to have much time for political protest; and that the middle class was worried about losing what advantages they had achieved in a once expanding and

---

18 Examples of the differing positions some scholars have taken over the relationship between the economy and democratization include:

(1) *a rising economy improves chances of democratization* because it improves socio-economic conditions that lead more people to demand reforms (Diamond 1999; Huntington 1991; Lipset 1959); it raises incomes (Geddes 1999; Przeworski and Limongi 1993; Przeworski and Limongi 1997; Przeworski et al. 1996); it strengthens the bourgeoisie (Moore 1963), the working class (Rueschmeyer, Stevens and Stevens 1992), the middle class (Dahl 1971; 1998);

(2) *a rising economy reduces chances of democratization* because it increases instability (Huntington 1968); leads to bureaucratic authoritarianism in some cases (O'Donnell 1973) or boosts the clout of the out-going authoritarian regime (Haggard, Kaufmann 1995);

(3) *a declining economy improves chances of democratization* by increasing the chances for authoritarian breakdown (Geddes 1999; Haggard, Kaufmann 1995; Przeworski, Limongi 1997);

(4) *a declining economy reduces chances of democratization* because it increases demands for an authoritarian regime (Dahl 1971); or it may lead to a prolonged economic crisis that weakens democracy (Diamond 1999).

19 Bratton and van de Walle, 36.

20 Diamond, Larry. 1999. *Developing Democracy: Toward Consolidation*. Baltimore. Johns Hopkins University Press; Huntington, Samuel P. 1991. *The Third Wave: Democratization in the Late Twentieth Century*. Norman, OK.: University of Oklahoma; Linz, Juan J. & Alfred Stepan. 1996. *Problems of Democratic Transition and Consolidation: Southern Europe, South America, and Post-Communist Europe*. Baltimore: The Johns Hopkins University Press; O'Donnell, Guillermo, and Philippe C. Schmitter. 1986. *Transitions from Authoritarian Rule: Tentative Conclusions about Uncertain Democracies*. Baltimore: Johns Hopkins University Press.

now declining economy. Yet there was considerable public agitation for change, for democratization.

Except in a sudden economic crisis, economies tend to move slowly upward or downward. The poor generally remain poor over a very long period, sometimes decades. It would be hard to show convincingly that at a particular point in economic trends, upward or downward, protests and demands by the poor stop or start as a result.[21] This study argues that the economy was a background factor of discontent but not a triggering device for protests. The trigger was regime behavior which led to active resistance by some individuals and organizations, drawing in more and more Kenyans to protest for a variety of reasons. Protection of human rights was the initial rallying cry in the resistance; then it was democratization; and finally outright calls for regime change.

Regardless of whether an economy is rising or falling, poor people have often joined political protests in Africa. If a declining economy improves chances of democratization by weakening an authoritarian regime,[22] then why were there not democratic transitions in all the sub-Saharan countries in the 1990s that had declining economies?

In their archival study, Bratton and Van de Walle concluded that popular resistance to authoritarian rule in Africa, according to admittedly "sometimes very weak national data," was "apparently no more likely to occur in relatively prosperous, diversified economies than in low-income, agrarian ones." They added ". . . the level of economic development and the frequency of political protest were essentially unrelated. Pro-democracy demonstrations occurred frequently in both very low-income African countries as well as in the richest, middle-income countries." The current Kenya study offers an explanation for why protests occur and the conditions under which they occur.

International Factors

After the Cold War the West began applying a somewhat tougher standard to the behavior of former non-Communist authoritarian regimes in terms of human rights

---

21 Anthropologist Angelique Haugerud (1995, 33–34) writes: "In Kenya, economic decline certainly played a part in the political upheavals in the early 1990s." She cites background data but does not suggest there was a triggering device in the economic bad news. Moi's decision to accept multiparty elections starting in 1992 was "a risky legitimizing device for a regime without fiscal options" (Holmquist, Weaver, Ford 1994).The declining economy of the 1980s had left the regime without the usual resources it used in a patrimonial system that rewarded friends and penalized opponents. With less money available, the system of buying support was weakened, according to such arguments. Yet when the regime needed more money to help win the contested 1992 election, it simply printed more, causing sharp inflation.

22 Haggard, Stephen, Robert R. Kaufman, eds. 1995. *The Political Economy of Democratic Transitions*. Princeton: Princeton University Press.

and democratization.[23] As we have seen in the two previous chapters, donors were generally supportive of the Moi regime during the late 1980s and up until a funding freeze in late 1991, despite documented use of torture by the state against political dissidents. The International Monetary Fund (IMF) imposed two other freezes, in 1997 and 2002, ostensibly for economic reasons, each time followed by protracted negotiations with the Kenyans to restore aid. Starting around 1990, bilateral donors put more pressure on the regime to democratize, but such pressure "did not inspire mass uprisings."[24]

Were people who came onto the streets to protest likely to consider beforehand the international funding position of donors? More likely encouragements to protest were the fall of the Berlin Wall in 1989, followed soon by the demise of several authoritarian heads of state in Eastern Europe; the release of Nelson Mandela from prison in 1990; and the wave of democratization that spread across much of sub-Saharan Africa in the early 1990s. Numerous Kenyan activists interviewed for this study cited these factors as encouraging their own activism.

For a few years in the early 1990s, there was a feeling that authoritarian regimes were on the run. In 1989, only five African states had what might be called democracy, with more than one political party and contested elections.[25] By 1995, three out of four African states had "competitive party systems" of one degree or another.[26]

Institutional Factors

If a regime chooses to use unrestrained brutality against a rising opposition, it is likely to crush it, though risking the start of an underground movement that might eventually lead to violent efforts to seize power. Such unrestrained brutality was seen in the late 1980s and early 1990s in the region in Somalia under Mohamed Siad Barre, Ethiopia under Mengistu Haile Mariam, and Sudan under Omar Al-Beshir. But Kenya under Daniel arap Moi was different.

Although President Moi had cracked down hard on suspected members of the underground movement Mwakenya in the 1980s, he continued to take a public stand as one who respected the rule of law. Yet the President was not against using the state security agencies to harass, intimidate, and arrest those he felt were pushing too hard for change that would threaten his own patrimonial base of power. Faced with

---

23 Kenyan activist attorney Gibson Kamau Kuria suggested that the West did have a Cold War interest in human rights but primarily as a means of critiquing Communist nations; in an interview with the author, July 2002, in Nairobi, Kenya.

24 Bratton and van de Walle, 136.

25 The five were Botswana, The Gambia, Mauritius, Senegal, and Zimbabwe. A military coup in The Gambia ousted the government in July 1994. Zimbabwe's leader Robert Mugabe later turned autocratic and abusive of human rights.

26 Wiseman, John A. 1996. *The New Struggle for Democracy in Africa*. Aldershot, Eng.: Avebury, 1–2. Wiseman defines a fully-fledged single-party state as one in which "only one political party is allowed, by law, to exist and, where elections take place, participation is confined to members of the party."

growing public resistance from individual and organizational activists and instances of public support for demands for greater human rights and democratization, a regime has four main choices:

Full Repression. This is something the Moi regime was reluctant to pursue. It claimed legitimacy both domestically and internationally as a representative regime based on rule of law. Although its critics soundly denied this, the fact that the regime claimed to be upholding democratic principles and laws made it difficult to justify all-out repression against opponents who were not taking up arms. Occasionally the regime claimed that a few dissidents had plans to mount an armed attack, but the claims were widely considered absurd by international human rights groups and domestic critics and were never able to gain much credibility at home or abroad. Thus full repression of its critics was not much of an option.

Full Reform. President Moi repeatedly stated that he would not be pushed into making reforms such as multiparty elections, which he contended were dangerous to the unity of the country. His critics read his opposition as a plan to retain power without competition. Moi resisted most reform proposals and never genuinely cooperated in efforts to achieve a new constitution with fewer Presidential powers and better protection of human rights. His acceptance in December 1991 of multiparty elections, as seen in chapter 4, came as the result of a convergence of domestic and international forces at a time when there was a rush across much of sub-Saharan Africa (as well as Eastern Europe) to replace authoritarian regimes with reformists.

Selective Repression. When an authoritarian regime at least pretends to subscribe to democratic principles and the rule of law, activism with public support is more likely to be met with selective repression. Full repression is likely to bring penalties too high for most regimes to handle in terms of both domestic pressure and international loss of support. Full reforms could lead to electoral defeat.[27]

    Part of the regime's strategy was selective repression. By continuing to target leading activists or activist organizations for punishment, the regime hoped to keep others off guard and from unifying to make greater demands. Although the regime reduced use of torture of dissidents and use of detention starting around 1987, both were still selectively used into the early 1990s. Even after Moi's presidential victory in 1992, the regime continued periodic pressure on activist politicians and journalists, including detention, arrest, banning publications temporarily, and sometimes seizing copies of critical issues.

Selective Reforms. This was the other part of the regime strategy. As many activists recalled in a series of interviews, the regime seemed to have learned to play the democratization game skillfully, giving in a little when pressure mounted; holding

---

27 The Moi regime's defeat in 2002 was through an election. It was not anticipated by the President, who fully expected to be able to help his handpicked candidate win.

firm when it slacked off, but never fully implementing any of the conceded reforms. Even as late as 1997 when the regime agreed to key reforms regarding freedom of speech and assembly, officials dragged their feet and sometimes blocked putting such measures into action.

In 1997, police and other security personnel were brutal in their attacks on civilian demonstrators. Did the public calculate in advance the risk of being beaten if they showed up at a public protest rally, most of which were declared illegal by the incumbent regime; did they worry about losing a government job if they were identified as a member of the opposition, or a government contract if they were in business? The likely answer to both questions is yes.

Yet the regime violence, instead of ending resistance, seemed to nourish it. Protests, never great in number but highly visible, had a snowballing effect, encouraging further demonstrations and public participation, according to interviews with activists and the record of protests. Risk-adverse individuals may be deterred by state threats but "coercion may have the opposite effect on others, indeed heighten their political activity.[28]

Civil Society

Civilian protestors played a role in the transition of a number of African countries in the early 1990s, including Mali, where students, union members and other groups confronted the forces of an authoritarian President with demands that escalated quickly from educational reforms to regime change. But public protests were not always successful; in Nigeria, for example, following the annulment of apparently free and fair elections for President in 1993, activism was met with severe repression by a military regime.

If one were to assume that a robust civil society lay behind the public protests in Kenya, then one might expect to find strong nongovernment organizations (NGOs) and opposition political parties in terms of personnel, planning, and financing. But in many cases this simply was not the case. Many of these were poorly staffed, under-equipped, and lacking independent sources of financing apart from foreign funding, which made them vulnerable to the agendas of their benefactors. "Donor agencies and NGOs have often tried to do too much with too little resources and the impact of civil education, especially in rural areas, has been exaggerated. The haphazard, ad hoc, and sporadic seminars and protests have not resulted in any meaningful constitutional or political change"; Political parties were often weakened by rivalries, divisions, and little focused on human rights or, except as a way to win office, on democratization. "Despite their ambitious rhetoric about democracy, good governance and economic reform, most of the political parties are not instruments

---

28 Andrain, Charles F., and David E. Apter. 1995. *Political Protest and Social Change: Analyzing Politics.* New York: New York University Press, 4.

for social transformation. They are vehicles for organizing the regional, tribal and clan votes."[29]

Mass Support for Activism: Theoretical Perspectives

Despite these structural and institutional barriers to protests, there was visible public support for activism and leadership in the resistance movement throughout most of the study period. To appreciate why, one must move beyond the long-standing structural constraints argument that still dominate the political process model, despite more recent attempts by the founders to add a cultural element to that model, an attempt still structurally-biased.[30]

One scholar suggests that emotion and passion can help explain why someone would support a resistance movement that involves "sometimes dangerous, and often risky, intense, and exhilarating activities." An analysis based on pure rationality would not able to capture such motivation. Gould argues that such a protester is not entirely irrational as some earlier behavior models suggested, overcome by emotion. Yet "in the now-dominant models we have rational actors who coolly calculate their grievances and pursue a strategic course of action, all the while apparently devoid of and certainly unaffected by, anger, fear, joy, pride, or any other emotion."[31] That seems unrealistic, he contends.

Gould makes a good argument. Given their fears, are protesters likely to coolly calculate the odds of getting arrested, the chance that their presence in a mass rally would somehow make a difference in the country's – and their own – future? If anything, a mass protest seems a perfect argument for Olson's free-rider argument:[32] stay home; one more demonstrator can't possibly make a difference.

But "optimism" that change is possible, as well as a disregard by some of danger helps bring people out onto the streets.[33] Such intangible motivations make it practically impossible to "predict the outcome of protest movements... What sort of scenario would we present to survey respondents? Could we expect their cost-

29 Murungi, Kiraitu. 2000. *In The Mud of Politics*. Nairobi, Kenya: Acacia Stantex, 204; 206.

30 Goodwin, Jeff, and James M. Jasper, eds. 2004. *Rethinking Social Movements: Structure, Meaning, and Emotion*. Oxford, U. K.: Rowman & Littlefield.

31 Gould, Deborah B. 2004. "Passionate Political Process." In *Rethinking Social Movements: Structure, Meaning, and Emotion*, eds. Jeff Goodwin and James M. Jasper. Oxford, U. K.: Rowman & Littlefield, 160–161.

32 Olson, Mancur. [1965] 1998. *The Logic of Collective Action: Public Goods and the Theory of Groups*. Cambridge, MA.: Harvard University Press.

33 In extreme cases such as the Iranian Revolution where some protestors were even "willing to face prison, torture, and death, or even welcome such fates, then repression will not faze them (Kurzman 2004, 116).

benefit calculations to be the same in the cool of the moment?"[34] In such cases an analysis based just on structural constraints, or on the threat of repression, is not very helpful.

From the previous discussion of structural constraints we can see that identifying the poor economy as a cause of the public protests is an uncertain endeavor. And it is unlikely that protesters were calculating the latest international donors' positions on Kenya before joining protests. According to Bratton and Van de Walle, "international and economic factors played supportive but essentially secondary roles in explaining political protest in Africa."[35]

Predisposed Dissent. Evidence that a significant portion of the public was predisposed against the regime is seen in the widespread disgruntlement with the 1988 queue voting (see below) and in the 1992 and 1997 election returns in which President Moi received approximately 37 and 40 percent of the vote, respectively.[36] Evidence that activism, not the strength of institutions provided opportunities for expression of dissent is seen in the turnout for entirely unplanned protests, spontaneous ones (see below) that had nothing at all to do with civil society organizations except that, in some cases, their leaders had been arrested and people took the opportunity to show support for them in the streets.

This predisposition against the regime meant that it was not the skill of human rights and democratization groups or opposition parties in framing messages that drew crowds to the streets for political protests. People turned out without having to be convinced of anything except that change was possible, something the resistance itself and the concessions won showed was the case. The Moi regime's limited but sometimes severe repression probably frightened many from taking part in public protests, but failed to keep others away. Civil society and political parties merit some credit for organizing protests, despite the fact that many were not strong financially or otherwise.

Shift of Norms. This study argues that the accumulation of resistance by individuals and later organizations facilitated a mental shift of norms.[37] People who were previously more impressed by the dangers of protests saw activists taking risks and

---

34 Kurzman, Charles. 2004. "The Poststructuralist Consensus in Social Movement Theory." In *Rethinking Social Movements: Structure, Meaning, and Emotion*, eds. Jeff Goodwin and James M. Jasper. Oxford, U. K.: Rowman & Littlefield, 117.

35 Bratton, van de Walle, 139.

36 Hornsby, Charles. 2001. "Election Day and the Results." In *Out for the Count: the 1997 General Elections and Prospects for Democracy in Kenya*, eds. Marcel Rutten, Alamin Mazrui, and François Grignon. Kampala, Uganda: Fountain Publishers, 139–140.

37 Hyden (2000, 9) suggests that democracy can be a "limiting" concept for analyzing the strength of state and society in Africa because it tends to focus primarily on the ways civil society tries to win control of the "democratic moment." A more useful way of analyzing political change, he suggests, would be to look at both the state and society as well as how rules and "norms" shape change.

surviving, and decided to join them. Though still fearing reprisals, many Kenyans turned out for protests, apparently convinced that their actions might help gain them what they felt they deserved – a better economic life, more political freedom, and an end to authoritarian rule. Where these members of the public had once been silent, they had evolved from deference to open defiance of the regime.

"There are moments and periods when large numbers of people step out of... their daily lives to participate in collective action – action that often entails sacrifice and risk."[38] There are other times when just a few step out to protest, sometimes spontaneously. Those who do show up can be divided into several categories: activist leaders who plan a protest; members of an organization who may have helped in the planning and sponsorship; sympathetic observers who come, perhaps at the last minute, perhaps with advance intent; and bystanders who may linger just out of reach of the police batons that often accompany illegal protests.[39]

Massive protests succeeded in Eastern Europe in 1989 because (1) people grew less afraid of the consequences as the momentum grew and they saw more protestors in their own group and other groups and an assumption that they might escape harm and win political change; (2) the regimes suffered from fragmentation, defections and loss of self-confidence. And they miscalculated that brute force would stop the protests; coming after the momentum for change was well underway, such force served only as a rallying cause for further protests.[40]

By comparison, in Kenya it was only shortly before the 2002 elections that defections from the ruling party became a major issue as the tide began turning in favor of the opposition, whose main presidential candidates attracted massive public support. Crowds provided a certain degree of anonymity to protestors compared to the more visible role activist leaders played. But the risk to activist leaders and the members of the public who supported them never went away.

Laying the Groundwork for Mass Participation

When public protests start, they may mark the beginning of a process that leads to a transition. "The outbreak of political protest signals to incumbent leaders that the regime faces a crisis of legitimacy...The persistence of political protest, even in the face of state repression, indicates that the old regime has begun to break down. And if unrest prompts incumbent leaders to make concessions, then protests have sparked the onset of a political transition."[41]

---

38 Flacks, Richard. 2004 "Knowledge for What? In *Rethinking Social Movements: Structure, Meaning, and Emotion*, eds. Jeff Goodwin and James M. Jasper. Oxford, U. K.: Rowman & Littlefield, 142.

39 Kurzman (2004, 142) stresses the importance of an analytical distinction between activists and mass participants.

40 Karklins, Rasma, and Roger Petersen. 1993. "Decision Calculus of Protesters and Regimes: Eastern Europe 1989. *The Journal of Politics*, 55(3):588–614.

41 Bratton and van de Walle, 129.

As activism progressed, its leaders would seek forums for attracting public support to show that their cause had some popular backing. But in the early phases of the resistance, activists exposed abuses of power without attempting to attract supportive crowds. Their actions had the effect of "exciting the masses" with the idea that the regime could be challenged.[42]

What follows are three brief examples which helped lay the groundwork for mass public participation in the resistance movement in Kenya.

1. *Voting Fraud Stirs Public Resentment.* In 1988 when the regime substituted for ballot box elections an open system of voting in which voters lined up behind the name of their candidate, a system known as queuing (*mlolongo* in Swahili), there was still only one party, but candidates within the party could contest a seat in Parliament. When members of the clergy and others helped document glaring cases of fraud in which candidates favored by the regime won despite having shorter voter lines, the abuse sent shock waves of resentment across much of the country, according to many of those interviewed for this study. Kenyan historian Macharia Munene describes this resentment as a starting point for resistance among a portion of the general public:[43]

"Before the mlolongo, rigging took place but you could always say well we don't know whether that's how the votes were. But with the mlolongo everybody saw. [It] was the turning point; the real turning point in Kenyan politics on the human rights issues. Because this is the time that it became normal to question the government and almost get away with it. Before that, before '88, everybody spoke in hushed tones."

One winner of the queuing election in 1988 denied even being a candidate. Some members of the public who complained openly about the rigging were arrested. After a national outcry about the rigging, the government was prepared to drop those cases. But some of those charged wanted to precede with the cases, exhibiting a "totally new attitude" toward the regime, one of defiance.[44] "The anger at the destruction of their neo-democratic heritage – their right to choose their leaders, if not change what they did once in office – was an important inspiration behind the popular protests of 1990–1991."[45]

The magazine *Beyond*, published by the National Council of Churches of Kenya (NCCK), exposed the voting fraud. It was the editor of *Beyond*, Bedan Mbugua, whose quiet determination to publish the facts, helped win public support for reform. The day the magazine published the exposé, magazine sales shot quickly up to 20,000 within a few hours. Sales continued to soar during the day as the printer rushed to meet the demand, reaching some 105,000 copies by late afternoon. Copies were

---

42 Activist Paul Muite, in an interview with the author in Nairobi, Kenya, July 2002.
43 Munene interview.
44 Munene interview.
45 Throup and Hornsby, 44.

selling for up to five times their normal price. "It became like a bomb. And people could not believe that anybody could express ideas so boldly."[46]

Late that afternoon the government issued an emergency banning order against the publication. Mbugua was arrested soon after. While in custody he was brought to State House, President Moi's official residence. There he recalled he met with two senior aides to the President and was told his case could be dropped if he blamed the NCCK for pushing him into publishing the article about the voting fraud. The President apparently was looking for something to hold against the NCCK, which was one of the few sources of criticism of his regime at that time.

But Mbugua refused the deal, saying it was he, not the NCCK who made the initiative to publish the exposé. He was taken to court and found guilty. After the verdict, he was whisked out a back entrance of the courthouse and taken to prison. He soon learned from newspaper clippings handed to him by sympathetic prison guards, that on the day of his judgment, large numbers of Kenyans had gathered in a prayer meeting on his behalf in front of the courthouse.[47]

2. *President's Authority Challenged.* In 1989 Dr. Wangari Maathai, an internationally-known conservationist and political activist, challenged the regime's plans to build a sixty-story headquarters complex for the ruling party, including a four-story statue of the President, in a downtown public park. The project was considered important to the ruling party but the issue soon became whether someone could challenge the President on a pet project, something practically unheard of in that period. Eventually the project was scrapped after donors balked at the cost. But even more significant, the public had seen how a supposedly all-powerful regime could be stymied and forced to retreat by the work of just one activist.

"And from that moment the opposition was on the way…everybody was so euphoric and felt like, 'Oh my God! It is possible to challenge [the regime]. It is possible for us to claim our rights.' And it was shortly after that [Oginga] Odinga launched his [opposition] party."[48]

There was no venue for mass public support in this case. Coming not long after the height of the use of torture by the regime against suspected dissidents in detention, the challenge by Maathai was at a time when public fear of speaking out was still high. Dr. Maathai carried out her battle in the newspapers which ran her statements and the condemnation of her by President Moi.

---

46 Bedan Mbugua, former editor of *Beyond*, in an interview with the author in Nairobi, Kenya, August 2002.

47 The courthouse protest was quickly organized by the chairman of the Board of *Beyond* in support of Mbugua. Mbugua said the Chairman of the NCCK, however, did not support him when he was arrested, even trying to distance himself from Mbugua, though others on the Board did back him.

48 Wangari Maathai, in an interview with the author in Nairobi, Kenya, September 2002.

In choosing to respond to the conservationist's challenges with words only, the President put himself in a position to lose some legitimacy. If he had been counting on the strength of his verbal attacks to silence her, he soon found out he was wrong. When donors later turned their back on the project and it was quietly shelved, Kenyans did not have to be reminded that not only was the project in question unpopular but the President had been challenged – and lost, something that put another crack in the President's intended wall of political invincibility and in the wall of silence around many Kenyans.

3. *Ethnic Violence Increases Awareness of Rights.* One of the regime's most violent responses to the pressures for reform may have helped raise public consciousness concerning the need for change. Politically-manipulated clashes broke out against members of ethnic groups not generally supportive of President Moi, namely the Kikuyu and Luhya, against the Kalenjin, Moi's ethnic grouping, in 1991-1993 in central Kenya and again in 1997 in a coastal region. There were many allegations of why the state allowed (or supported) ethnic violence, but a common explanation was that the state wanted to drive out potential rival voters from electoral areas it hoped to control.[49] There was an unintended consequence, however, though they terrorized thousands of poor, rural residents, the clashes "radicalized" many Kenyan rural residents into opposition against the regime and damaged regime "credibility," according to human rights attorney and early activist Gibson Kamau Kuria.[50]

"There may be different perspectives but for me it [the clashes] really accelerated democratization because it heightened human rights awareness. Because peasants thought they were not involved in politics [but] they were being killed, they were losing their land. [They] became aware...that the government was evil," said Kuria.

Another unintended consequence of the clashes was an explosion in 1993 of a form of cultural protests: use of clandestine musical tapes describing the deaths and destruction of property in the clash areas that the regime had sealed off from the public. The tapes were the work of Kenyan musicians and several activists who snuck into the closed areas. They were produced in Nairobi.

The making of the tapes marked an expansion of the resistance in Kenya to include clandestine publishers and artists working to expose the abuses of the regime. The playing of the tapes in matatus (mini-van taxies) and their popularity was another crack in the culture of fear and silence. It was an important step in the public awareness of Kenyans concerning the abuse of human rights. "Music and theater became important avenues through which criticisms of the ruling regime

---

49 The clashes in early 1992, after the first multiparty presidential election, were seen by some as a form of punishment for Kikuyu communities that had supported the opposition (Throup and Hornsby 1998, 197).

50 Gibson Kamau Kuria, in an interview with the author in Nairobi, Kenya, September 2002.

coalesced, influencing individual consciousness as the opposition grew wider and became more public by late 1991 and early 1992."[51]

Different Kinds of Mass Support for Resistance

Just as the previous chapters have disaggregated activism in order to better understand its phases, dynamics, and strategies, so too, one can disaggregate mass support for resistance. Mass participation is an essential ingredient in the establishment of a culture of resistance. But to view it as some kind of amorphous whole does not allow the kind of insights that are possible when it is examined more closely. As Table 6.1 below indicates, there were discernible patterns in the mass public participation.

In Kenya, mass public support for resistance from 1987–2002 tended to happen under three sets of circumstances, each with their own characteristics and dynamics: (1) spontaneous event organized by or involving individual activists; (2) mobilized event led by individual activists; (3) mobilized event led by organizational activists. Each category represents a different expression or forum for dissent; different risk levels for participants; and is the result of different strategies on the part of the activists.

Table 6.1   Mass public participation in resistance movement in Kenya 1987–2002

Mobilized Participation

	Informal protests; large crowds illegal; high risk	Formal rallies large crowds; legal; illegal; high risk
Individual Activism		Organized Activism
	Informal protests small crowds illegal; high risk to low	

Spontaneous Participation

Note: in the absence of reliable estimates of crowd size, the categories used are very broad: small (dozens); large (hundreds to thousands).

What follow are analyses and examples of the three categories of mass participation shown in Table 6.1 and the role they play in a resistance movement. In the analyses

---

51 Haugerud, Angelique 1995. *The Culture of Politics in Modern Kenya.* Cambridge, U.K.: Cambridge University Press, 28.

individual and organizational activism is considered an independent variable; mass participation is considered a dependent variable – dependent on activism to provide an opportunity to express their resistance, not dependent on structural or institutional constraints.

Individual Activism/Spontaneous Participation

As this study has documented, the initial phases of resistance are often carried out by individual activists who challenge regime authority and, by their example, encourage others to join the resistance. Because they receive no support or only minimal support from any organization, they often are not in a position to mobilize crowds, even informally. Much of what they do is considered illegal by the regime. At this early stage in the resistance, activists try to make use of state institutions such as courts and seek to get what they can into the independent media, which is still practicing a high degree of self-censorship.

Thus the mass public participation they attract is almost accidental, unplanned, and spontaneous. Though such protests would be considered illegal, the risk to participants depends on the length of the event. If a sympathetic crowd assembles in support of an activist, as they did outside courthouses when some leaders were arrested after a thwarted rally in 1991, the crowds have a fair chance of escaping before police move in. But if the event lasts a while, as the mothers' protests did, supporters risk becoming victims of police violence, as many did in that case.

Often the individual activists themselves are trying to avoid arrest; and when arrested, trying to avoid conviction – or at least turn their courtroom appearances into spontaneous forums for public dissent. Such was the case of four activists convicted in court in 1991 for sedition. The case illustrates how members of the public, when given the opportunity, were ready to express their support of activists in opposition to the regime. Three examples follow.

1. *Courtroom Drama*. A year after the Saba Saba rally of 1990 was thwarted by police, some members of the public spontaneously demonstrated their support for several individual activists as they were sentenced in open court for sedition. It was becoming clearer that the regime was unable to control outbursts of public expression – not in a public park, not even in its own courts. The momentum of public expression of support for activism was growing.

The regime was seeking to win the chess game of tactics with human rights and democratization activists and especially to limit expressions of public support for them. Given the four choices mentioned earlier (full or partial repression or concessions), the regime continued to choose partial repression and partial concessions. But the strategy seemed to have little effect on stopping spontaneous, unplanned public demonstrations.

The lengthy trial of the four activists ended with guilty verdicts in July 1991, an intense political year in Kenya when both domestic and international pressure on the Moi regime was growing to allow multiparty elections.[52] In the trial there were nearly two dozen defense attorneys, another tactic activists used to help draw attention to human rights cases. Amnesty International, PEN, and Human Rights Watch, among others, issued statements critical of Kenya's human rights during this time. The trial stirred public opposition to the regime. Public norms were already shifting, partly as a result of individual activists like George Anyona, one of the defendants and other activists who had spoken out against the government when most still were afraid to do so.

The regime's rigid response to demands for reform, and its show of force at venues such as the Saba Saba rallies in 1990 and 1997, instead of deterring the public, was having a reverse effect; they were igniting public support for the activists and their cause. As the guilty verdict was read in the Anyona trial, for example, instead of gloom, an air of jubilation filled the courtroom. *Weekly Review*, in a nine-page cover story with numerous photos, described it as "the most sensational act of political defiance ever seen in a Kenyan court: [53]

> Almost as one, the hundreds of spectators in the overflowing courtroom rose up to give the four men in the dock a thunderous cheer, flashing the two-finger salute of multiparty advocacy. The four accused stood with upraised arms to acknowledge the cheers, and were still returning the two-finger salute as they were herded out of the court by nervous prison warders.

In a statement aimed at stirring public support for their cause, Anyona described the verdict as influenced by the Executive Branch and as "the darkest and saddest day in a judicial and political history." He continued, "[we] the accused are imbued with the knowledge that a new dawn is breaking on the eastern horizon of our political panorama. Liberty will come and with it the advent of pluralism." Co-defendant Augustus Njeru Kathangu, reading part of Anyona's statement, quoted the closing words in the trial of Nelson Mandela that he believed in the principles of democracy, equality, freedom and justice, 'ideals for which we are prepared to die." Clearly the intended audience was not just those in the courtroom but all Kenyans seeking reform.[54]

---

52 The activists were George Anyona, former Member of Parliament, charged with sedition, along with Njeru Kathangu, Edward Oyugi and Ngoto Kariuki. They were released on bail in February 1992 in the aftermath of the regime's acceptance in December 1991 of multiparty politics.

53 *Weekly Review* July 12, 1991.

54 *Weekly Review* July 12, 1991.

2. *Mothers' Protest.* A second example of spontaneous support for individual activists that stirred much of the Kenyan public and brought harsh international condemnation for its brutal disruption, was the case of the elderly mothers of Kenyan political prisoners. When they started their protest in March 1992 they were not supported by any organization other than their own informal network among half a dozen or so mothers. Although they made no concerted effort to attract crowds, they soon had the nation's attention. People began showing up spontaneously at their open-air camp in Uhuru (Freedom) Park.

The protest for release of their sons was in the tradition of the Mothers of the Plaza de Mayo in Argentina asking where their disappeared loved ones had gone, and other mother's protests in Latin America. From modest backgrounds, lacking much education, and without the benefit of any formal organization or political party, the Kenyan mothers posed a challenge that in some ways was more threatening to the regime than the daring deeds of elite activists.

Their protest is also an example of what an earlier scholar termed symbolic politics.[55] Mothers symbolized the traditional virtues and values of society. When pitted against an authoritarian regime they were placing themselves in what detractors of the regime could see as a kind of good vs. evil battle. It became "the most celebrated strategy for influencing democratic change" in Kenya in the decade, inspiring many Kenyans and helping increase pressure for democratization.[56]

Their lack of fear and clarity of purpose gave the mothers power. "I decided to go there because I felt my son would be hanged. My [son] had been grabbed by Moi, and I was very annoyed," said one of the protesting mothers.[57] Their lack of organization helped the mothers: they offered a less formal target for regime efforts to foil their intentions. The mothers offered the public an unusual opportunity to show their support. Freedom Corner,[58] where the mothers gathered in the Park, became a rallying point for individuals who felt aggrieved by the regime. People began stopping by there to air their own stories of oppression.

"People started their story and it was like there was an opening here, a free place where people were talking about things they had never talked about... They were shouting! 'I'm a victim! I have been tortured!' And I thought to myself, what a

---

55 Edelman, Murray. 1964. *The Symbolic Uses of Politics.* Urbana, Ill.: University of Illinois Press.

56 Nzomo, Maria. 1998. "Kenya: The Women's Movement and Democratic Change." In *The African State at a Critical Juncture: Between Disintegration and Reconfiguration,* eds. Leonardo A. Villalón and Phillip A. Huxtable. Boulder, CO.: Lynne Rienner, 179.

57 Milcah Kinuthia, mother of Rumba Kinuthia, in an interview with the author, Nairobi, Kenya, October 2002.

58 It was named by Wangari Maathai after the ruling party dropped its plans to build a skyscraper party headquarters in the park, a decision made after opposition by Maathai and publicity which led to donor pressure on the regime to drop the project.

freedom place…where people are saying things that had never been said for years in this country."[59]

After a few well-publicized days of protest by the mothers in the park, riot police chased them away. But the mothers simply continued their demonstration for a year in the basement of the nearby All Saints Cathedral. In the end, they took credit for the release of all but one of some fifty political prisoners locked up when they began the strike.[60] But more than winning release of their sons, the mothers had stirred the imaginations of many Kenyans.

3. *Riots*. Activists seeking greater human rights and democracy led a non-violent resistance movement. But there was plenty of violence on the part of the regime. At times some Kenyans reacted to this with violence of their own. Riots became a variation of informal protests linked to the resistance movement, spontaneous displays of anger with regime behavior. There were riots after the funeral in Nairobi in February 1990 of popular Cabinet Minister Robert Ouko, whose body was found near his rural home shot and burned. There were riots after police violently disrupted a mass demonstration calling for multiparty government in 1991. After the mother's strike was temporarily broken up with force by the police, there were more riots in parts of the country.[61]

It is always difficult to trace back from a riot which side started things. With tensions high at political protests, and with police under orders to prevent them, often – but not always – with force. In reaction most demonstrators fled the batons, teargas and sometimes police shooting. Some Kenyans on the scene or in other parts of the country reacted with their own violence as a way to express their anger. Some other Kenyans at protests were opportunistic thieves or unemployed youth willing to engage the police in pitched battles or to commit offenses they hoped would go unnoticed in the chaos.

Riots enforced a perception that public order was at risk of breaking down. Unrest was growing among the poor and the middle class amidst demands for multiparty politics which many hoped would bring better economic conditions as well as more political freedom.

---

59 Wangari Maathai, who participated in the mothers' protest, in an interview with the author in Nairobi, Kenya, September 2002.

60 Release Political Prisoners (RPP), a nongovernment organization, later reported that the number of Kenyans which they claimed had been arrested for political reasons began an upward climb soon after the release of the prisoners.

61 Most of the riots were in areas populated by Kikuyu, according to the *Weekly Review* (July 13, 1990). Most of the mothers involved in the protest were Kikuyu.

Individual Activism/Mobilized Participation

This more aggressive category of mass public participation brings with it added risks. Events are announced in advance to draw a crowd. That gives police plenty of time to organize, too, which they are likely to do since the event will be considered illegal. Here the regime's threats are intended at keeping the size of the turnout low to try to discredit the activists and their cause. Thus participation is considered very dangerous, a fact that is likely to keep many from taking part. But with no legal forums open to them, activists take the chance that enough people will brave the risks and show up.

The July 7 (Saba Saba) 1990 national political rally in favor of multiparty elections discussed in an earlier chapter was the first example in the study period of a planned mass demonstration against the regime. Individual activists until then had challenged the regime on their own, primarily in court or in publications. Hundreds of Kenyans showed up even after organizers themselves called it off at the last minute for lack of a government permit for the event.[62] Police turned out in force to break up the rally and the riots that broke out in Nairobi and parts of central Kenya after the protest was blocked.

The term Saba Saba had an immense effect on the political awareness of the nation. "From that time you could see people openly speaking not in hushed tones the way they used to, but saying anything they want and they didn't care who was listening."[63] Its very name became a symbolic term for defiance, "preserving in public consciousness a particular significance for a public rally the government had forbidden." The Moi regime quickly grasped the significance of the spreading resistance and the importance of the term Saba Saba, officially banning its use.[64]

Organizational Activism/Mobilized Participation

Organizational activism tends to draw larger crowds. Because it is an organization sponsoring the event there is likely to be a group of planners who can attend to more details than one or two individual activists could be expected to do. Until concessions have been won allowing such events, they are normally considered illegal by the authoritarian regime. They may be more dangerous for the public to attend than ones individual activists try to organize because police will be alerted more in advance. The police may choose to arrest the whole leadership of the organization, as they attempted in 1991. Demonstrations sponsored by organizational activists pose a

---

62 It is difficult to imagine that either individual activist actually assumed a permit would be forthcoming. The regime made it clear from the moment the event was announced that it was illegal and would be blocked. A more reasonable assumption is that both men wanted to expose neither themselves nor their followers to what was certain to be a brutal attack by police if the rally went ahead.

63 Munene interview.

64 Haugerud, 23.

greater threat than ones attempted by individual activists because they involve a wider network of activists and their supporters.

While highly risky, the organizational activism behind such an event has a better chance of drawing a sizeable crowd. Members of the organization are likely to have followings of their own that they can call on to participate. After legalization of competitive parties in Kenya starting in 1992, the new parties were the main organizer of rallies aimed at drawing supportive crowds. Despite the supposed legality of such rallies, the regime from 1992-1997 often refused permission for the parties to hold them. Even after this was officially changed in 1997, authorities still dispersed some rallies. Legal or not, the rallies consistently drew large crowds, especially in election years, as the following two examples illustrate.

> *Pro-Multiparty Demonstration.* The public protest rally in favor of multiparty politics scheduled at the Kamakunji grounds in Nairobi in November 1991 offered the public the first opportunity to support a unified opposition effort aimed at replacing the Moi regime. As noted, representatives of the main ethnic groups had united to start the Forum for the Restoration of Democracy (FORD), which soon emerged as the main opposition party. As in 1990, hundreds, perhaps thousands of Kenyans showed up for the event, many of them actually assembling on the rally grounds despite a heavy police presence. Riot police moved in with tear gas and batons, but huge crowds assembled in the immediate area, dispersing when chased, reassembling informally when the attacks abated.[65]

When the arrested organizers were sent up country for trials in their home districts, the huge crowds that gathered spontaneously at the courthouses were further signs that public consciousness and norms were shifting. By sending the leaders to their home towns, the regime unintentionally helped nationalize the resistance against it, providing not one but a series of rally points around the country for the opposition.

> "Word had gotten out that everyone had been flown to their home areas. So the turnout all over in different parts of the country was huge. As we were being escorted by the police there were thousands of people turning out. They were waving and shouting words of encouragement. "We shall overcome," things like that. So I think the state realized that it was a miscalculation. It was transporting or exporting a broad and bold political dissent from the capitol to the provinces."[66]

> *Mass Demonstration; Mass Violence.* In 1997, five years after the regime agreed to competitive politics again, no permission was given for a series of nonviolent marches in favor of a new constitution. The police struck marchers with a vengeance, killing more than a dozen and wounding many others. But the marches continued.

---

65 The author witnessed some of these events first-hand from near the intended rally site.

66 James Orengo in an interview with the author in Nairobi, Kenya, July 2002.

The push for a new constitution in 1997, an election year, was described in the previous chapter. As important as the citizens' Constitutional Convention was, however, it is an argument of this study that without the mass participation at public demonstrations supporting the demands, the Convention might have gone down as simply a good example of civil society organization.

Middle Class Participates. More than in the demonstrations of 1990 and 1991, members of the middle class, in particular professionals were drawn into participation in the 1997 protests, perhaps moved as much by concerns such as water and electric shortages and other economic hardships as by the ideal of democratization. Their participation was an important breakthrough in the resistance movement in Kenya, according to activist Willy Mutunga.

> In 1997 we were almost getting there because the accountants would come to the mass action. They park their little cars very far; they take off their ties and they march with everybody. So we were moving to a stage where the professionals, the middle class in Kenya were convinced that there was need to agitate for changes because they were suffering [from] power rationing, [shortages] of water, a decayed infrastructure...[67]

But if material concerns could draw some middle class supporters to mass protests, the violence that ensued when police attacked could drive others away. Business leaders who had supported the demonstrations began backing away from them once the confrontations began. "They were issuing statements condemning this, saying this [violence] is pandemonium and it is discouraging investors...without saying that the government is banning people from exercising their freedom and rights."[68]

The 1997 marches marked a major point in the establishment of a culture of resistance in Kenya, helping win key constitutional reforms regarding human rights and encouraging a further push for a new constitution in the period leading up to the 2002 general election, which a united opposition won. If there was a litmus test for the proposition that an aroused public will continue to demonstrate openly against an authoritarian regime in the face of less than all-out, but still harsh repression, the 1997 marches for a new constitution was it for Kenyans. Despite being tear-gassed, clubbed with police batons (some protesters were chased into a local church and beaten there), and despite a number of demonstrators being shot dead by police, crowds continued to march periodically.[69] It was this determination to keep on

---

67 Willy Mutunga, Executive Director of the Kenya Human Rights Commission and an organizer of the constitutional Convention, in an interview with the author in Nairobi, Kenya, September 2002.

68 Cyprien Nyamwamu, a youth organizer, in an interview with the author in Nairobi, Kenya, November 2002.

69 Had the pro-constitutional marches been legal, permitted, and protected by the police, they probably would have drawn even larger crowds, though if they had become too routine, it is possible public interest could have gone the other way and dropped off. It is worth noting,

marching that helped achieve the reforms the regime agreed to late that year. The regime realized "it can not imprison everybody; it can not kill everybody."[70]

The willingness of a segment of the public to keep protesting despite regime violence helped convince the President to make key concessions, including allowing the 2002 election to go ahead on schedule. The crowds that opposition candidates drew in the months leading up to the election were massive. By then resistance had become the norm for many Kenyans.

Human Rights Watchdogs Become the Watched in a New Regime

The defeat of President Moi by his one-time Vice President Mwai Kibaki in December 2002 brought into government some key human rights and democracy activists who had been targeted by the previous regime. It also resulted in some dramatic reforms.

The High Court Chief Justice accused of "complicity in torture and cruel, inhuman and degrading treatment of suspected [dissidents]" in the late 1980's was forced out of office. A major reform program was launched in the judiciary, police and prison services; and numerous judges accused of corruption were forced to resign. Past government scandals were investigated, and the press and electronic media flourished, including FM radio, a trend that began in the late 1990s and accelerated after 2002.[71]

But the constitution remained unchanged. Repressive colonial-era powers inherited by Kenya's first President and much abused under President Moi, were still intact. President Kibaki showed no signs of wanting to reduce them. This presented a "continuing danger to sustainable human rights in Kenya." On July 3, 2004, police used water cannons and tear gas to break up peaceful protests in Nairobi in support of a new constitution. In Kisumu, police fired on crowds, killing one person and injuring several demonstrators on July 7, 2004, the traditional protest day in Kenya since the 1990s.[72]

A repressive law passed in the final year of the defeated regime to try to restrict anti-government commentaries in the press remained on the books. The new Minister of Information opened an investigation against an outspoken radio station. Torture was still practiced by police, not on political dissidents, but on ordinary criminals. Prison conditions remained appalling.

Freedom House, an independent monitoring agency in New York that rates countries had given Kenya a "partly free" rating on political rights and civil liberties

---

however, that in Eastern Europe as Communism was collapsing in most those states, illegal rallies got bigger and bigger, often becoming so massive it was far beyond the ability of the state to try to stop them.

70 Muite interview.
71 Human Rights Watch World Report 2005.
72 Human Rights Watch World Report 2005.

before 1986; then from 1987–1991 it ranked Kenya as "not free." Except for 1992, the year of the first multi-party election when the rating moved back up to "partly free," Kenya stayed "not free" through the 1990s. In 2003, Kenya was ranked as "partly free" and stayed there into 2006.

Maina Kiai, a founder of the private, Kenya Human Rights Commission, later worked for Amnesty International in London and then a U.S. human rights organization. But in 2003, he moved back to Kenya to head the government's human rights office. He, and others who had remained in the private NGO network of human rights groups, found themselves watching the conduct of government officials who, in numerous cases, had been leading the activists' charge for more human rights and democratic freedoms. In Kenya, people had won not only a new President but had laid the groundwork for continued "small victories…expanding the political space. Civil society will continue making its demands," said Kiai.[73]

Implications of Public Support for a Resistance Movement

An actor without an audience is not very convincing; neither are activists without a turnout to support them and the events they stage. Public participation is an essential element in the establishment of a culture of resistance. For Kenyans among the nearly two-thirds of voters opposed to President Moi and his regime, activism provided another venue, a forum for expression of their discontent. This participation, in turn, sent a signal to the rest of the public that resistance was growing, and to the President that the resistance was more than the work of a small group of bold individuals.

Public participation in Kenya occurred despite a general weakness of the organizations in civil society and political society. Public support for individual activists was not dependent on the strength of the organization and in some cases not dependent on an organization at all. Each major protest laid the ground for the next; the accumulation of resistance encouraged still more resistance and public support. As indicated in previous chapters, activism had its lulls and peaks, but when it occurred, it drew large crowds despite the regime's violent response.

Mass participation should not be analyzed as an indivisible unit. Close analysis reveals several distinct categories of public support for activists and the events they sponsored. Each category has its own dynamics, risks and purposes. The sophistication of the planning grows as resistance shifts from individual to organizational activism, but if the regime continues authoritarian rule, demonstrations and other protests remain dangerous.

---

73   Maina Kiai, in a telephone interview with the author, September 2003.

Unlike the massive protests of Eastern Europe in conjunction with the demise of Communism, the protesters in Kenya had little chance to overcome their fear of reprisals even when large crowds turned out. The regime continued sporadic violent repression of demonstrators throughout the study period with the general exception of the months leading up to the election in 2002. By then the threat of more mass protests if the President tried to delay or rig the election was sufficient to forestall such tactics. Public participation in protests had become so common by then that for many Kenyans it had become the norm, marking an important shift from earlier deference to open defiance.

Chapter 7

Conclusion

This study offers a much more optimistic assessment of the ability of people to shape their own destinies than much of the literature on social movements or democratic transitions. The optimism is not based on hope, though that is an important ingredient in political reform movements, but on the research findings in Kenya.

As we have seen, establishing a non-violent, overt *culture of resistance* under an authoritarian regime involves public challenges to the abuse of power by a visible segment of individuals, organizations and the general public. The process by which all three attempt to advance human rights and democracy is a political one that challenges the legitimacy of a regime.

In the first phase of resistance, individual activists successfully, though at considerable risk, challenged the regime in the courts, through the alternative media, in attempted public rallies and in public statements to improve human rights and allow pluralism. Once the regime met the later demand, allowing multiparty elections, political activists continued to pressure the regime to broaden democratic participation through constitutional changes. Though only partially successful, this phase of activism drew in thousands of people to organized rallies and other demonstrations, adding currency to claims of public discontent and adding pressure for democratic elections.

Kenya went from a country whose government tortured suspected dissenters to one in which the ruling party gave up power for the first time in some forty years after losing an election. This book has shown that a relatively small number of determined people using nonviolent methods can help bring about significant improvements in human rights and democracy in an authoritarian state under very adverse conditions, not through a change in external circumstances but mostly through their own efforts.

Human rights can also be used by an opposition as a tool to advance their own interests. The struggle for advancing human rights and democratic freedoms in Kenya involved risks for many of the early activists, risks some activists took for idealistic reasons. For others, however, and especially for some political opposition leaders, human rights were a way of eroding the legitimacy of the incumbent regime and advancing the opposition's chances of assuming power.

Once in power, do human rights activists continue to promote rights or simply use their new power for their own interests? That issue is beyond the scope of this study, but interviews in Kenya in December 2005 and January 2006, some three years after the Moi regime was ousted in an election indicated that a number of positive changes had been made. Several human rights activists had been placed in senior positions in government. Reforms had been taken in police training; and a number of corrupt judges had been weeded out. Freedom of expression was vibrant. The repression of the Moi years was largely a thing of the past.

But there were complaints about high-level government corruption in the new regime and slowness in addressing past government corruption cases. A new generation of younger human rights activists who were not a part of the new government complained that police abuses continued. They added that some former activists who had been appointed to office (several were later ousted in a Cabinet reshuffle), were either arrogant or inefficient in office and that the government had not lived up to expectations for further reforms. The usual jockeying for political power among leaders of the coalition that won power in 2002 had eclipsed much of the earlier focus on human rights. And lack of institutional changes, including failure to adopt a new constitution with reduced presidential powers, left the potential for serious human rights abuses.[1]

Advancing and safeguarding human rights and democratic freedoms is a never-ending process. Even if the advocates for reform win power, someone has to take their place as the new advocates for human rights: even former watchdogs need watching. The initial enthusiasm over victory by the opposition can weaken a resistance movement, as it has in Kenya, especially after some activists were named to government posts. It can take time before abuses in a new regime lead to a revival of a human rights movement outside of government. But the lessons of past resistance movements can serve as guideposts for new ones.[2]

---

1   Human Rights Watch noted in a report in 2004: "The current human rights situation in Kenya is one of few serious abuses. However, the potential is growing for serious problems in the future as much of the repressive state machinery from the Moi era remains intact."

2   This study ends in December 2002 when the Moi regime was defeated at an election and a new team, headed by President Mwai Kibaki took power. With numerous human rights activists elected to power or joining the new government, one question was how effective civil society would be as a watchdog for the new regime's performance on human rights and democracy?

Many of the key human rights and democratization advocacy organizations functioning by around 1992 were still operating as of 2006. Some activists said the organizations would continue to function effectively because Kenyans were much more aware of their rights than a decade or so earlier. Beyond basic political rights such as the right of expression and assembly and the right not to be tortured, were a host of other critical issues such as land and property rights and womens' legal rights.

But the role of the activists had grown more routine in the 1990s. And as social movement and interest group literature remind us, the danger of social movements becoming too formalized, too institutionalized, too much a pattern of everyday life, is that they lose their punch and effectiveness. They risk becoming bureaucracies themselves, more a part of the system than a force knocking at the door of power and demanding accountability. And when the 'enemy' is defeated, when an incumbent regime is ousted, for example, the risk is that some of the steam of a reform movement can dissipate, as it had in Kenya by 2006. Protests had become a common occurrence over many issues, in part a legacy of the earlier activists.

The Kenya research involved a combination of agency, institutional, structural and other analyses, including political process, rational choice, and altruism or community motivations. It has not been a singular focus, but the emphasis has been on an area seldom examined in such detail, human rights activism, and how this not only started a resistance movement but how that movement grew and led to a culture of resistance. No prediction was offered as to whether such activism leads to democracy or a new election, though it certainly helped do so in Kenya.

No sweeping claims were made about the generalization of the Kenya findings to other countries. But it is suggested that a similar study in other authoritarian settings may well detect a phenomenon highlighted in this work: individual activism. And it also may reveal how a culture of resistance is established in places where a regime does not stamp it out completely or does not crack down with brutal effectiveness, disregarding any international outcry, as in Zimbabwe, for example.

Study Questions Answered

As noted in the first chapter, the Kenya investigation began with several questions: why did a reluctant authoritarian regime make some key concessions in terms of greater practice of human rights and democracy; and how did individuals and organizations in civil society resist an authoritarian government and pressure it to make concessions? Under what conditions do elements of civil society win concessions in human rights and democratization; and what conditions prevent further gains? The question of conditions will be addressed more fully in the section below on literature, but it is worth noting here that conditions, both external (in terms of international support) and internal (in terms of repression) were very adverse when individual activism emerged in the late 1980s in Kenya.

The answers to these and other questions posed can be stated in terms of the model of resistance presented earlier and based on the research findings.

Individual Activism. In terms of the model, the resistance begins with individual activism in response to regime abuses. Individual activists, or *early resisters*, often acting without an overall strategy, step forward to challenge the regime in a variety of ways, such as lawsuits aimed at halting specific abuses, and critical commentary in legal publications. These early resisters, if allowed to survive, reveal a vulnerability of the authoritarian regime, especially if they are able to win some concessions. In this first phase, individual activists and relatively safe organizations such as churches, press for reforms.

In Kenya, primarily in the capitol city, Nairobi, a group of human rights advocates, many of them attorneys, began representing dissidents and challenging the regime on their treatment and on other points of law. There was no overall strategy. In fact the resistance had an air of chaos at times, with attorneys and others striving not only to file numerous law suits aimed at bringing public attention to alleged abuses, but also simply trying to avoid arrest themselves. At times this meant temporarily hiding when it was learned that the regime security forces had been ordered to arrest them.

This first stage is a critical one. Activists in the first phase proceed at great risk and against great odds, even in a setting such as Kenya, where the regime at least pretended to subscribe to the rule of law and made efforts to keep international support. An intransigent regime willing to pay a potential price of international isolation and condemnation may either crush the resistance or use enough force to intimidate activists.

In Kenya, if the regime had chosen to clamp down with excessive force, perhaps not only jailing all known activist attorneys and others but also executing some, the resistance might well have been halted, or driven underground. It is an argument of this book that a nonviolent culture of resistance can persist and grow only if a regime avoids massive repression. In cases such as Ethiopia, where no dissent was tolerated for years under Mengistu Haile Mariam, a culture of resistance can only mature underground, as it did there in the form of an armed rebellion that later swept Mengistu from power.

The Kenyan regime did arrest numerous activists, though it did not execute them; and as the resistance grew, fewer and fewer spent any time in prison. Activists used to their advantage the regime's pretense at upholding the rule of law, challenging the regime in court and in public statements on points of law related to human rights and democracy. The model of resistance suggests that such pressure can maneuver a reluctant regime into a corner where they make a few initial concessions, perhaps to avoid greater ones, as happened in Kenya. None of the concessions in Kenya, however, were fully implemented.

What motivated domestic activists to take high risks? As the research showed, a rational choice explanation failed to explain why early resisters such as attorneys would risk their own safety for the sake of a little extra money from dissident clients, or small publishers in the alternative media would risk arrest and their family wealth for the sake of selling extra copies of their publication. Later the range of possible motivations was broader, including employment, political power, or ideological promotion, as activism opened more opportunities through opposition parties and a proliferation of nongovernmental organizations promoting human rights and democracy.

Organizational Activism. In a second phase of the model, organizational activists emerge using the opening or opportunities created by the individual activists in terms of concessions, bolstered by the knowledge that the regime can be challenged. Many individual activists continue their resistance with the support of advocacy organizations, which gives them greater resources with which to work.

In Kenya, this second phase of activism saw the emergence of opposition political parties even before an official acceptance of them by the ruling party, an acceptance by the President that came only after mass public demonstrations, some riots, and additional pressure from international donors. Organizational activists, backed to some degree by their organizations or parties (often limited by lack of resources), were able to employ a broader range of resistance tactics, including mobilized public rallies. The role of individual activism as a catalyst was no longer needed and faded almost entirely in this phase; but most individual activists became organizational activists.

Activists in Kenya were disheartened when a fragmented political opposition lost the multiparty elections in 1992 and 1997 to President Moi, who used unfair practices in an electoral system designed to favor his party. Organizational activism faded sharply after the 1992 election, but picked up again as the 1997 and 2002 elections approached, a pattern which revealed fresh nuances to the theory of a cycle of resistance (see below).

Mass Participation. The author asked what role the mass public has in the establishment of a culture of resistance. Without this third element, mass participation, a culture of resistance in Kenya might not have been established. The participation of a segment of the general public in mass opposition rallies and other demonstrations gives credence to claims of activists that they represented more than just a small band of brave dissidents.

Activists provided the general public in Kenya with an opportunity to express predisposed frustration and anger with the regime. These members of the public shifted from a norm of deference to defiance of the regime's abuse of power. Where they were once fearful and silent, they were now open in their resistance, though still fearful since the regime could strike back at anyone, anytime, as it did.

International Pressure. The investigation also asked what role donors and international agencies play in the advancement of human rights and democracy in an authoritarian state. Activists' ties to international agencies provided some measure of protection through publicity, especially when they were arrested or threatened by the regime. Kenyan advocacy nongovernmental organizations (NGOs) also received much of their funding from international sources, including bi-lateral donors. This enabled organizational activists to accomplish more in terms of information, challenges, and events that put additional pressure on the regime. Twice, in a coordinated manner, international donors froze new funds to the regime, thus supporting domestic demands for reforms.

But as the research has shown, the timing of international donor actions such as freezing funds, put the donors in a supportive, not an initiating role, in terms of pressure for reforms. And on closer inspection, it was seen that donors often were inconsistent in terms of reducing, holding firm, or increasing funding, sending mixed signals to the regime as to just how much and what type of reforms it was supposed to make.

Also, often overlooked in analyses of donors' role in helping bring about reforms in Kenya are the regime's own actions which indicated that it was responding more to domestic than international pressure. For example, it was not simply a funding freeze but mass demonstrations that preceded the decisions by the regime to make significant political reforms in 1991 and 1997. Such demonstrations and other signs of public unrest posed a greater threat to the regime's survival than a temporary cutoff of aid. Further evidence of this is the delays by the regime after each funding freeze to negotiate a resumption of aid. Had it been responding primarily to international pressure to make reforms, the regime logically would have rushed to restore funding.

Political Synergy Achieved

A culture of resistance as a whole has a greater effect than the sum of the three main elements of which it is comprised (individual activism, organizational activism, and mass participation). Individual activists can only do so much in their role as ice-breakers in the reform process. Organizational activists build on their advances but need the presence of members of the public at their events to make a serious bid for reforms. The public in turn needs the forums of the activists to express their discontent. Together the resistance sends signals to the regime, the public and international officials and agencies that the demands for change have substantial and visible public support.

Any one element of the resistance alone has much less impact and poses less of a threat to the regime than the whole and can be dealt with more easily. Once a culture of resistance is established, it is harder to crush and is likely to spawn additional resistance in various parts of the country, as happened in Kenya. The regime is forced into deciding whether to respond to the resistance with partial or full reforms, or partial or full repression, each decision carrying its own set of repercussions domestically and internationally for the regime as well as the people.

The process of resistance as revealed through extensive interviews in Kenya of activists and others turned out to be a rather messy one. In the early stages of resistance, activists demonstrated less of an overall strategy and more day-to-day survival tactics and uncoordinated challenges to the regime.

A process of political learning took place in which both the regime and activists sought advantages over the other and tried to block moves by the other side. The Kenyan regime and activists played a kind of tactical chess game over human rights and democratic reforms. The stakes were higher during the organizational activism phase when not just a few laws, but the presidency itself was at stake. At such a point a regime is likely to step up pressure or diversionary tactics to try to derail the opposition. In Kenya, the regime initiated or allowed a series of mass raids on ethnic groups not seen as supporting the President.

Contribution to Social Movement Literature

This work builds on the rich pioneering efforts of such social movement scholars as Charles Tilly, Doug McAdam, Sidney Tarrow and others who have helped us understand so much about the nature of how people try to change the political conditions they live under. But it also differs with key aspects of the predominant social movement literature, including theirs, in several ways.

1. *Greater Emphasis on People's Power to Resist Authoritarian rule: Agency vs. Structure.* The Kenya findings come amidst a growing debate among social movement scholars over whether initiative (agency) or societal conditions (structure) is more influential in determining how a movement begins. The findings suggest that a key element in establishing a culture of resistance is human initiative, choices made by people, and that this can be the primary (though certainly not the only) force behind a social movement.

It is not necessary for activists to wait until societal or international conditions or circumstances are more conducive to action. Activists, this study has shown, can create their own opportunities. In other words, the often-cited concept of a "political opportunity" is not necessarily exogenous but endogenous, not dependent on external conditions beyond the control of the challengers but on internal conditions and opportunities primarily of their own making.[3]

This is in sharp contrast to Tilly, McAdam and Tarrow who presented a heavily structural basis of opportunity, especially in their earlier works. Tilly, for example[4], designed a model that linked social movements to an "opportunity-threat to challengers and facilitation-repression by authorities", as Tarrow[5] summarizes it. In other words Tilly linked the success of contentious politics to the state and argued that a movement's success would vary with the nature of the particular state.[6] This moved beyond the earlier grievance theories of why people might be inclined to join a movement,[7] and beyond the analysis of movements based on their resources (resource mobilization theory). Tarrow notes [8] that given Tilly's background in European social thought, "Tilly's model was resolutely structural (i.e., it focuses on conditions that cannot be molded to actors' purposes)."

McAdam synthesized various political approaches to social movements in his work on the American civil rights movement into what became known as a "political

---

3   Goodwin and Jasper (2004, 4) note that the term "political opportunity structure" has gradually given way to "apparently more fluid concepts" such as "process" and "opportunities."

4   Tilly, Charles. 1978. *From Mobilization to Revolution*. Reading, MA: Addison-Wesley, chapters 3; 4; 6.

5   Tarrow, Sidney. 1998. *Power in Movement: Social Movements and Contentious Politics*. 2nd ed. Cambridge, U. K.: Cambridge University.

6   On two points the Kenya study agrees with Tilly's linkage of social movement success to the state: without state repression, there would have been no need for the kind of activism that developed. And if a state is repressive enough to wipe out resistance, it can probably do so, though at the risk of international isolation and transforming overt, nonviolent resistance into covert, violent resistance, a price many state leaders may not want to pay.

7   Gurr, Ted Robert. 1970. *Why Men Rebel*. Princeton: Princeton University Press.

8   Tarrow, 18.

process model" of social movement mobilization.[9] But as seen below, his, too, was strongly biased toward a structural explanation of political change. The political process model, which Goodwin and Jasper criticize, claims that "social movements result when *expanding political opportunities* [emphasis in original] are seized by people who are formally or informally organized, aggrieved, and optimistic that they can successfully redress their concerns."[10] This puts activists in the position of waiting for a shift in political opportunities. In Kenya, the resistance that emerged openly in the late 1980s occurred when there was no dramatic shift of external opportunities.

Tarrow makes what he describes as "the most forceful argument" of his study: "that people engage in contentious politics *when patterns of political opportunities and constraints change* [emphasis added] and then, by strategically employing a repertoire of collective action, create new opportunities, which are used by others in widening cycles of contention." This can lead to "sustained interactions with opponents – specifically, in social movements." Tarrow identified political opportunity as "emphasizing resources *external* [emphasis in original] to the group."[11]

The Kenya study takes quite a different view, identifying opportunities for a resistance movement as primarily *internal*, and within control of the activists. For Tarrow, activists "respond to opportunities…" in Kenya activists largely created their own opportunities, as explained above.

In his 1982 work, McAdam identified structural conditions that led to opportunities for a social movement to advance as including "wars, industrialization, international political alignments, prolonged [economic woes], and widespread demographic changes." But with one exception, such structural conditions showed no major shifts during the period in which a culture of resistance was established in Kenya. The exception was the end of the Cold War, but as this book has shown, the resistance in Kenya which began several years earlier, was only partially aided by a related shift in donor attitudes, and was largely supplanted in importance toward the end of the 1990s by the massive public participation in opposition rallies and other demonstrations as a force for change. In Kenya the activists did not wait for structural conditions to shift in their favor; they took the initiative.

In the past few years, some of the architects of the structural opportunity thesis, including Tilly, Tarrow, and McAdam, have attempted to broaden their arguments. Goodwin and Jasper, however, argue that in one attempt to incorporate more of a cultural explanation about social movements,[12] there is still a strong structural bias. McAdam laments about the strict structural bias with which his concept has been

---

9 McAdam, Doug. 1982. "The Political Process Model." In *Political Process and the Development of Black Insurgency*. Doug McAdam. Chicago: University of Chicago.

10 Goodwin, Jeff, and James M. Jasper, eds. 2004. *Rethinking Social Movements: Structure, Meaning, and Emotion*. Oxford, U. K.: Rowman & Littlefield, 17.

11 Tarrow, 20.

12 McAdam, Doug, John D. McCarthy, and Mayer N. Zald. eds. 1996. *Comparative Perspectives on Social Movements: Political Opportunities, Mobilizing Structures, and Cultural Framings*. Cambridge: Cambridge University Press.

developed by others. But he also adds "…most shifts in POS [political opportunity structure] are themselves responses to broader change processes." Then in offering examples of the kinds of events and processes he meant, he returned to the same list of structural factors cited in his 1982 work.[13]

But Tarrow counters that in their more recent work, they have tried to break away from what he calls the "static" nature of the so-called political process model and look more at the dynamics of political change.[14]

2. *The Importance of Individual Activism.* The Kenya study applies a dynamic version of the political process model and social movement theory to a developing country, something Tarrow noted has seldom been done outside of the "liberal democracies of the West.[15] In so doing, it reveals a process that begins with individual activism, not organizations, something that is practically overlooked in the literature. Although Tarrow makes a few references to "early resisters," he does not develop the concept.

This is a critical difference with the mainstream social movement literature which does not focus heavily on how movement dynamics begin. This book suggests that without such a focus, an important initial phase of movement dynamics is missing. Coupled with the study's findings that the dynamics of the movement were primarily self-generated, not dependent on external conditions, the Kenya study offers fresh insights into how social movements work.

A Missing Focus in the Literature. What the Kenya study shows that most of the mainstream social movement literature does not address is how a movement actually starts, the first steps taken, in this case not by organizations, but by individual activists. It was only later that activists began networking and starting new organizations of resistance such as human rights groups. Most studies of social movements assume there is already a movement for activists to join.

One could ask whether a social movement that challenges a regime is the same as one that addresses specific policy concerns. In the case of Kenya, the answer can be found in the political process that occurred. Most individual activists did not set out originally to challenge the regime but specific policies centered on the treatment of political prisoners and freedom of speech. Later, however, activists shifted their

---

13 McAdam, Doug. 2004. "Revisiting the U.S. Civil Rights Movement: Toward a More Synthetic Understanding of the Origins of Contention. In *Rethinking Social Movements: Structure, Meaning, and Emotion.* Goodwin, Jeff, and James M., Jasper. Oxford, U. K.: Rowman & Littlefield, 213.

14 Repeating part of Tarrow's November 2005 e-mail to the author noted in chapter 1, Tarrow said…[T]he goal of the revised political process theory in *Dynamics of Contention* [2001] and related work by McAdam, Tilly and myself, is a serious attempt to transcend the sterile division between agency and structure by a REAL [emphasis in the e-mail] focus on process, and particularly on the social mechanisms that bring about change…

15 Tarrow, 19.

goals to regime change, not through violence but through elections, a goal usually associated with political parties. In this book, the term *resistance movement* is used to describe the dynamics of a resistance that involved both individual and organizational activists, as well as opposition political parties and mass public support.

Cycles Theory Revisited. This book takes note of Tarrow's ground-breaking concept of "cycles of contention," involving a rise and fall of social movements but finds that a more accurate term to describe the resistance in Kenya is "waves" of contention. Tarrow uses this term, too, at several points but his analysis emphasizes a one-time rise and fall of social movements and not the mini-cycles the Kenya study found to have occurred over the period examined. In Kenya there was an ebb and flow of activism with peaks during election years; but the resistance never died out completely, and the push for a new constitution kept activism at a higher level than it might have been without such a drive.

Contribution to Democratic Transition Literature

The book also contributes to the literature on democratic transitions with its focus on activism as a key variable. While the Kenya study does not veer entirely away from the structure-related literature, it clearly joins those arguing for a close look at agency or human initiatives as a key element in political reforms and democratization. But it also differs from some of the agency-focused transition literature, which can be sub-divided into two categories: agency/economy and agency/institutions. The former correlates economic conditions and prospects for transition, with some scholars arguing that an improvement of economic conditions favors transitions while others hold that a decline in economic conditions encourages a change. The Kenya research found that economic conditions were negative for most citizens during the period covered (1987–2002), but without the kind of sudden change that key political process/ social movement scholars such as McAdam have long argued is necessary for launching of a social movement.

The Kenya research instead found an explanation for resistance not in economic conditions but in the determination of a few (at first) activists, to win improved freedoms despite enormous risks. The agency-institutions explanations come closer to describing what happened in Kenya than an agency-economy approach, yet even here there are important differences. For example, one of the most often-cited agency/institution studies on transitions points to transitions based on pact making and negotiations between elite reformists and members of a changing regime.[16] There were no such negotiations in Kenya other than indirect bargaining through pressure tactics and countermoves by the regime.

---

16 O'Donnell, Guillermo, and Philippe C. Schmitter. 1986. *Transitions from Authoritarian Rule: Tentative Conclusions about Uncertain Democracies*. Baltimore: Johns Hopkins University Press.

The Kenya findings build on the literature that point to civil society as an active agent of change. As Diamond notes, civil society has often played "a crucial role if not the leading role, in producing a transition to democracy."[17] But in Africa, particularly, there have been few comprehensive studies that have looked closely at just how civil society actually takes such a leading role in transitions. One of the broadest studies of transitions (Bratton, van de Walle 1997) offered an archival assessment that pointed to an active role by civil society. But as an archival work, it did not attempt to present a close-up of any particular transition that could shed light on just how elements of civil society initiate and support a transition process.[18] Bratton and van de Walle's ground-breaking book was a top-down look; the Kenya case study is done from the ground up, offering detail that helps us understand the dynamics of resistance and transition movements.

Another important contribution of the Kenya investigation to this literature was to identify the role of individual activism in preparing the ground for a democratic transition. This is a stage that, where it occurs, is almost entirely overlooked in the transition literature as it is in most of the social movement literature. A few studies offer political psychological profiles of activists. This book does not attempt to provide such profiles in any depth; that is beyond the scope of the study.

International Support for Domestic Resistance. Some recent literature has pointed to the importance of international (also called transnational) networks in supporting domestic resistance to authoritarian rule. This literature suggests there is a strong influence of so-called international norms of human rights that can lead to their eventual adoption with the help of domestic and international pressure.[19] Such literature recognizes the importance of domestic resistance but argues that the primary factors influencing political change are international. The Kenya investigation, however, while recognizing international pressures as important has shown that such pressure was a secondary factor after domestic resistance.

Beyond Kenya

The findings and methodology of this research have wide potential applicability in similar authoritarian countries because they describe a process of resistance rather than only the details of a single country. The findings will not all apply to similar settings: historical, political and cultural circumstances vary from place to place.

---

17 Diamond, Larry. 1999. *Developing Democracy: Toward Consolidation.* Baltimore. Johns Hopkins University Press, 235.

18 Bratton, Michael, and Nicolas van de Walle. 1997. *Democratic Experiments in Africa: Regime Transitions in Comparative Perspective.* Cambridge: Cambridge University Press.

19 Risse, Thomas, Stephen C. Ropp, and Kathryn Sikkink, eds. 1999. *The Power of Human Rights: International Norms and Domestic Change.* Cambridge: Cambridge University Press.

But the methodology for locating and interviewing activists (see Appendix) and the general premises of the Kenya study can help detect a process by which a culture of resistance is established in regimes that at least pretend to subscribe to the rule of law and democratic principles and are not prepared to crush domestic resistance. This work suggests that in both historical studies and contemporary investigations, researchers using a similar methodology and analysis in broadly similar settings are likely to discover patterns similar to those in Kenya. But the study does not predict similar outcomes, which depend on a great a variety of factors.

Findings in similar authoritarian settings that would differ from the findings in Kenya might include ones that found a domestic resistance with no evidence of individual activism;[20] a domestic resistance that did not show a pattern of progression from early resisters to broader, organized resistance involving mass participation; or cases in which a regime was forced to make reforms without any significant domestic resistance.

Future research possibilities include studies of rural activism (the Kenya study was mostly urban-focused and did not attempt to document or analyze rural activism); the role of women in activist resistance; and further testing of the proposition that agency can be more influential than structure in establishing a culture of resistance.

In Latin America in recent years there have been numerous resistance movements. In several Latin American countries, popular uprisings resulted in the forced departure of several heads of state. In Sub-Saharan Africa, the wave of democratization that swept across much of the continent in the early to mid-1990s did not push every country into the democratic column. By 1995 when the surge had peaked, three out of four African states had competitive political systems,[21] but in many of them democracy was still a fairly shallow institution. In others there have been setbacks (e.g., Zimbabwe) or non-transitions (e.g., Togo).

There are ample grounds – and need – for future research of domestic resistance movements. The state of human rights in the world today is "lamentable;" there are more countries where fundamental human rights are regularly violated than where they are effectively protected.[22] Despite near-global endorsement of the United Nations Universal Declaration of Human Rights, the number of states committing one of the most serious abuses, torture, is actually rising.[23] According to the 2006

---

20 In countries where regime repression comes after establishment of advocacy organizations and does not force these to close, resistance is likely to be led by organizational activists, not individual activists, unless such organizations are crushed by the regime.

21 Wiseman, John A. 1996. *The New Struggle for Democracy in Africa.* Aldershot, Eng.: Avebury, 2.

22 Robertson, A. H., and J. G. Merrills. 1996. *Human Rights in the World: An introduction to the Study of the International Protection of Human Rights*, 4th ed. Manchester, U. K: Manchester University Press.

23 William F. Schulz, Executive Director of Amnesty International USA, cited in an article by Matt Kantz in the *National Catholic Reporter*, July 2, 1999. Schulz reported that in Amnesty's survey of 142 nations, the percentage of countries where torture and other abuses occurred increased from 55 percent to 66 percent between 1988 and 1998. He also reported

report of Freedom House, 49 nations, including China and Russia, were "not free," representing 36 percent of the world's population; another 58 nations were only "partly free," representing another 19 percent of the world's population. In other words, 54 percent of the world's population still has significant restrictions on their freedom.[24] Putting this another way, more than half the countries in the world are either "not free" or only 'partly free." The struggle for human rights and democratic freedoms is far from over.

Summary of Findings and Implications for Future Research

1. Human rights and democracy activists helped establish a generally non-violent culture of resistance in an authoritarian state. This political process began primarily with individual activism, which opened opportunities for organizational activists by helping obtain some initial concessions. The organizational activists in turn gained the support of a visible segment of the mass public and benefited from some international help.

Implications: Using the Kenya model of resistance and applying it to other authoritarian settings could help determine the existence and scope of a culture of resistance and how it was formed. Most analyses of democratization and political reform overlook the contribution from activists, especially individual activists as opposed to organizational activists; and most analyses focus on institutional change.

The Kenya model captures the energy, impact, and political importance of human rights and democracy activism in helping transform a society from one of passive and reluctant acceptance of authoritarianism to active and effective resistance to it, a cultural transformation that is most traceable through field research. The model and the methodology introduced in this book have practical application to both past and present settings.

2. The resistance was not crushed; the regime claimed to abide by the rule of law. Activists used the law to press their demands. Thus the resistance was not driven underground but managed to survive and grow openly as activists used a variety of tactics.

---

that the countries responsible for deaths from torture and for "disappearances" of individuals increased over the same decade.

24 Freedom House. 2005. *Freedom in the World 2005: The Annual Survey of Political Rights and Civil Liberties*. New York: Freedom House. By comparison, the number of "free" countries had increased from 76 (40%) to 89 (46%) from 1994 to 2004. Freedom House measures four main categories of civil liberties: freedom of expression and belief; associational and organizational rights; rule of law; personal autonomy and individual rights.

Implications: It is important to note in looking for comparative or contrasting cases regarding the establishment of a culture of resistance, that a ruthless regime can block creation of such a culture. A regime that really doesn't care how it looks internationally or at home and that is willing to use enough force can drive a budding resistance movement underground. The risk, of course, is that such an underground movement can erupt into armed rebellion, which is one incentive for authoritarian leaders to not try to squash resistance but to delay it, defuse it, derail it if possible.

This is why an examination of tactics is critical to understanding how both a state and activists learn from each other in what some scholars call institutional learning. It is a chess game of tactics, with each side probing the other for weaknesses and trying to detect ways to block the other while learning what to anticipate from the other. In Kenya this learning process was early evident in the courts. In other countries, the learning or adaptation may take place through other venues.

3. Activists proceeded mostly on their own initiative without the benefit of favorable domestic or international circumstances. In other words, contrary to much of the social movement literature, they created their own opportunities for action by pressing forward despite dangerous and difficult conditions.

Although activism was a dependent variable in terms of state repression or to some extent international factors, it was even more an independent variable, capable of pressuring the regime and winning concessions. After the Cold War ended and Western governments and international financial institutions began paying more attention to human rights abuses and limits on democratic freedoms, activists received some support. But most of their support came from Kenyans willing to resist the regime openly.

Implications. Social movement theory is always evolving. Political opportunity theory, for example, suggested movements progress most rapidly when societal conditions (negative or positive) open the way for a popular reaction against some political or social condition. Newer thinking suggests that there are more entities involved than the state and a particular movement: political parties, relations among activists and other forces are involved. But the concept has persisted that activists do best when something beyond their control favors their activism and encourages others to support it. The Kenya research showed quite a different picture: activists can create their own 'opportunities' and push a resistance movement forward pretty much on their own initiative.

These findings suggest another reason why it is worth taking a second look at both contemporary and historic cases where a repressive state currently opposes or has opposed reform and where activists are pushing or have pushed for political change, to see whether the activism involved was dependent on external circumstances or fairly self-generated. If the later, then we need to recognize such resistance and be willing to grant credit to those who lead or develop it. Where it is found, this kind of activism invites a more positive appraisal than is often made of what man is capable of doing in harsh circumstances.

4. Informal organizations were as important as formal ones, especially in the initial phase of resistance. The early resistance was often carried out without the benefit of organizational support; even the organizations formed later were often weak, under-financed, and ineffective.

Implications. This finding encourages further research into the kind of informal groups and networks that often play a key role in political change. One way to sort out from the multitude of organizations which ones played an essential role is to shift the focus of an investigation from organizations to the process by which a culture of resistance is established.

This involves looking at the individual players in a resistance movement and not so much at the groups they belonged to, if any. Spending too much time focusing on the organizations can be misleading, especially in places where formal, institutional strength is often modest at best, as it is in many parts of the developing world. Instead, the researcher can look more closely at informal institutions and customs as well as social and political networks of the activist opposition leaders who often play a lead role in establishing and advancing a resistance movement. This approach can also help the researcher avoid the time-consuming process one runs into when the focus is mostly on organizations: trying to sort out which human rights and democracy organizations are genuine and which are mostly trying to take advantage of international funding. This is a separate and valid field of research.

5. The democratic transition was not dependent on pact making and negotiations between elites inside and reformists outside a regime but resulted primarily from domestic pressures.

Implications. The pacting model stems from analyses of a number of Latin American regimes and was probably never intended to be as widely referred to as it is. The Kenya transition was, however, largely a bottom-up phenomenon in terms of pressures on the regime. It was also a top-down phenomenon in terms of concessions. Without the pressure from below, the concessions would have been much slower in coming, if they came at all.

6. The cost of activism in the early phase of resistance far exceeded likely personal benefits to activists; but activists kept taking high risks to advance human rights and democracy. Their actions contradicted the argument that people act only out of self-interest.

Implications. The suggestion here is not that we throw out rational choice as an analytical tool, though the danger of an over-reliance on it, as Lawrence Dodd has pointed out, is that it promises predictable behavior where such predictions may not be accurate. Rather, the findings show that it makes sense to consider that while some early activists may engage in resistance out of self-interest, others do so out of a sense of community and on principle.

7. International donors and international human rights agencies played an important, but secondary, role in bringing about a democratic transition in Kenya. The Kenya findings show donors were inconsistent and often late in their efforts to use aid as leverage for reform. But international demands and a spotlight on abuses helped protect some activists and added to the pressures on a reluctant regime to allow reforms.

Implications. The assumption often is made that international pressures force a bad government to bend. That is true. But it is also true, as the Kenya study has shown, that strong activism can oblige a reluctant regime to make reforms. It is never all of one or the other; deciding where the dividing line comes is a difficult thing to judge. Quantitative and historical correlations give some ideas; but in-depth field research, including interviews can also reveal patterns and strength of activism not easily detectable from afar. This book offers an appreciation and close assessment of human rights and democracy activism.

Considerable attention in recent years has been devoted to the concept of networks of activists between nations [sometimes referred to as transnational networks] and their impact on winning political reforms. Certainly in the age of cell phones and web pages, such networks are thriving and have an important impact. But a case such as Kenya, where domestic activism, not transnational networks, appears to have provided the primary pressure on the regime, cautions us to approach the research of human rights and democratization modestly, using a variety of methods and theories to help us, and with a willingness to discover new insights on political change.

Finally, the way individual and organizational activists and members of the public who supported them, with some international help, stubbornly and daringly wrested reforms out of an abusive regime is more than a story of human rights; it is also a testament to the human spirit.

APPENDIX A
METHODOLOGY

Table A.1   Kenyan human rights/democracy activists 1987–2002

Rank	Activist	Work	Phase 1 87-91	Phase 2 91-2002	Interviewed for this study
1	Muite, Paul	attorney	I/O	O	√
2	Imanyara, Gitobu	attorney	I	O	unavailable
3	Orengo, James	attorney	I	O	√
4	Kuria, Gibson	attorney	I	I/O	√
5	Mutunga, Willy	attorney		O	√
6	Njoya, Timothy	clergy	I/O	I/O	√
7	Murungi, Kiraitu	attorney	I	O	√
8	Kariuki, Mirugi	attorney	I	O	√
9	Maathi, Wangari	biologist	O	O	√
10	Nowrojee, Pheroze	attorney	I	O	√
11	Kinyatti, Maina wa	academic			√
12	Nyong'o, Peter A.	academic	I/O	O	√
13	Mbugua, Bedan	journalist	O	O	√
14	Khaminwa, John	attorney	I	I	√
15	Odinga, Raila	activist	I	O	√
16	Wamwere, Koigi	activist	I	I/O	√
17	Karua, Martha	attorney	I	O	√
18	Muge, Alexander	clergy	O		deceased
19	Kibwana, Kivutha	academic	I/O	O	√
20	Odinga, Oginga	politician	I	O	deceased
21	Kababere, Njeri	business	I	O	√
22	Matiba, Kenneth	business	I	O	√
23	Rubia, Charles	business	I	O	√
24	Kariuki, GBM	attorney	I	O	√
25	Kiai, Maina	attorney		O	√
26	Buke, Wafula	activist	I	O	√
27	Gitari, David	clergy	O	O	√
28	Lamba, Davinder	architect		O	√
29	Nzeki, Ndingi	clergy		O	√
30	M'Inoti, Kathurima	attorney	I	O	√

Note: phase 1 was primarily individual activism; phase 2 was primarily organizational.
I = individual activist; O = organizational activist. Some activists carried out resistance in both categories at different times. Most individual activists later became organizational activists as more organizations, including opposition parties, started up. "Unavailable:" After a brief initial interview, he was not available despite repeated attempts to make an appointment. But archival records on his activities were used.

How Activist Interviewees were Selected

All but a few of the interviews with Kenyan activists were conducted by the author during 2002; several were conducted in 2003 and 2004. Almost all were conducted face to face; all but two interviews took place in Kenya. Interviewees were selected using a snowball method. Initially a number of well-known activists and some non-Kenyan analysts were asked who they considered as activists in the study period. As additional activists were interviewed they, too were asked to name other key activists.

A second verification of activism came through archival research with *The Weekly Review*, a moderate, independent magazine published during most of the study period. This provided corroboration that the activists interviewed had been engaged in public challenges to the regime. A third check was the author's own personal knowledge of activists and activism during the years 1987-1995 when he lived in Nairobi and reported on some of the resistance.

When the snowballing technique appeared to be leading almost exclusively to men, the author made an effort to include several female activists who also played important roles in the mounting pressure against the regime. In one case, a female activist had recently died (of natural causes) and was not being mentioned on anyone's list of activists. When I added her name to a possible list of activists, she frequently was identified as one of the important active activists. The weakness of the snowball interview technique is that some people, such as this woman, can be overlooked.

Ranking

The ranking shown in Table A.1 was achieved by asking each interviewee and some of the 45 or so others who were interviewed regarding events in Kenya (Kenyans and some non-Kenyans) to suggest which Kenyans on the list they considered as important activists. Interviewees were also asked to put an asterisk beside the few they considered the most active in the struggle to bring greater human rights and democracy to Kenya. This resulted in a rolling ranking, ending in the above ranking once all interviews were completed.

The Psychology of Interviewing

The author used a semi-structured form of interviewing. Questions were prepared in advance, though not read to the interviewee in advance and introduced without referring to a written list. In other words, I was prepared and knew what I wanted to know, but I was also alert to answers that provided new leads, new threads to follow in a complex, inter-woven tapestry of activism.

In one interview, for example, a Kenyan activist casually mentioned well into the interview that she and several other activists had met frequently at a 'war room' in downtown Nairobi to map out day-by-day tactics against the regime. Instead of just noting that statement and proceeding, I followed the new information, asking what a 'war room' meant (it was an attorney's office), how often they met, what they talked about, who was there, etc. What emerged as a result was another insight on the nature of the activism in Kenya during the early part of the study period, before the regime made a concession of allowing multiparty elections. This was a period when activists were often arrested. The attorney's explanations became part of the evidence of the lack of overall plan and the predominance of day-to-day tactics instead, tactics which were aimed at keeping the regime off guard with a flurry of lawsuits, and at keeping themselves from being arrested and in or seeking release of activists who were picked up. The 'war' room example became part of the evidence of the importance of informal networks in lieu of formal organizations in the individual activism phase. If I had not veered off to pursue this lead, that evidence might have gone unnoticed, unrecorded.

I ended interviews by giving the interviewees a chance to add any thoughts on any aspect of the topic. For example, at the end of my third interview with Kenyan attorney Gibson Kamau Kuria, stretching over nearly three hours and a period of about two weeks, I asked such an open-ended question. It led to my mentioning a scholarly paper by a non-Kenyan on the lack of coordination among human rights groups in Kenya. He disagreed and mentioned a network of human rights activists during the period I was studying. Until that moment I had not heard of that network.

Long Interviews

The initial request was for an interview lasting no more than one hour, but many of them lasted much longer. Sometimes an activist would agree to a brief interview of 15 to 20 minutes then go much longer with no persuasion on my part. Often the interview lasted two hours; a few were interviewed more than once; and one key activist spent five hours detailing what had happened and how.

Often, activists ended an interview thanking me for the opportunity to allow them a chance to think back over what they had done during a fairly dangerous period on behalf of human rights. This was true even in several cases where the interviewee described physical torture at the hands of the regime. The interview, it seemed, helped those past victims of state repression explain why they had done what they had done. In no case did any of them say they had regrets for their activism which often had led them into conflict with the state. The details of such accounts were easy to corroborate with human rights reports from international agencies and archival accounts. In only one case was there a hint of exaggeration. Usually those activists who had been tortured were rather matter-of-fact about their ill treatment, responding to questions rather than volunteering information about it. Overall, most interviewees were quite modest, though obviously proud, concerning what they had done.

The Mechanics of Interviewing

All but one interview was taped, always with the written permission of the interviewee. A tape recording allowed for much more accurate capturing of the words of the interviewee. While some interviewees spoke slow enough to allow me to keep up with note taking, most spoke much too rapidly to take verbatim notes. My hand-written notes showed partial sentences, sometimes just a few words, as interviewees raced along from one point to another. There was no way I could keep up; I would have lost a considerable portion of the remarks. The taped interviews allowed me to follow more closely the nut of the ideas being discussed, the logic, and the analysis being offered. Taping, even though I also took some notes, left me more relaxed, confident that what my notes did not show, the tape would. It gave me a greater chance to mentally prepare my next questions. But it is still worth taking even partial notes in case the tape recorder or the tape is damaged.

But the tape recorder may formalize the interview more than one would like. Facing a recorder only inches away might lead the interviewee to assume a more formal voice, to give a stiffer kind of response than otherwise. In the case of the Kenyan activists, I may never know if they would have felt more at ease and perhaps more reflective – less self-conscious without a tape recorder. It was my impression, however, that the recorder, a small, inexpensive one, which had to be set very close to those who spoke in a soft or low voice, had little, if any effect on their remarks or reflections. Few looked at it or spoke in a more formal voice once the recorder was turned on. Many had been interviewed before by journalists, no doubt with tape recorders, if not TV cameras during some of the more dramatic years of confrontation with the government.

Taking Notes during Interviews

One might think that tape recording an interview would be sufficient and that note taking would not be necessary. Both have advantages and disadvantages:

1. *Advantages*. The tape recorder might fail to record – which it did a few times. Such instances make it useful to check the tape from time to time, stopping it, reversing, and playing it aloud for a few seconds to make sure the recording is continuing. I wanted to use the notes as a kind of index to the tape, noting key sections so I could skip portions of the tape and go directly from one key point to another. Even sketchy, incomplete notes were enough to flag my attention to major points.
2. *Disadvantages*. When taking notes, I momentarily lost eye contact with the interviewee. Often they kept talking. Eye contact is important, especially in a country such as Kenya, where people prefer not to talk to each other while looking away. Keeping in contact is important in the Kenyan culture, even on the telephone. For example, a speaker on the telephone will almost certainly seek verification that you are still on the line if you make no audible response

for more than a few seconds. Often a speaker will stop their conversation if you are unresponsive and say "hello?" to elicit confirmation that you are there. The normal response to avoid such interjection is to utter "hmm," or "uh huh," or some variation that indicates you are following the other speaker. (One finds a similar back and forth interaction in the United States in African American pentecostal churches where a preacher's comments are met with "yes," or "say it," or "tell it.")

Tracking down Interviewees

It is good to start very early compiling you own telephone list. Most developing nations have a phone directory but many numbers are likely to be out of date and some not working. With the switch to cell phones or mobile phones as they are called in Kenya, even listed numbers are not so helpful in locating prospective interviewees. I found in Nairobi that, to my surprise, many of the human rights activists of recent years did not have up-to-date phone numbers of fellow activists. One church activist, well-known by everyone I spoke with, was particularly hard to find. It took me several hours and many local calls to finally trace him to his last church post (he was retired) and from there to a cell phone of his wife, who invited me to call her husband that evening at home. Later, during the interview (some distance from Nairobi), he expressed mild surprise at the fact that I had found him at all. A month or so into the research, I took a couple of days to transfer the bits and pieces of papers and notations of numbers in various notebooks onto a master telephone list which I used extensively.

Cell Phones

A local cell phone is a necessary investment. I waited more than a month to get one and finally was convinced to buy one (about $60) when I heard that a few people had tried in vain to reach me. My phone in the apartment had no answering machine, which costs more than a cell phone. One of the big changes in Kenya between my field work in 2002 and a preliminary research visit in 1999 was the widespread use of cell phones. Even a former gardener I knew had one.

Preparing for the Interview

I used an archival review to collect information on activism. This proved useful in suggesting questions; and it served as a useful reference for the interviewee in recalling some of the many actions they had taken. It is essential to know the accomplishments of an interviewee and general events in order to know when to pursue a point. For example, I asked one activist if a mass demonstration had occurred (it had):

Interviewer:

"Do you have any estimates of the number of people who turned out for that?"

Activist:

"Oh my God, you see we didn't even have the rally."

Under further questioning, he said the police blocked all routes to the rally. That could have been the end of it; but I continued asking questions; he mentioned that some people were injured.

Interviewee:

"Tires were burning; wooden planks were burning. Shops had been stoned. The whole place was stoned. A lot of police were hurt. A lot of civilians, people were clobbered very badly; injured. Vehicles [of] elite were put on fire. The whole place was fire; there was no going there [downtown]. So it was stone throwing the whole day; tear gas lobbing."

In other words, what at first response appeared to be a non-event was actually a major event. Without some prior knowledge on the part of the interviewer regarding what had happened in Kenya, the interview might have shed no light on the event.

Transcriptions

In order not to fall too far behind, I hired an assistant to transcribe many of the interviews. This was tedious work, especially for the longer ones, but it is good to keep up as much as possible to avoid weeks of transcribing back home. Still, I fell far behind.

Early transcripts helped reflection. Transcriptions offer ideas for follow-up actions such as books or articles to track down, people to call, new questions to ask and new people to interview. It became clearer as I did the transcriptions which questions would be the most useful for the next interviews. But more importantly, themes began to emerge from the transcription process. I began to see links between what one person said and others had said; patterns took shape. As themes emerged, I would type THEME, or THEORY, as well as TACTIC of the regime or activist. I then copied paragraphs from these categories onto a separate file for further analyses.

APPENDIX B
HUMAN RIGHTS TREATIES IN KENYA

Table B.1   United Nations treaties in force in Kenya: 1976–2004

Treaty	Year entered in force in Kenya	Years Late in reports to UN
International Covenant on Civil and Political Rights[a]	1976	18
International Covenant on Economic, Social and Cultural Rights[a]	1976	4
Convention on the Elimination of All Forms of Discrimination against Women	1984	3
Convention on the Rights of the Child	1990	6
Convention Against Torture and Other Cruel Inhuman or Degrading Treatment or Punishment	1997	6
International Convention on the Elimination of All Forms of Racial Discrimination	2001	1
Convention on the Prevention and Punishment of the Crime of Genocide	-	-

Source: *United Nations High Commissioner for Human Rights*, 2004

Note: [a] These two treaties, along with the Universal Declaration of Human Rights, adopted by the United Nations General Assembly in 1948, are known informally as the International Bill of Rights (Henkin et al. 1999, 320-321). The Declaration did not require ratification. But it took 28 years for the two Covenants to come into effect in 1976.

APPENDIX C
SOCIO-ECONOMIC PROFILES OF KENYA

Table C.1   Socio-economic profiles of Kenya: 1990 and 2003

	1990	2003
Population	24,639, 261	31,639,091
Population growth rate	3.80%	1.27%
Infant mortality	60 per 1,000 live births	63 per 1,000
Life expectancy	62 male/67 female	45 both[a]
Fertility rate	6.5 children per woman	4.4
Literacy	59.20%	85.1[b]
Labor force	9 million est.	10 million est.
Workforce in agriculture	78% est.	75-80% est.
Unemployment	"high" (no figures)	40% (2001)
GDP	$8.5 billion	$32.9 billion
GDP per capita	$360	$1,100
GDP growth rate	5.2% (1986-1988)	1.10%
Inflation rate	8.3% (1988)	1.90%

Source: *CIA World Fact Book* (1990 and 2003), except 2003 fertility rate, which is an estimate by the Population Reference Bureau in Washington

Note: 1990 is the earliest available on-line archival edition of the CIA World Fact Book. It includes some earlier data and provides useful comparison data for the study period.
[a] 15% of the population was estimated to have AIDS or the AIDS virus.
[b] age 15 and over who can read and write.

APPENDIX D
REPRESSION AND TORTURE IN KENYA

The brief descriptions of torture of several activists in this study do not adequately portray the very crude and widespread use of physical abuse and torture during the study period (1987-2002). This practice, exposed to some extent in the local media, in human rights reports by private Kenyan organizations and international watchdogs, and in a United Nations report (excerpts below) is relevant to the study.

The risks posed by such practices amounted to repression against reform as well as systemic police brutality unchecked by the regime. Prominent activists early on faced this risk, though less so later as the reform movement gained strength. But ordinary citizens who chose to come out and support activism knew they risked mistreatment at the hands of a police force that routinely tortured the accused. Despite the risks, activists and their supporters stepped forward in Kenya, helping bring about change.

The following are excerpts from a report on a visit to Kenya by a Special Rapporteur of the United Nations in pursuant to a 1999 resolution on Kenya by the United Nations Commission on Human Rights. The report was issued in March 2000. Although Kenya had finally signed the UN Convention Against Torture in 1997, as of 2004, it had yet to file the required reports on progress in implementing the treaty. And as noted in Appendix B, Kenya was 18 years behind in its required reporting on implementation of the International Covenant on Civil and Political Rights.

Excerpts from UN Report on Torture in Kenya

Constitutional Protesters Attacked. The Special Rapporteur has received information on three rallies organized by the National Convention Executive Committee (NCEC) in 1997, which were reportedly dispersed by the police, using force. On 3 May 1997, NCEC reportedly organized a rally at the Kamukunji grounds in Nairobi. According to the information received the meeting was called to discuss constitutional reforms and to discuss resolutions of the Limuru Convention held between 3 and 6 April 1997. The meeting was reportedly disrupted before it commenced at 10 a.m... According to the information received, police officers armed with pangas [machetes] and whips were stationed from 8 a.m. about a kilometre from the meeting at the Machakos Country Bus Station. Two preachers, the Reverend Timothy Njoya and Samuel Njoya were reportedly the first to be stopped by police at the Country Bus Station. They were allegedly whipped in full view of the police before walking to the Kamukunji grounds, which police had allegedly sealed off, blocking all entries. While he was arguing with the police, the Reverend Njoya's robe was allegedly grabbed and torn by an officer.

The two men were then reportedly taken to the middle of the Kamukunji grounds and held there for more than seven hours without having a chance to leave or to address the attendants. Thereafter, a number of NCEC officials reportedly entered the grounds from different directions. Among the group was Peter Ndwiga, who was allegedly "hit" by more than six police officers as he made his way through a human barrier that had been erected. Willy Mutunga, NCEC Co-Convenor and Vice-Chairman of the Kenya Human Rights Commission, was allegedly slapped as he tried to enter the grounds.

The police officers then reportedly held the leaders in the middle of the grounds and allegedly used tear gas and beat several people present. Members of the Shauri estate were reportedly among the group of people allegedly beaten by the police. According to the information received, at around 4 p.m., the Reverend Njoya and two other men led members of the public out of the Kamukunji grounds. Upon reaching the Country Bus Station, the group reportedly encountered a contingent of regular and General Service Unit police officers. The police officers allegedly exploded tear gas canisters and used whips, batons and machetes to disperse the group. Many people reportedly began to disperse, however at least one man was arrested, James Orengo, an opposition Member of Parliament, who was later released.

Journalists were also reportedly injured during the confrontation. It is reported that Govedi Atsusa, a photographer for the *Daily Nation* sustained an injury to his arm. Another journalist, Karen Shaw, who was working with the Kenya Human Rights Commission, was allegedly hit by a club by a police officer as she took photographs of what was happening. She reportedly wrote a letter to the Commissioner of Police but there has allegedly been no response.

Protest Rally Attacked

A second NCEC constitutional reform rally reportedly took place on 31 May 1997, also in Nairobi. According to the information received, many participants present at the rally reportedly sustained serious injuries and were later admitted to various hospitals when the rally was allegedly disrupted by police at Central Park, which had been cordoned off by police at around 8 a.m. The rally reportedly commenced at St Andrews Church near the University of Nairobi and then proceeded to Central Park, where people were reportedly blocked from entering. According to the information received, police officers allegedly threw stinging teargas canisters into the crowd and allegedly started beating people indiscriminately when prayers were led by Reverend Njoya. People reportedly scattered and trampled on each other and police allegedly beat several people present.

The following individuals were reportedly amongst those harmed: Muturi Kigano, the Chairman of the Safina party, was allegedly hit on the head by police. He was reportedly admitted to Nairobi Hospital for treatment. Saulo Busolo, Ford-Kenya MP for Webuye, reportedly sustained a broken arm after he tried to stop police batons allegedly aimed at his head. He was reportedly admitted to Nairobi Hospital for treatment. Eddah Rubia, reportedly a Ford-Asili activist, suffered a fractured leg after a police officer allegedly hit her repeatedly with a baton. Kiraitu Murungi, Member of Parliament (MP) for Imenti South, was reportedly injured on the head when a teargas canister exploded on his head. Njuguna Muthahi, a Kenya Human Rights Commission official, was reportedly running from police officers when he fell to the ground, where he was allegedly beaten on the head and elbows. He was reportedly later treated at a local clinic.

On 10 October 1997, a third NCEC rally, of around 5,000 people, reportedly took place in the Kamukunji grounds, Nairobi. It was reportedly interrupted by heavily armed police officers who allegedly entered the venue and boxed, kicked and whipped persons present. The officers were reportedly acting under the control of the Buru Buru divisional police chief. According to the information received, police officers lobbed tear gas canisters into the crowd, which resulted in several injuries. Some people were also reportedly injured by rubber bullets. The following individual cases have been brought to the Special Rapporteur's attention: Henry Ruhiu, MP for Embakasi, who is a recovering stroke victim, was reportedly beaten in front of around 40 local and international journalists. The police chief allegedly descended upon him with sticks, kicking his ribs after knocking away his walking stick. Paul Muite, also an MP, was allegedly kicked and punched before being held firmly on the neck and dragged for several metres. Other MPs allegedly beaten and/or tear-gassed are Aloo Ogeska, Otieno Mak Onyango, Benjamin Ndubai, Kamau Icharia, Philip Gitonga, Safina members Muturi Kigano, Richard Leakey and Ngengi Muigai of FORD-Asili.

Human Rights Monitor Attacked

John Kamanda, a Kenya Human Rights Commission monitor in Nairobi, was reportedly on his way home from Muthaiga, on 17 February 1997, where he had been collecting signatures for a Commission petition against police killings, when he was reportedly stopped by policemen. The officers allegedly grabbed him by the collar and accused him of being a thug who was harassing residents at night. A second police officer allegedly grabbed an envelope he was carrying. Upon noticing that it contained material on the KHRC "Campaign against police killings" and other documents on human rights violations in Kenya, the officer allegedly hit him hard and accused him and the KHRC of defending "criminals". He was allegedly kicked and slapped several times and when he reportedly refused requests to hand over his materials, he was allegedly hit more vigorously. He was reportedly then ordered to leave, amid insults and verbal abuse.

Accused Criminals Tortured and Killed

Mohammed Sheikh Yahya was reportedly arrested at his home at about 5:30 p.m. on 13 June 1998 by military officers who allegedly suspected him of having killed a herdsman during a bandit attack in Boka. Military officers allegedly tied him to the back of a Land Rover and dragged him for about two kilometres to a nearby forest. He was reportedly killed in the forest. According to the information received, when his body was found, his eyes had been gorged out and one of his ears cut off. A post mortem examination was reportedly performed which revealed that he had suffered cuts to his chest, back, legs and head. His upper torso had also reportedly been partly burnt and both of his wrists had been broken. The results of the post mortem examination were allegedly ordered to be covered up by security officers.

George Gacheru Muchiri was reportedly arrested on 31 March 1997 at a petrol station where he was working, in Banana town, Kiambu district. He was reportedly arrested by two plain clothes policemen on suspicion of having stolen some money. He was taken to Karuli police station, where he reportedly stayed for two days. He was then transferred to Kiambu police headquarters, where he was tied to a wooden stick and hung between two tables. He was then allegedly beaten with wooden sticks on the legs and on the soles of the feet. He reportedly spent one night in Kiambu police station before being transferred to Mai Mahi forest, near Narok, where, along with two other detainees who had been arrested on suspicion of having stolen the money in the same petrol station, he was severely beaten after having been hung up on a tree. He allegedly had a shot fired above his head, which is said to have impaired his hearing. His private parts were allegedly tied up and beaten. The two others were allegedly subjected to the same treatment.

Select Bibliography

Africa Watch. 1991. *Kenya: Taking Liberties*. New York: Human Rights Watch.

Africa Watch. 1993. *Divide and Rule: State-Sponsored Ethnic Violence in Kenya*. New York: Human Rights Watch.

Almond, Gabriel A. 1990. *A Discipline Divided: Schools and Sects in Political Science*. Newbury Park, CA.: Sage Publications.

Almond, Gabriel, and Sidney Verba. [1963] 1989. *The Civic Culture: Political Attitudes and Democracy in Five Nations*. Newbury Park, CA.: Sage Publications.

Amnesty International. 1987. *Kenya: Torture, Political Detention and Unfair Trials*. London: Amnesty International.

Anderson, Leslie E. 1994. *The Political Ecology of the Modern Peasant: Calculation and Community*. Baltimore: Johns Hopkins University Press.

Andrain, Charles F., and David E. Apter. 1995. *Political Protest and Social Change: Analyzing Politics*. New York: New York University Press.

An-Na`Im, Abdullahi Ahmed, and Francis M. Deng, eds. 1990. *Human Rights in Africa: Cross-cultural Perspectives*. Washington: Brookings Institution.

Barkan, Joel. 1992. "The Rise and Fall of a Governance Realm in Kenya." In *Governance and Politics in Africa*, eds. Goran Hyden and Michael Bratton. Boulder, CO.: Lynne Rienner Publishers.

Barkan, Joel D. 1993. "Kenya: Lessons from a Flawed Election." *Journal of Democracy* 4(3):85–99, July.

Barkan, Joel D. 2001. "U.S. Human Rights Policy and Democratization in Kenya." Manuscript.

Barkan, Joel D. 2004. "U.S. Human Rights Policy and Democratization in Kenya. In *Implementing U.S. Human Rights Policy*, Debra Liang Fenton, ed., Washington: United States Institute of Peace.

Bates, Robert H. 1981. *Markets and States in Tropical Africa: The Political Basis of Agricultural Policies*. Berkeley, CA.: University of California Press.

Bates, Robert H., Avner Greif, Margaret Levi, Jean-Laurent Rosenthal, and Barry R. Weingast. 1998 *Analytic Narratives*. Princeton, NJ.: Princeton University Press.

Berlin, Isaiah. 1991. *The Crooked Timber of Humanity: Chapters in the History of Ideas*, ed. Henry Hardy. New York: Knopf.

Berman, Bruce. 1992. "Bureaucracy & Incumbent Violence: Colonial Administration & the Origins of the 'Mau Mau' Emergency. In *Unhappy Valley: Conflict in Kenya & Africa; Book Two: Violence and Ethnicity*, Bruce Berman and John Lonsdale. London: James Currey.

Berman, Sheri. 1998. *The Social Democratic Movement: Ideas and Politics in the Making of Interwar Europe*. Cambridge, MA: Harvard University Press.

Brantley, Cynthia.1981. *The Giriama and Colonial Resistance in Kenya, 1800–1920*. Berkeley: University of California Press.

Bratton, Michael. 1989. "Beyond the State: Civil Society and Associational Life in Africa." *World Politics* 41(3):407–430, April.

Bratton, Michael, and Nicolas van de Walle. 1997. *Democratic Experiments in Africa: Regime Transitions in Comparative Perspective*. Cambridge: Cambridge University Press.

Brown, Stephen. 2000. "Donors' Dilemmas in Democratization: Foreign Aid and Political Reform in Africa." PhD dissertation. New York University.

Brown, Stephen. 2001. "Authoritarian Leaders and Multiparty Elections in Africa: How Foreign Donors Help to Keep Kenya's Daniel Arap Moi in Power." *Third World Quarterly* 22 (5):725–739.

Burke, Fred G. 1969. "Public Administration in Africa: the Legacy of Inherited Colonial Institutions." In *Journal of Comparative Administration* 1(3).

Callaghy, Thomas M. 1984. *The State-Society Struggle: Zaire in Comparative Perspective*. New York: Columbia University Press.

Carothers, Thomas. 1999. *Aiding Democracy Abroad: The Learning Curve*. Washington: Carnegie Endowment for International Peace.

Central Intelligence Agency. 1990. *CIA World Fact Book*. Washington: Central Intelligence Agency.

Central Intelligence Agency. 2003. *CIA World Fact Book*. Washington: Central Intelligence Agency.

Chazan, Naomi, Robert Moritmer, John Ravenhill, and Donald Rothchild. 1992. *Politics and Society in Contemporary Africa*, 2nd ed. Boulder, CO.: Lynne Rienner.

Chege, Michael. 1994. "What's Right with Africa? *Current History*. May.

Chege, Michael 1997. *Liberal Democracy and Its Malcontents: Contrasting Perspectives of a Democratic Capitalist World Order From Sub-Saharan Africa in the 1990s*. Cambridge, MA.: Weatherhead Center for International Affairs.

Clayton, Anthony. 1976. *Counter-Insurgency in Kenya: A Study of Military Operations against Mau Mau*. Nairobi, Kenya: Transafrica Publishers.

Crain, Mary. 1990. "The Social Construction of National Identity in Highland Ecuador," *Anthropological Quarterly* 63:43–59, January.

Dahl, Robert A. 1971. *Polyarchy: Participation and Opposition*. New Haven, Conn.: Yale University Press.

Diamond, Larry. 1999. *Developing Democracy: Toward Consolidation*. Baltimore. Johns Hopkins University Press.

Dodd, Lawrence. 1991. "Congress, the Presidency and the American Experience: A Transformational Perspective." In *Divided Democracy*. James Thurber. Washington: Congressional Quarterly.

Dodd, Lawrence C. 1994. "Political Learning and Political Change: Understanding Development Across Time," In *The Dynamics of American Politics: Approaches & Interpretations*, eds. Lawrence D. Dodd and Calvin Jillson. Boulder, CO.: Westview Press.

Downs, Anthony. 1957. *An Economic Theory of Democracy*. New York: Harper & Row.

Eckstein, Harry. 1975. "Case Study and Theory in Political Science." In Handbook *of Political Science,* Vol. 3, eds. Fred Greenstein and Nelson Polsby. Reading, MA: Addison-Wesley.

Edelman, Murray. *1964. The Symbolic Uses of Politics.* Urbana, IL.: University of Illinois Press.

Eisinger, Peter K. 1973. "The Conditions of Protest Behavior in American Cities." *American Political Science Review* 67:11–28.

Elgström, Ole, and Goran Hyden. 2002. *Development and Democracy: What have we learned and how?* London. Routledge.

Etzioni, Amitai. 1988. *The Moral Dimension: Toward A New Economics.* New York. Free Press/Macmillan.

Femia, Joseph. 1987. *Antonio Gramsci's Political Thought.* Oxford: Clarendon Press.

Ferree, Myra Marx. 1992. The Political Context of Rationality: Rational Choice Theory and Resource Mobilization. In *Frontiers In Social Movement Theory*, eds. Aldon D. Morris and Carol McClurg Mueller. New Haven, CN.: Yale University Press.

Flacks, Richard. 2004 "Knowledge for What? In *Rethinking Social Movements: Structure, Meaning, and Emotion*, eds. Jeff Goodwin and James M. Jasper. Oxford, U. K.: Rowman & Littlefield.

Foweraker, Joe. 1995. *Theorizing Social Movements.* London: Pluto Press.

Freedom House. 2006. *Freedom in the World.* New York: Freedom House.

Gamson, William A., David S. Meyer. 1996. "Framing Political Opportunity." In *Comparative Perspectives on Social Movements: Political Opportunities, Mobilizing Structures, and Cultural Framings*, eds. Doug McAdam, John D. McCarthy, and Mayer N. Zald. Cambridge: Cambridge University Press.

Geddes, Barbara. 1999. "What Do We Know About Democratization After Twenty Years," *Annual Review Political Science* (2):115–144.

Gitari, Bishop David. 1996. In Season and Out of Season: Sermons to a Nation. Carlisle, U. K.: Regnum.

Giugni, Marco, Doug McAdam, and Charles Tilly, eds. 1999. *How Social Movements Matter.* Minneapolis. University of Minnesota Press.

Goodwin, Jeff, and James M. Jasper, eds. 2004. *Rethinking Social Movements: Structure, Meaning, and Emotion.* Oxford, U. K.: Rowman & Littlefield.

Gould, Deborah B. 2004. "Passionate Political Process." In *Rethinking Social Movements: Structure, Meaning, and Emotion*, eds. Jeff Goodwin and James M. Jasper. Oxford, U. K.: Rowman & Littlefield.

Gurr, Ted Robert. 1970. *Why Men Rebel.* Princeton: Princeton University Press.

Gutto, Shadrack B. O. 1993. *Human and People's Rights for the Oppressed: Critical Essays on theory and Practice from Sociology of Law Perspectives.* Lund, Sweden: Lund University Press.

Haggard, Stephen, Robert R. Kaufman, eds. 1995. *The Political Economy of Democratic Transitions.* Princeton: Princeton University Press.

Harbeson, John W., Donald Rothchild, and Naomi Chazan, eds. 1994. *Civil Society and the State in Africa.* Boulder, CO.: Lynne Rienner.

Haugerud, Angelique 1995. *The Culture of Politics in Modern Kenya*. Cambridge, U. K.: Cambridge University Press.

Havel, Vaclav. "The End of the Modern Era," *New York Times*, 1 March 1992.

Hawking, Stephen. [1988] 1995. *A Brief History of Time: From the Big Bang to Black Holes*. Toronto. Bantam.

Hay, Colin. 2002. *Political Analysis: A Critical Introduction*. Houndmills, U. K.: Palgrave.

Hempstone, Smith.1997. *Rogue Ambassador: An African Memoir*. Sewanee, TN.: University of the South Press.

Hipsher, Patricia L. 1998. "Democratic Transitions as Protest Cycles: Social Movement Dynamics in Democratizing Latin America." In *The Social Movement Society: Contentious Politics for a New Century*, eds. David S. Meyer and Sidney Tarrow. Oxford, U.K.: Rowman & Littlefield.

Hirschman, Albert O. 1970. "The Search for Paradigms as a Hindrance to Understanding." *World Politics* 22 (3):163–177.

Hobbes, Thomas. [1651] 1997. *Leviathan*. New York: Norton.

Holmquist, Frank W., Frederick S. Weaver, and Michael D. Ford. 1994. "The Structural Development of Kenya's Political Economy." In *African Studies Review*. 37(1):69–105, April.

Hornsby, Charles. 2001. "Election Day and the Results." In *Out for the Count: the 1997 General Elections and Prospects for Democracy in Kenya*, eds. Marcel Rutten, Alamin Mazrui, and François Grignon. Kampala, Uganda: Fountain Publishers.

Hsin-Huang, Michael Hsiao, and Hagen Koo. 1997. "The Middle Classes and Democratization." In *Consolidating the Third Wave Democracies: Themes and Perspectives*, eds. Larry Diamond, Marc F. Plattner, Yun-han Chu, and Hung-mao Tien. Baltimore: Johns Hopkins University Press.

Human Rights Watch. 2001. *World Report 2001: Kenya*. http://www.hrw.org/wr2k1/africa/kenya.html. New York: Human Rights Watch.

Human Rights Watch. 2002. *World Report 2002: Kenya*. http://www.hrw.org/wr2k2/africa6.html. New York: Human Rights Watch.

Human Rights Watch. 2003. *World Report 2003: Kenya*. http://www.hrw.org/english/docs/2003/12/31/kenya7271.htm. (January 2004) New York: Human Rights Watch.

Human Rights Watch. 2004. *Human Rights Overview: Kenya* http://hrw.org/english/docs/2003/01/13/kenya7271.htm (January 2004). New York: Human Rights Watch.

Human Rights Watch. 2005. World Report 2005: Kenya http://hrw.org/english/docs/2005/01/13/Kenya9831.htm.

Huntington, Samuel P. 1968. *Political Order in Changing Societies*. New Haven, CN.: Yale University Press.

Huntington, Samuel P. 1991. *The Third Wave: Democratization in the Late Twentieth Century*. Norman, OK.: University of Oklahoma.

Hyden, Goran. 2000. "The Governance Challenge in Africa." In *African Perspectives on Governance*, eds. Goran Hyden, Dele Olowu, Hastings W. O. Okoth Ogendo. Trenton, N. J.: Africa World Press, 2000.

Hyden, Goran. 2002 "Development and democracy: An Overview." In *Development and Democracy: What have we learned and how?* eds. Ole Elgström and Goran Hyden. London: Routledge.

Hyden, Goran, Dele Olowu, and Hastings W. O. Okoth Ogendo, eds. 2000. *African Perspectives on Governance*. Trenton, NJ.: Africa World Press.

Inglehart, Ronald. 1977. *The Silent Revolution: Changing Values and Political Styles Among Western Publics*. Princeton, NJ.: Princeton University Press.

Inglehart, Ronald. 1988. "The Renaissance of Political Culture." *American Political Science Review*, Vol. 82(4), December.

Inglehart, Ronald. 1990. *Cultural Shift in Advanced Industrial Society*. Princeton: Princeton University Press.

International Bar Association on Kenya. *Report on the Legal System and Independence of the Judiciary in Kenya*; November 1996.

International Commission of Jurists (Kenya Section). 2001. *State of the Rule of Law in Kenya 2000*. Nairobi: International Commission of Jurists (Kenya Section).

International Human Rights Working Party of the International Committee of the Law Society of England and Wales: *Report on a Visit to Kenya 27–31 January 1997*. Gerald Shamsh, Andy Unger, and Katherine Henderson.

Jackson, Robert H. and Carl G. Rosberg. 1982. *Personal Rule in Black Africa: Prince, Autocrat, Prophet, Tyrant*. Berkeley, CA: University of California Press.

Jervis, Robert. 1999. *System Effects: Complexity in Political and Social Life*. Princeton, NJ.: Princeton University Press.

Joseph, Richard A.1987. *Democracy and Prebendal Politics in Nigeria: The Rise and Fall of the Second Republic*. Cambridge: Cambridge University Press.

Jung, Hwa Yol. 1973. "A Critique of the Behavioral Persuasion in Politics: A Phenomenological View." *Phenomenology & The Social Sciences* vol. 2. Evanston, IL.: Northwestern University Press.

Kabira, Wanjiku Mukabi, and Patricia Ngurukie, eds. 1997. "Our Mothers' Footsteps: Stories of Women in the Struggle for Freedom." Nairobi, Kenya: The Collaborative Centre for Gender and Development.

Kakwenzire, Joan. 2000. "Human Rights and Governance." In *African Perspectives on Governance*, eds. Goran Hyden, Dele Olowu, Hastings W. O. Okoth Ogendo. Trenton, NJ.: Africa World Press.

Kanogo, Tabitha. 1992. *Dedan Kimathi: A Biography*. Nairobi, Kenya: East African Educational Publishers.

Karklins, Rasma, and Roger Petersen. 1993. "Decision Calculus of Protesters and Regimes: Eastern Europe 1989." The Journal of Politics 55(3):588–614.

Kasfir, Nelson, ed. 1998. *Civil Society and Democracy in Africa: Critical Perspectives*. London: Frank Cass.

Keck, Margaret E. and Kathryn Sikkink. 1998. *Activists Beyond Borders: Advocacy Networks in International Politics*. Ithaca: Cornell University Press.

Kershaw, Greet. 1997. *Mau Mau from Below*. Oxford. James Currey.

Kihoro, Wanyiri. 1998. *Never Say Die: The Chronicle of a Political Prisoner.* Nairobi, Kenya: East African Educational Publishers.

Kinyatti, Maina wa, ed. 1987. *Kenya's Freedom Struggle: The Dedan Kimathi Papers.* London: Zed Books.

Kirigia, Rev. Joyce Karuri, ed. 2002. *Eight Great Years: October 1994 to September 2002, To God be the glory great things He has done; Achievements of the ministry of the retiring Archbishop The Most Rev. Dr. David Mukuba Gitari as the 3rd Archbishop of the Anglican Church of Kenya.* Nairobi, Kenya: Anglican Church.

Kirk-Greene, A.H.M., ed. 1979. *Africa In the Colonial Period. III. The Transfer of Power.* Oxford: University of Oxford Inter-Faculty Committee for African Studies.

Kloop, Jacqueline Maria. 2001. *Electoral Despotism in Kenya: Land, Patronage and Resistance.* PhD dissertation. McGill University (Canada).

Kuhn, Thomas S. [1962] 1966. *The Structure of Scientific Revolutions.* 3rd ed. Chicago: University of Chicago Press.

Krasner, Stephen. 1984 "Approaches to the State: Alternative Conceptions and Historical Dynamics." *Comparative Politics* (16):223–246.

Kurzman, Charles. 2004. "The Poststructuralist Consensus in Social Movement Theory." In *Rethinking Social Movements: Structure, Meaning, and Emotion,* eds. Jeff Goodwin and James M. Jasper. Oxford, U. K.: Rowman & Littlefield.

Laitin, David D. 1995. "The Civic Culture at 30," *American Political Science Review* 89(1):168–173, March .

Lakatos, Imre. 1970. "Falsification and the Methodology of Scientific Research Programmes." In *Criticism and the Growth of Knowledge,* eds. Imre Lakatos and Alan Musgrave. Cambridge: Cambridge University Press.

Lane, Ruth. 1997. *The Art of Comparative Politics.* Boston: Allyn and Bacon.

Lijphart, Arend. 1971. "Comparative Politics and the Comparative Method," *American Political Science Review* 65(3):682–693, September.

Lijphart, Arend. 1975. "The Comparable-Cases Strategy in Comparative Research," *Comparative Political Studies* 8 (2) 158–177.

Lindberg, Staffan. 2002. "Problems of measuring democracy: Illustrations from Africa. In *Development and Democracy: What have we learned and how?* eds. Ole Elgström and Goran Hyden. London: Routledge.

Linz, Juan J. & Alfred Stepan. 1996. *Problems of Democratic Transition and Consolidation: Southern Europe, South America, and Post-Communist Europe* Baltimore: Johns Hopkins University Press.

Lipset, Martin Seymour. 1959. "Some Social Requisites of Democracy: Economic Development and Political Legitimacy." *American Political Science Review* 53(1):69–105, March.

Lonsdale, John. 1992. "The Moral Economy of Mau Mau: Wealth, Poverty & Civic Virtue in Kikuyu Political Thought." In *Unhappy Valley: Conflict in Kenya & Africa; Book Two: Violence and Ethnicity,* Bruce Berman and John Lonsdale. London: James Currey.

Lonsdale, John. 1997. "Foreword" In *Mau Mau from Below*. Greet Kershaw. Oxford: James Currey.

Macrae, Donald G. 1974. *Max Weber*. New York: Viking Press.

March, James G., and Johan P. Olson. 1989. *Rediscovering Institutions: The Organizational Basis of Politics*. New York: Free Press.

McAdam, Doug. 1982. "The Political Process Model." In *Political Process and the Development of Black Insurgency*. Doug McAdam. Chicago: University of Chicago.

McAdam, Doug, John D. McCarthy, and Mayer N. Zald. eds. 1996. *Comparative Perspectives on Social Movements: Political Opportunities, Mobilizing Structures, and Cultural Framings*. Cambridge: Cambridge University Press.

McAdam, Doug, Sidney Tarrow, Charles Tilly. 2001. *Dynamics of Contention*. Cambridge: Cambridge University Press.

McAdam, Doug. 2004. "Revisiting the U.S. Civil Rights Movement: Toward a More Synthetic Understanding of the Origins of Contention." In *Rethinking Social Movements: Structure, Meaning, and Emotion*. Oxford, U.K.: Rowman & Littlefield.

Melucci, Alberto.1994. "A Strange Kind of Newness: What's "New" in New Social Movements?" In *New Social Movements: From Ideology to Identity*, eds. Laraña, Enrique, Hank Johnston, and Joseph R. Gusfield. Philadelphia: Temple University Press.

Meyer, David S. 2004. "Tending the Vineyard: Cultivating Political Process Research. In *Rethinking Social Movements: Structure, Meaning, and Emotion*, eds. Jeff Goodwin and James M. Jasper. Oxford, U.K.: Rowman & Littlefield.

Meyer, David S., and Sidney Tarrow. 1998. *The Social Movement Society: Contentious Politics for a New Century*. Lanham, MD.: Rowman & Littlefield.

Miller, Norman, and Rodger Yeager. 1994. *Kenya: The Quest for Prosperity*. Boulder, CO.: Westview Press.

Monga, Célestin.1996. *The Anthropology of Anger: Civil Society and Democracy in Africa*. Boulder: Lynne Rienner.

Moore, Barrington, Jr. [1966] 1993. *Social Origins of Dictatorship and Democracy: Lord and Peasant in the Making of the Modern World*. Boston: Beacon Press.

Morton, Andrew. 1998. *Moi: The Making of an African Statesman*. London: Michael O'Mara Books.

Mueller, Susanne D. 1984. "Government and Opposition in Kenya, 1966–9." *The Journal of Modern African Studies* 29(3):399–427.

Munene, Macharia. 2001. *The Politics of Transition in Kenya: 1995–1998*. Nairobi, Kenya: Quest & Insight Publishers.

Murphy, John F. 1986 "Legitimation and Paternalism: The Colonial State in Kenya. *African Studies Review* 29(3):55–65, September.

Murungi, Kiraitu. 2000. *In The Mud of Politics*. Nairobi, Kenya: Acacia Stantex.

Mutahi, Nguyi. 2001. *Transition without Transformation: Civil Society and the Transition Seesaw in Kenya*. Working paper 003/2001. Nairobi Kenya: SARET.

Mutunga, Willy. 1999. *Constitution-Making from the Middle: Civil Society and Transition Politics in Kenya, 1992–1997*. Nairobi, Kenya: SARET.

Mwangi, Paul. 2001. *The Black Bar: Corruption and Political Intrigue within Kenya's Legal Fraternity*. Nairobi, Kenya: Oakland Media Services.

Nelson, Harold D. 1984. *Kenya: A Country Study*. Washington: American University/ Department of the Army.

Nzomo, Maria. 1998. "Kenya: The Women's Movement and Democratic Change." In *The African State at a Critical Juncture: Between Disintegration and Reconfiguration*, eds. Leonardo A. Villalón and Phillip A. Huxtable. Boulder, CO.: Lynne Rienner.

O'Brien, F. S., and Terry C. I. Ryan. 2001. "Kenya." In *Aid and Reform in Africa*. Washington: World Bank.

Ochieng' W. R., ed. 1989. *A Modern History of Kenya*. London: Evans Brothers.

O'Donnell, Guillermo, and Philippe C. Schmitter. 1986. *Transitions from Authoritarian Rule: Tentative Conclusions about Uncertain Democracies*. Baltimore: Johns Hopkins University Press.

Ogot, B.A. 1995. "The Politics of Populism." In *Decolonialization & Independence in Kenya 1940–93*, B.A. Ogot and W. R. Ochieng'. London: James Currey.

Ogot, B.A., and W. R. Ochieng'. 1995. *Decolonialization & Independence in Kenya 1940-93*. London: James Currey.

Okullu, Bishop Henry. 1997. *Quest for Justice: An Autobiography of Bishop John Henry Okullu*. Kisumu, Kenya: Shalom Publishers and Computer Training Centre.

Olson, Mancur. [1965] 1998. *The Logic of Collective Action: Public Goods and the Theory of Groups*. Cambridge, MA.: Harvard University Press.

Orvis, Stephen. 2001. "Moral Ethnicity and Political Tribalism in Kenya's 'Virtual Democracy.'" *African Issues* 24 (1,2).

Ottaway Marina, ed. 1997. *Democracy in Africa: The Hard Road Ahead*. Boulder, CO.: Lynne Rienner.

Oxhorn, Phillip. 1994. "Where Did All the Protestors Go? Popular Mobilization and the Transition to Democracy in Chile." *Latin American Perspectives* 21(3):49-68.

Payne, James L. 1968. *Patterns of Conflict in Columbia*. New Haven: Yale University Press.

Peters, Ralph-Michael. 2001. "Civil Society and the Election Year 1997 in Kenya." In *Out for the Count: the 1997 General Elections and Prospects for Democracy in Kenya*. Kampala, Uganda: Fountain Publishers.

Piven, Frances Fox, and Richard Cloward. 1977. *Poor People's Movements*. New York: Vintage.

Polsby, Nelson. 1968. "The Institutionalization of the U.S. House of Representatives." *American Political Science Review* 62(1):144-168, March.

Popkin, Samuel. 1979. *The Rational Peasant: The Political Economy of Rebellion in Southeast Asia*. Berkeley, CA.: University of California Press.

Popper, Karl [1934] 1985. "Scientific Method." In *Popper Selections,* ed. David Miller. Princeton: Princeton University Press.

Popper, Karl. 1968. *The Logic of Scientific Discovery*. London: Hutchinson.

Popper, Karl. 1972. "Of Clouds and Clocks: An Approach to the Problem of Rationality and the Freedom of Man." In *Objective Knowledge: An Evolutionary Approach*. Oxford: Clarendon Press.

Population Reference Bureau. 2003. *2003 World Population Data Sheet*. Washington: Population Reference Bureau.

Press, Robert M. 1999. *The New Africa: Dispatches from a Changing Continent*. Gainesville, FL.: University Press of Florida.

Przeworski, Adam. 1991. *Democracy and the market: Political and Economic Reforms in Eastern Europe and Latin America*. Cambridge: Cambridge University Press.

Przeworski, Adam, Michael Alvarez, José Antonio Cheibub, and Fernando Limongi. 1996. "What Makes Democracies Endure?" *Journal of Democracy* 7(1): 39–55, January.

Przeworski, Adam, Fernando Limongi. 1993. "Political Regimes and Economic Growth," *Journal of Economic Perspectives* 7(3):51–69, Summer.

Przeworski, Adam, and Fernando Limongi. 1997. "Modernization: Theories and Facts." *World Politics* 49:155–183, January.

Przeworski, Adam and Henry Teune. [1970] 1982. *The Logic of Comparative Social Inquiry*. Malabar, FL.: Robert E. Krieger.

Putnam, Robert D. 1993. *Making Democracy Work: Civic Traditions in Modern Italy*. Princeton: Princeton University Press.

Riessman, Catherine Kohler. "Analysis of Personal Narratives." In *Handbook of Interview Research: Context and Method*. Jaber F. Bubrium and James A. Holstein, eds. Thousand Oaks, CA.: Sage Publications.

Risse, Thomas, Stephen C. Ropp, and Kathryn Sikkink, eds. 1999. *The Power of Human Rights: International Norms and Domestic Change*. Cambridge: Cambridge University Press.

Robertson, A. H., and J. G. Merrills. 1996. *Human Rights in the World: An introduction to the Study of the International Protection of Human Rights*, 4th ed. Manchester, U. K: Manchester University Press.

Rosberg, Carl G., Jr., and John Nottingham. 1966. *The Myth of Mau Mau: Nationalism in Kenya*. London: Stanford Praeger.

Rothstein, Bo. 1996. "Political Institutions: An Overview." In *A New Handbook of Political Science,* eds. Robert E. Goodin and Hans-Dieter Klingemann. Oxford: Oxford University Press.

Rueschemeyer, Dietrich, Evelyne Huber Stephens and John D. Stephens. *1992. Capitalist Development and Democracy.* Chicago: University Press of Chicago.

Rule, James, and Charles Tilly. 1975. "Political Process in Revolutionary France, 1830–1832." In *1830 in France,* ed. John M. Merriman. New York: New Viewpoints.

Rustow, Dankwart. 1970. "Transitions to Democracy: Toward a Dynamic Model." *Comparative Politics* 2(3):337–363.

Rutten, Marcel, Alamin Mazrui, and François Grignon. 2001. *Out for the Count:*

The 1997 General Elections and Prospects for Democracy in Kenya. Kampala,
   Uganda: Fountain Publishers.
Salman, Ton. 1994. "The Different Movement: Generation and Gender in the
   Vicissitudes of the Chilean Shantytown Organizations, 1973–1990." *Latin
   American Perspectives* 21(3):8–31.
Schmidt, Siegmar, and Gichira Kibara. 2002. *Kenya on the Path Toward Democracy?
   An Interim Evaluation: A Qualitative Assessment of Political Developments
   in Kenya Between 1990 and June 2002.* Nairobi, Kenya: Konrad Adenauer
   Foundation.
Schmitz, Hans Peter. 1999. Transnational Activism and Political Change in Kenya
   and Uganda." In *The Power of Human Rights: International Norms and Domestic
   Change*, eds. Thomas Risse, Stephen C. Ropp and Kathryn Sikkink. Cambridge:
   Cambridge University Press.
Schmitz, Hans Peter. 2001. "When Networks Blind: Human Rights and Politics in
   Kenya." In *Intervention and Transnationalism in Africa: Global-Local Networks of
   Power*, eds. Thomas Callaghy, Ronald Kassimir, and Robert Latham. Cambridge:
   Cambridge University Press.
Schneider, Cathy. 1999. "Mobilization at the Grassroots: Shantytowns and Resistance
   in Authoritarian Chile." *Latin American Perspectives* 18(1):92–112.
Scott, James C. 1985. *Weapons of the Weak: Everyday Forms of Peasant Resistance.*
   New Haven, CN.: Yale University Press.
Sikkink, Kathryn. 1991. *Ideas and Institutions: Developmentalism in Argentina and
   Brazil.* Ithaca, NY.: Cornell University Press.
Skocpol, Theda. 1979. *States and Social Revolutions: A Comparative Analysis of
   France, Russia, and China.* Cambridge: Cambridge University Press.
Snow, David E., and Robert Benford. 1992. "Master Frames and Cycles of Protest."
   In *Frontiers in Social Movement Theory*, eds. Aldon Morris and Carol McClurg
   Mueller. New Haven, CN,: Yale University Press.
Snow, David, E., Burke Rochford, Steven Worden, and Robert Benford. 1986.
   "Frame Alignment Processes, Micromobilization, and Movement Participation."
   American Sociological Review 51(4):464–81.
Steinmo, Sven H. 1994. "American Exceptionalism Reconsidered: Culture
   or Institutions?" In *The Dynamics of American Politics: Approaches and
   Interpreations*, eds. Lawrence C. Dodd and Calvin Jillson. Boulder, CO.:
   Westview Press.
Tarrow, Sidney. 1998. *Power in Movement: Social Movements and Contentious
   Politics.* 2nd ed. Cambridge, U. K.: Cambridge University.
Thiong'o, Ngugi wa. 1987. "Foreward." In *Kenya's Freedom Struggle: The Dedan
   Kimathi Papers*, ed. Maina wa Kinyatti. London: Zed Books.
Throup, David W. 2001. "Kenya: Revolution, Relapse, or Reform?" *Africa Notes.*
   Washington: Center for Strategic and International Studies.
Throup, David, and Charles Hornsby. 1998. *Multiparty Politics in Kenya: The
   Kenyatta and Moi States & the Triumph of the System in the 1992 Election.*
   Oxford: James Currey.

Tilly, Charles. 1978. *From Mobilization to Revolution*. Reading, MA: Addison-Wesley.

Tilly, Charles. 1984. "Social Movements and National Politics." In *State Building and Social Movements*, ed. W. Bright and S. Harding. Ann Arbor: University of Michigan Press.

Tilly, Charles. 1999. "Conclusion." In *How Social Movements Matter.* eds. Marco Giugin, Doug McAdam, Charles Tilly. Minneapolis: University of Minnesota Press.

Tilly, Charles. 2000. "Processes and Mechanisms of Democratization." *Sociological Theory* 18(1):1–16.

Tocqueville, A. de. 1955. *The Old Regime and the French Revolution*. Translated by S. Gilbert. Garden City, NJ.: Doubleday.

United Nations Commission on Human Rights. 2000. *Civil and Political Rights, Including Questions of Torture and Detention: Report of the Special Rapporteur, Sir Nigel Rodley; submitted pursuant to resolution 1999/32: Visit of the Special Rapporteur to Kenya.E/CN.4/2000/9/Add.4.* United Nations Economic and Social Council.

United States Department of State. 2001 *Annual Report on Kenya: Country Reports on Human Rights*. Washington: Department of State.

Wallerstein, Immanuel, ed. 1966. *Social Change: The Colonial Situation*. New York.

Wamwere, Koigi wa. 2002. *I Refuse to Die: My Journey for Freedom*. New York: Seven Stories Press.

Weaver, R. Kent, and Bert A. Rockman, eds. 1993. *Do Institutions Matter? Government Capabilities in the United States and Abroad*. Washington: Brookings Institution.

Weber, Max. [1930] 1992. *The Protestant Ethic and the Spirit of Capitalism*. London: Routledge.

Wiseman, John A. 1996. *The New Struggle for Democracy in Africa*. Aldershot, UK.: Avebury.

Womack, John. 1969. *Zapata and the Mexican Revolution*. New York: Knopf.

World Bank. 1995. *African Development Indicators* 1994–1995. Washington: World Bank.

World Bank. 1999. *African Development Indicators* 1998–1999. Washington: World Bank.

Young, Crawford. 1994. *The African Colonial State in Comparative Perspective*. New Haven, CN: Yale University Press.

Zamosc, Leon. 1994. Agrarian Protest and the Indian Movement in the Ecuadorian Highlands. *Latin American Research Review* 29(3):237-252.

Index